HOW TO READ A
NAUTICAL
CHART

SECOND EDITION

A Complete Guide
to Understanding and Using
Electronic and Paper Charts

Nigel Calder

INTERNATIONAL MARINE / McGRAW-HILL

Camden, Maine ▪ New York ▪ Chicago ▪ San Francisco ▪ Lisbon ▪ London ▪ Madrid ▪ Mexico City
Milan ▪ New Delhi ▪ San Juan ▪ Seoul ▪ Singapore ▪ Sydney ▪ Toronto

Also By Nigel Calder

Boatowner's Mechanical and Electrical Manual: How to Maintain, Repair, and Improve Your Boat's Essential Systems, 3rd edition

The Cruising Guide to the Northwest Caribbean: The Yucatan Coast of Mexico, Belize, Guatemala, Honduras, and the Bay Islands of Honduras

Cuba: A Cruising Guide

How to Read a Nautical Chart, Quick Guide

Marine Diesel Engines: Maintenance, Troubleshooting, and Repair, 3rd edition

Nigel Calder's Cruising Handbook: A Compendium for Coastal and Offshore Sailors

Refrigeration for Pleasureboats: Installation, Maintenance, and Repair

Repairs at Sea

The McGraw-Hill Companies

2 3 4 5 6 7 8 9 10 11 12 13 14 15 QVR/QVR 1 9 8 7 6 5 4 3

Library of Congress Cataloging-in-Publication Data is available for this title.

ISBN 0-07-177982-5
EISBN 0-07-177983-3

Permissions and art credits may be found on page 7.

Questions regarding the content of this book should be addressed to www.internationalmarine.com

Questions regarding the ordering of this book should be addressed to
The McGraw-Hill Companies
Customer Service Department
P.O. Box 547
Blacklick, OH 43004
Retail customers: 1-800-262-4729
Bookstores: 1-800-722-4726

NOTICE: The information, charts, and illustrations contained in this book are not for navigational purposes. All material in this book is subject to change at any time.

Hoping this will keep you off the rocks!

■ ■ ■

This book is dedicated to
hydrographers and chart-makers,
the unsung heroes of the navigational world,
and to Molly Mulhern,
production boss extraordinaire
at International Marine,
whose idea it was.

■ ■ ■

Contents

Acknowledgments
TO THE SECOND EDITION

FOR THIS SECOND EDITION, I need to thank Ben Ellison, the world's preeminent marine electronics journalist, for his input on the latest happenings in the world of electronic charting and for pointing me in the direction of "user-generated content," which is likely to revolutionize charting (see chapter 4). Jeffrey Siegel provided detail and illustrations of the Active-Captain approach.

At the time I wrote the first edition, the University of New Hampshire, with funding from the National Oceanic and Atmospheric Administration (NOAA), had recently launched the Center for Coastal and Ocean Mapping (CCOM). A small team was working on everything from the cutting edge of surveying technologies and associated software to radical explorations of the interface between humans and navigational products. Since then, this acorn has grown into an oak tree which has placed the CCOM at the forefront of a number of emerging technologies and concepts in the hydrographic world, including the "Chart of the Future" that I have included in this edition. My thanks to the staff, and particularly Captain Ben Smith, for their enthusiasm in sharing what they do.

Michel Huet and Tony Pharoah from the International Hyrdrographic Organization (IHO) in Monaco have once again contributed their expertise.

And from the private sector my thanks go to Bill Washburn at Nobeltec, Dave Pennington at Garmin, Tim Sullivan at NV Charts, and Ken Cirillo at C-Map. Jonathan Bailey of Clipper Ventures Plc shared with me details of the loss of the *Cork Clipper* on an Indonesian reef.

Acknowledgments to the First Edition

Writing this book has been a fascinating odyssey through the world of chart-making. I am indebted to many "tour guides" who provided information, helped me understand difficult concepts, and commented on various drafts for the book. I thank all of them, and in particular:

At the British Admiralty, Chris Smith, Patrick Nealon, Rex May, and Jim Nichols.

At the National Oceanic and Atmospheric Administration (NOAA), National Ocean Service (NOS), and National Imagery and Mapping Agency (NIMA), Captain Nick Perugini, Dave Enabnit, Mike Brown, Jerry Mills, John Bailey, Fanny Powers, and Barbara Hess.

At the International Hydrographic Organization (IHO), Michel Huet and Tony Pharoah.

At the Hydrographic Society (based in the U.K.), Michael Boreham.

In the private sector, Dick Davis of Soft Chart, Dennis Mills of the Capn, and David D'Aquino and Ken Cirillo of C-Map.

I am particularly indebted to the IHO for supplying various manuals and giving me permission to quote from them, notably *M4—Chart Specifications of the IHO* (now renamed S4, and available from the IHO website at www.iho-ohi.net). I am similarly indebted to NOAA (U.S.) for all the work entailed in compiling *Chart No. 1* and the *Nautical Chart User's Manual*; the first has been included in this book more or less in its entirety, and the second I frequently referred to in the course of my labors (both are now available on-line at www.nauticalcharts.noaa.gov). I also used NOAA's version of *M-4*, the *Nautical Chart Manual*, 7th (1992) edition, volumes 1 and 2, and the British Admiralty's chart *5011 (INT-1): Symbols and Abbreviations Used on Admiralty Charts*.

Various people have reviewed sections of the book and provided useful feedback. In particular, my thanks to staff at the Italian Hydrographic Office, Maptech, Navionics, and especially Rex May at the British Admiralty.

Then there is the team at International Marine, with whom it has always been and continues to be a pleasure to work.

Finally, there is my family—Terrie, Pippin, and Paul—who continue to tolerate my somewhat compulsive work habits with minimal complaint!

Art Credits

The artwork on the following pages has been reproduced from *The Mariner's Handbook, Publication NP 100*, and from copyrighted British Admiralty charts, by permission of the Controller of Her Majesty's Stationery Office and the U.K. Hydrographic Office (www.ukho. gov.uk): pages 18, 19, 20 (bottom), 21 (top right), 22 (bottom left), 33 (top), 35 (left and right), 60 (lower left and upper right), 82, 84, 93 (bottom), 94, 106 (bottom), 120, 128, 134, 143, 145 (bottom), 146, 147, 149, 154, 155, 167, 173, 199, 208, 209, 210, 211, 212, 216, 228. NOTICE: No National Hydrographic Office has verified the reproduced data and none accept liability for the accuracy of the reproduction or any modifications made thereafter. No National Hydrographic Office warrants that this product satisfies national or international regulations regarding the use of the appropriate products for navigation. Additional copyrighted chart material supplied by Imray, Laurie, Norie and Wilson (pages 23 [right], 98, 106 [bottom], 145 [bottom], 146, 153 [bottom], 205, 206, 220), and Stanfords Charts (pages 97, 106 [top], 217) and the Russian Hydrographic Office (pages 107 [both], 207, 217).

Additional credit is due to these agencies:
Australian Hydrographic Office: page 86.

DMA/NIMA: pages 13, 21 (left), 24, 25, 27, 30, 62 (left), 64, 69, 93 (left), 113, 138, 145 (top), 151, 153 (top), 162, 171 (right), 175, 182 (bottom), 187, 196 (right).

FEMA: page 70 (left).

IHO: page 87, reproduced from Colour and Symbol Specifications for ECDIS, SP-52.

Library of Congress: page 72 (both).

National Geodetic Survey: pages 16, 17.

NOAA: pages 15, 49, 60 (lower right), 65, 66 (right), 90, 91, 93 (top right), 95, 96, 99, 100, 101, 105, 109 (bottom), 117, 119, 123, 126, 133, 136, 137, 139, 141, 144, 152, 156, 163, 164, 169, 171 (left), 174, 176 (top), 177, 181, 182 (top), 183, 185, 189, 196 (left), 197, 202, 203, 214, 215 (left), 219, 231.

NMSI: page 14 (bottom).

Swedish Hydrographic Office: page 86 (bottom left).

United States Coast Guard: pages 36, (top), 60 (top left), 92, 218.

And to these:
ActiveCaptain: page 80.

Associated Press: page 70 (right).

CCOM: pages 36 (lower), 77 (right).

Clipper Ventures, Plc./Jonathan Bailey: pages 23 (top left), 51.

Brett and Priscilla Donham: pages 14 (top), 15 (bottom), 20 (top).

Ben Ellison: pages 74, 75, 78, 81.

Lou Evans: page 71 (top).

Explorer Charts: page 48 (bottom left and right).

Maptech: page 56 (bottom right).

John Neal and Amanda Swan-Neal: page 22 (right).

Nobeltec: pages 13, 40, 46, 48 (top left and right), 52, 53, 54, 55, 56, 57 (left), 58 (left), 66 (left), 88 (middle and bottom), 109 (top).

NV Charts: pages 57 (right), 58 (right), 73 (lower), 77 (left), 86 (right), 88 (top right).

The CapN: page 47.

All other photos by Nigel Calder.

Introduction
TO THE SECOND EDITION

AT THE TIME OF WRITING the first edition of this book (2001), we were in the midst of the massive upheaval in the charting world created by the introduction of electronic charting. The private sector had leapt in with enthusiasm and digitized worldwide suites of charts from existing paper products using a variety of off-the-shelf and proprietary software processes. It was an exciting but chaotic situation. The official hydrographic offices had been struggling for the better part of 15 years to agree on a set of common standards to govern the digitization and display processes. These standards had more-or-less gelled by then, but the inevitably slow process of achieving consensus at an international level had substantially slowed the process of developing electronic charts. The private sector appeared to be running rings around the public sector.

Looking back, we can now see that 2000 was a turning point for the public sector. The various standards under development for raster and vector charts (more on the distinctions and standards later), and for rules governing their display, had developed to the point where they were sufficiently refined to give the national hydrographic offices a firm platform on which to build their digitization processes. These standards changed very little in the subsequent decade, and they have increasingly come to govern the digitization processes in the private sector. This standardization is a benefit to all navigators, both commercial and recreational.

Based on these standards, initially, the hydrographic offices digitized their existing charting products, with all the errors inherent in those products (see chapter 2), but a steady stream of fresh, and inherently more accurate, data has been added to the mix, although there is still a good deal of confusion as to how to integrate this data into charting products. The private sector has drawn on this database and greatly expanded it with all kinds of "added-value" products. There has been a lot of fascinating activity here, but fundamentally the world of charting has not changed —all of this output has been tied to a traditional, two-dimensional, chart, albeit in an electronic format.

We are now on the cusp of another profound revolution in the way charts and navigational products are created, and the manner in which they are displayed and used. At the official hydrographic level, the combination of differential GPS (DGPS), modern survey technologies, and newly created software algorithms is opening up the possibility of generating and processing vast amounts of highly accurate data much faster and more cheaply than was ever possible in the past. Massive amounts of data are also becoming available from other sources (Google Earth is an obvious example). Within the private sector, mechanisms are emerging that will enable all sailors to incorporate user-generated content (UGC) to navigational products and share this with other sailors. We can harness the user base in a way that has never been possible before. We are still in the early stages of learning how to manage these capabilities (quality control is an obvious issue), but I feel certain they will revolutionize the process of creating and using navigational products. I have added a chapter on "Regulations and Revolution" that explores these issues.

These developments raise fundamental issues concerning information management—how do you process all this data and select from it what is critical for navigational decision making as opposed to overwhelming the navigator? Traditional two-dimensional cartography is being supplemented with all kinds of innovative approaches. On the display side, 3-D is moving from a gimmick into a useful technology. Innovative interactions with navigators are being explored. We are gravitating from traditional two-dimensional charting into a three-dimensional world. And in fact, with the addition of real-time depth and weather information, we can have interactive charts that will adjust all soundings for the state of the tide, display the anticipated depths at an estimated time of arrival based on a boat's current location and speed, and so on, in which case we move from a three-dimensional to a four-dimensional (time-based) navigational environment. The traditional 2-D paper chart and its electronic derivative have evolved over hundreds of years whereas the astonishing pace at which computer technology is now evolving is moving us from 2-D toward 4-D in a matter of decades.

These are exciting times in the world of chartmaking. I have tried to reflect these developments in the first half of this new edition. However, at the end of the day, we still need symbols to display features on whatever navigational products and devices we use, and so far this symbology has not changed. As a result, the second half of the book has only minor corrections and additions.

Introduction to the First Edition

I have been sailing and reading charts for well over thirty years. In addition to using them as a necessary navigational tool, I have something of a love affair with them. I now have hundreds, ranging from photocopies of the British Admiralty's 1830s charts of Belize that I found in the admiralty's archives (these charts are not global positioning system [GPS] accurate but, nevertheless, have more useful inshore detail than more recent charts) to the latest editions of the National Oceanic and Atmospheric Administration (NOAA) charts of the east coast of the United States. Many of these charts are works of art. The sense of history associated with some that I have been lucky

enough to handle—such as an original Gerhard Mercator atlas from the sixteenth century and charts drawn by Captain Cook in the eighteenth—has given me goose bumps.

Despite my familiarity with charts and chartmaking (including making charts for the Belize region and Cuba while writing two cruising guides), there are still numerous details and symbols on modern charts that I do not immediately recognize. There are other technical issues that underlie chart construction—the knowledge of which is important to a proper interpretation of the material presented—that I have only come to understand in recent years, and that I know many of my fellow navigators do not understand. It has seemed to me for some time that a small book explaining these details, written and presented in a format accessible to amateur sailors like myself, is long overdue. This is what you now have in your hands. I hope it proves both interesting and useful.

I have divided this book into two parts: the first deals with theoretical and background information underlying the construction of charts, both paper and electronic; the second concentrates entirely on the symbols used on charts, serving as a handy reference to anyone trying to decipher an unfamiliar symbol.

Although the user can jump right into part 2, using it as a reference guide, I encourage a reading of part 1, especially if using electronic charts. The modern chart summarizes an extraordinary amount of detail, some of it quite technical. The more the user understands about how it was put together, the more he or she will get out of it. Beyond this, in this age of satellite positioning systems and pinpoint navigation, the tools with which we navigate are significantly more accurate than those used to conduct most of the surveys on which our charts are based. Our tools may also be more accurate than the tools and techniques used to draw those charts (whether paper or electronic).

To a much greater extent than was the case for navigators in earlier times, the contemporary navigator needs to have an intuitive grasp of the limits of chart accuracy (both paper and electronic) and of satellite-based positioning systems relative to these charts. I believe that the best way to develop the necessary understanding is to delve into the somewhat esoteric details of surveying and chart-making—such things as horizontal and vertical datums, chart projections, the limits of surveying and charting accuracy, and the potential errors inherent in developing electronic charts. At the end of the day, there is little need to remember the details presented as long as an intuitive feel for the limits of charting technology (both paper and electronic) remains embedded in the navigator's consciousness, and with it a necessary degree of caution when using the information presented on a chart.

Part 2 of this book is essentially an annotated version of a U.S. government publication known as *Chart No. 1, United States of America: Nautical Chart Symbols, Abbreviations, and Terms.* This was formerly published in the United States by NOAA (National Oceanic and Atmospheric Administration),* but it is no longer in print (it can, however, be downloaded from www.nauticalcharts.noaa.gov/mcd/chartno1.htm). Almost identical publications are produced in other countries: in the United Kingdom, the British Admiralty's *Chart 5011 (INT 1): Symbols and Abbreviations Used on Admiralty Charts*; in Germany, *Karte 1*; in France, *Ouvrage 1*; and so forth. All are derivations of a publication produced by the International Hydrographic Organization (IHO) and known as *INT-1*. In my opinion, all these publications lack an explanation of some of the underlying conventions used in compil-

ing charts, and also some of the symbology; they assume the reader has a greater familiarity with hydrographic terms and techniques than is the case for most recreational boaters and even for many professionals.

I have added explanatory notes and additional detail where I believe they are needed or worthwhile. Perhaps of more use, I have inserted a large number of illustrative segments from a wide variety of charts to give you an opportunity to test your chart-symbol recognition skills. The chart segments are printed at the same size as they appear on the charts from which they came, so they are fully representative of what you will see in real life.

In summary, *this is not a book about how to navigate* (for a detailed description of basic piloting and navigation techniques, see *Nigel Calder's Cruising Handbook*, chapter 8).** How to Read a Nautical Chart *is a book about how to read a chart (both paper and electronic) and understand the wider significance of the information contained on the chart.* How this information is incorporated into your navigational practices is your business! I hope that what I have produced is more interesting, instructive, cautionary, and ultimately user-friendly than *Chart No. 1* and similar publications.

Nigel Calder
Newcastle, Maine

---

* NOAA is in charge of paper and electronic charts of U.S. coastal waters, with NOS (the National Ocean Survey) and OCS (the Office of Coastal Survey) under its aegis. The NGA (National Geospatial Intelligence Agency), the successor to NIMA (the National Imagery and Mapping Agency), is in charge of U.S.-produced charts of overseas regions.

** Published as the Boatowner's Practical and Technical Cruising Manual by Adlard Coles Nautical in the United Kingdom.

Part 1

The Limits
OF
Accuracy

Fundamental Chart-Making Concepts

UNTIL RECENTLY, there has been little need for chart users to understand the technology of chart-making, particularly its limitations, because the tools used by navigators to determine the position of their vessels were inherently less accurate than those used to conduct and display the surveys on which charts are based. Realizing the limits of accuracy of their tools, navigators tended to be a cautious crowd, giving hazards a wide berth and typically taking proactive measures to build in an extra margin of safety for errors and unforeseen events.

Knowing this, and knowing that navigation in inshore waters was by reference to landmasses and not astronomical fixes, surveyors were more concerned with depicting an accurate relationship of soundings and hydrographic features relative to the local landmass (coastline) than they were with absolute accuracy relative to latitude and longitude. The surveyor's maxim was that it is much more important to determine an accurate least depth over a shoal or danger than to determine its geographical position with certainty. Similarly, the cartographer, when showing an area containing many dangers (such as a rocky outcrop), paid more attention to bringing the area to the attention of the navigator, so it could be avoided by a good margin, than to accurately showing every individual rock in its correct position.

All this changed with the advent of satellite-based navigation systems—notably the global positioning system (GPS). Now a boat's position (latitude and longitude) can be fixed with near-pinpoint accuracy and, in the case of electronic navigation, accurately displayed on a chart in real time. This encourages many navigators (myself included) to "cut corners" more closely than they would have done in the past. With such an attitude, it is essential for the navigator to grasp both the accuracy with which a fix can be plotted (whether manually or electronically) and the limit of accuracy of the chart itself—together they determine the extent to which it is possible to cut corners in safety.

The next chapter discusses factors that affect the limits of chart accuracy. However, I first want to explore the extent to which electronic navigation devices actually give us the plotting accuracy we believe they do. This is best done by understanding the basic concepts of mapmaking and chart-making.

A Little History

As early as the third century b.c., Erastothenes and other Greeks established that the world is a sphere, created the concepts of latitude and longitude, and developed basic mapmaking skills. It was not until the sixteenth century a.d. that there were any advances in mapmaking techniques, which occurred largely as a result of steady improvements in the equipment and methods used for making precise astronomical observations and for measuring distances and changes in elevation on the ground. From this time, instruments were available for measuring angles with great accuracy.

The core surveying methodology that developed is noteworthy because it remained essentially unchanged until recent decades—for both cartographic and inshore hydrographic surveys—and is the basis of many of the charts we still use. A survey started from a single point whose latitude and longitude were established by astronomical observations. For accurate surveys, these observations required heavy, bulky, and

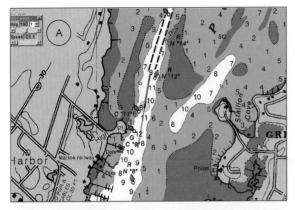

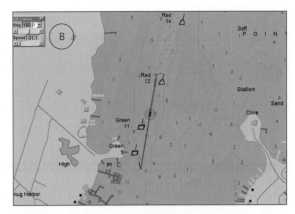

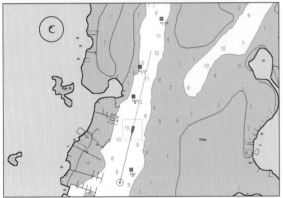

The incredibly precise real-time positioning of a boat that is possible with electronic charts and charting systems can tempt a navigator to follow a course closer to hazards than would have been the norm in the past. Here we have three different examples of electronic charts of the same area; all display the boat's position with great precision in real time. **A.** *NOAA raster scan.* **B.** *NIMA (now NGA) vector chart.* **C.** *Transas vector chart.*

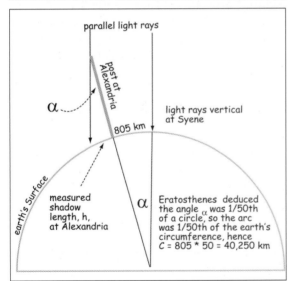

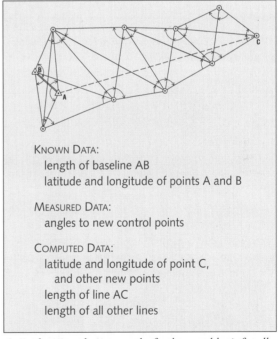

KNOWN DATA:
   length of baseline AB
   latitude and longitude of points A and B

MEASURED DATA:
   angles to new control points

COMPUTED DATA:
   latitude and longitude of point C,
      and other new points
   length of line AC
   length of all other lines

Eratosthenes's method for determining the size of the earth, and the world as he knew it.

A simple triangulation net, the fundamental basis for all surveying until recent decades.

expensive equipment, as well as multiple observations by highly trained observers over a considerable period of time. From the starting point, a long baseline was precisely measured using carefully calibrated wooden or metal rods or chains. The surveyors measured all changes in vertical elevation in order to be able to discount the effects of them on the horizontal distances covered. In this way, a precise log of horizontal distances was maintained, resulting in baseline measurements that were accurate to inches—sometimes over a distance of many miles. The process was slow and painstaking, and often took years to complete.

Once a baseline had been established, angular measurements were taken from both ends to a third

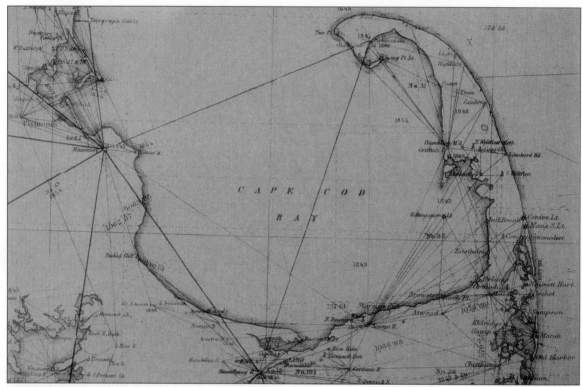

A nineteenth-century triangulation net for Cape Cod Bay off the coast of Massachusetts.

Astronomical observations used in early geodetic surveys.

position. Knowing the length of the baseline and the two angles, spherical trigonometry established the distances to the third point without having to make field measurements. The sides of the triangle thus es-tablished were now used as fresh baselines to extend the survey, again without having to make actual dis-tance measurements in the field. The measured base-lines plus the process of triangulation provided the horizontal distances on the ground. With one or more precise astronomical observations at a different point to the original one, it was possible to mathe-matically establish a latitude and longitude frame-work and apply it to the results of the survey—there was no need to obtain astronomical fixes for all the intermediate points, thereby avoiding the time, ex-pense, and difficulties involved.

By the seventeenth century, it was possible to make sufficiently accurate astronomical observations and distance measurements to discover that in one part of the world a degree of latitude as measured as-tronomically (i.e., with reference to the stars) does not cover the same distance on the ground as it does in another part of the world. This would be impossi-ble if the world were a perfect sphere.

From Sphere to Ellipsoid

How to model this nonspherical world? This was more than an academic question. To make maps, na-tional surveyors now universally used an astronomi-cally determined starting point and a measured baseline, working away from the beginning point by the process of triangulation (see art page 13).

As the surveyors progressed farther afield, if the mapped latitudes and longitudes were to be kept in sync with the occasional astronomical observations (i.e., real-life latitudes and longitudes), there had to be a model showing the relationship between the distance on the ground and latitude and longitude, and indicating how this relationship changed as the surveyors moved away from their astronomically determined starting point. This model had to be such that with available trigonometrical and computational methods, the mapmakers could adjust their data to accurately calculate changing latitudes and longitudes over substantial distances—in other words, the model had to be mathematically predictable.

The model that was adopted, and which is used to this day even with satellite-based mapmaking and navigation, is an *ellipsoid* (also called a *spheroid*). In essence, an ellipsoid is nothing more than a flattened sphere, characterized by two measurements: its radius at the equator and the degree of flattening at the poles. Clearly, the key questions become: What is this radius, and what is the degree of flattening?

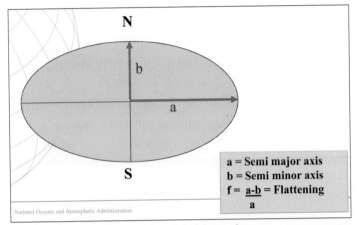

a = Semi major axis
b = Semi minor axis
$f = \dfrac{a-b}{a}$ = Flattening

National Oceanic and Atmospheric Administration

The ellipsoid, a mathematical model of the earth.

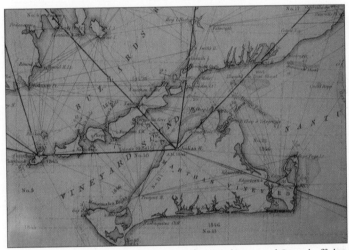

Nineteenth-century survey of Buzzards Bay and Vineyard Sound off the Massachusetts coast, showing the triangulation net.

During the nineteenth century, the continents were first accurately mapped based on this concept of the world as an ellipsoid. For each of the great surveys, preliminary work extending over years used astronomical observations and measured baselines to establish the key dimensions of the ellipsoid that was to underlie the survey. In the United Kingdom, a *geodesist* (a person who does this type of research) named Sir George Airy developed an ellipsoid (known as Airy 1830) that became the basis for an incredibly detailed survey of the British Isles. His ellipsoid is still used today (2012) for the British Isles, since it fits the actual shape of this part of the world very well (better than modern satellite-derived ellipsoids, which are described later in this chapter).

Using this ellipsoid, the surveyors commenced at a precisely determined astronomical point on Salisbury Plain, measured a baseline, and triangulated their way across the British Isles. The accuracy of the survey work and the ellipsoid was such that when western Ireland was reached decades later, and the original baseline was checked by computation from the Irish baseline 350 miles away, the two values differed by only 5 inches!

Another British geodesist, Alexander Clarke, went to the United States and was instrumental in developing the ellipsoid that has underlain the mapping of North America. Known as the Clarke 1866 ellipsoid, it was the basis of mapmaking and chartmaking on the North American continent until the advent of satellite-derived ellipsoids. Later, Clarke developed an ellipsoid for mapping France and Africa (Clarke 1880).

Using the Clarke 1866 ellipsoid, and commencing at a single astronomically derived point and a measured baseline at the Meades Ranch in Osborne County, Kansas, the American surveyors from the U.S. Coast and Geodetic Survey (now the National

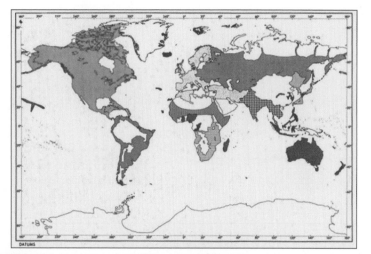

Geodetic Survey) fanned out, establishing triangulation points and mapping the entire continent as they went. This combination of an underlying ellipsoid, a specific astronomically determined starting point, and a measured baseline, together with some clever mathematics, is known as a *geodetic datum*; in this case, it is now known as the *North American Datum of 1927* (*NAD 27*). Such is the accuracy of the NAD 27 surveys and the correlation of the Clarke 1866 ellipsoid with the real world that at the margins of the survey (the northeast and northwest United States—those areas in the lower forty-eight states farthest from the starting point), the discrepancies between mapped and astronomically derived latitudes and longitudes are no more than 40 to 50 meters (130–165 ft.).

From Ellipsoid to Geoid

By the end of the nineteenth century, there were numerous ellipsoids in use, all of them differing slightly from one another. This raised another interesting question: Surely, they couldn't all be correct, or could they?

The answer lies in a more sophisticated understanding of our planet. The individual ellipsoids closely model the shape of the world in the areas in which the surveys were conducted, producing a close correlation between mapped and astronomically de-

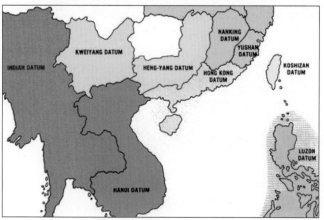

Major geodetic datum blocks still in use around the world, forming the basis for map and chart datums; within these, there are a number of subdivisions (e.g., the U.K.'s Airy 1830).

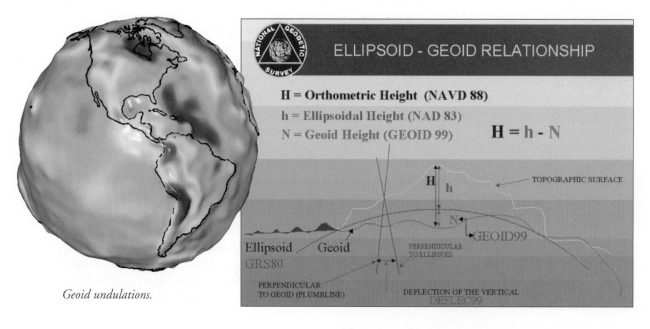

Geoid undulations.

rived positions, even at the margins of the survey. Nevertheless, although these ellipsoids are based on very accurate measurements over large areas of land, these are still only small areas of the world. When extrapolated to the globe as a whole, the ellipsoids produce increasingly serious discrepancies between ellipsoid-derived latitudes and longitudes and astronomically derived positions. Geodesists realized that not only is the world not a sphere, but it is also not an ellipsoid. In fact, it does not have a geometrically uniform shape at all, but rather has numerous irregular humps and hollows.

Another concept was needed to deal with this shape. It is the *geoid*, which is defined as the real shape of the surface of the world if we discount all elevations above sea level. In other words, if we were to bulldoze the mountains and valleys to sea level, we would have the geoid. In effect, this is the two-dimensional world as surveyed by mapmakers because the vertical element in the earth's topography is discounted when measuring baselines and other distances—which are all painstakingly reduced to the horizontal, using sea level as the base elevation. Whereas an ellipsoid is a mathematically defined regular surface, the geoid is a very irregular (mathematically unpredictable) shape. Regardless of the ellipsoid used to model the world, at different times the surface of the geoid will be above or below that of the ellipsoid, a phenomenon known as *geoid undulation*, or *geoid-spheroid separation*.

If we take two positions on an ellipsoid and define them in terms of latitude and longitude, the distance between them can be mathematically determined. However, no such relationship holds with the geoid. If the geoid undulates above the ellipsoid, the horizontal distance between the two points is greater than the corresponding distance on the ellipsoid; if the geoid undulates below the ellipsoid, the horizontal distance is less.

Astronomically derived positions are real-life points on the surface of the earth that have been determined relative to observable celestial phenomena. As such, they are referenced to the mathematically unpredictable geoid, as opposed to mapmakers' po-

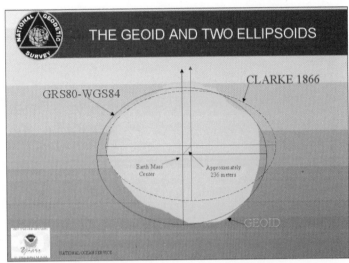

An illustration (grossly exaggerated) of how the "best-fit" datum in one part of the world will not be the best fit elsewhere.

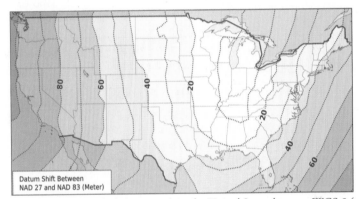

Longitude datum shift (in meters) in the United States between WGS 84 and NAD 27.

sitions that are mostly derived from a mathematical model (an ellipsoid) of the world. Because of the mathematically unpredictable nature of the geoid, *there is no mathematical relationship between astronomically determined positions and positions determined by reference to an ellipsoid.* The only way to correlate the two is either through individual measurements or by modeling the geoid and ellipsoid and measuring the offsets.

What this means is that there can be no ellipsoid that produces a precise correlation between ellipsoid-derived latitudes and longitudes and those derived astronomically. This is why we currently have more than twenty different ellipsoids in use around the world, each of which forms the basis for a different map datum, and none of which are compatible. In their own areas, these ellipsoids and datums create a "best fit" between latitudes and longitudes derived from the ellipsoid and those derived astronom-

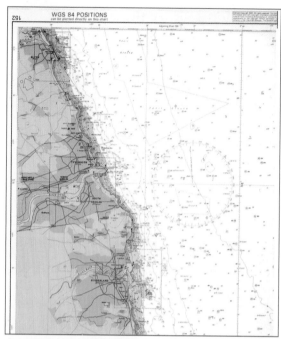

A modern chart, clearly indicating that it is based on the WGS 84 datum. On many older charts, the datum is hard to find, and is sometimes not given at all.

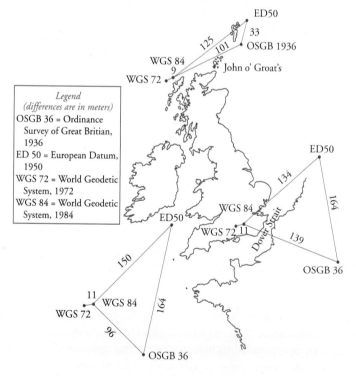

Position differences (in meters) relative to astronomical positions that result from using different datums at three different points around the British Isles. Note, in particular, the 130+ m shift in the Dover Straits, an exceedingly congested area with narrow, clearly defined shipping lanes.

ically (those referenced to the geoid). However, when expanded to worldwide coverage, latitudes and longitudes based on these ellipsoids exhibit increasingly large discrepancies from those derived astronomically.

A New Age

Geodesists have long tried to resolve these problems. In the eighteenth century, British and French surveyors coordinated the lighting of flares on both sides of the English Channel to establish triangulation data that would enable the national surveys to be brought into sync. More recently in North America, sightings were made off aircraft to tie surveys of Greenland, Cuba, and other outlying areas into the NAD 27 grid. With the advent of radio, electronic methods of accurately measuring relatively long distances on land or across seas allowed further improvements to be made by strengthening the triangulation networks with *trilateration*. However, until the satellite age, it was not possible to bridge the distances between continents in a way that would eliminate the inevitable discontinuities in mapmaking from one continent to another.

Today, all this has changed. Satellites and space-age technology (e.g., electro-optical distance-measuring devices such as lasers) have finally unified the globe, from a surveyor's perspective. In the past five decades, an incredible mass of geodetic data has become available from all parts of the world. On this basis, a succession of World Geodetic Systems (WGS) was developed (e.g., WGS 66, WGS 72), culminating in WGS 84. (The "66," "72," etc., refer to the year in which the system was developed.)

Each has been closer to the truth, allowing further measurements to be made with even more accuracy. The shift between WGS 72 and WGS 84 was just plottable at a scale of 1:50,000; it is likely that the magnitude of any further change from WGS 84 will diminish below the threshold of importance, in which case WGS 84 will be with us for a long time to come (the center of the WGS 84 ellipsoid is estimated to be less than 2 cm from its reference point, which is the earth's center of mass). (Note that in the United States, NAD 83—see page 23—is used for some map- and chart-making. For all intents and purposes, it is the same as WGS 84.)

WGS 84 is another ellipsoid; however, this one was developed as a best fit with the geoid (real-life sea-level world) as a whole, as opposed to having a best fit with just one specific region of the geoid. The irony in this is that, given the irregularities in the geoid, the divergence between WGS 84 and the geoid is actually greater in many areas than the divergence between older ellipsoids and the geoid. For example, in North America, the difference between the Clarke 1866 ellipsoid and the geoid is generally less than 10 meters (33 ft.), whereas with WGS 84, it is at least 15 meters (49 ft.) and often 30 to 35 meters (100–115 ft.). What this means is that the difference between map-derived and astronomically derived latitudes and longitudes is greater on a WGS 84–based map than it is on a NAD 27 map. But, on a worldwide scale, WGS 84 makes a better fit than Clarke 1866 (NAD 27).

However, almost no one uses astronomically derived position-fixing anymore because, with the advent first of Transit (NavSat) and then GPS and GLONASS (the Russian equivalent of GPS), after 2,500 years we have finally broken the umbilical cord that tied our mapmaking to the stars. In the new age, we have our own artificial stars (satellites) and satellite-based survey techniques that relate surveyed positions to the WGS 84 ellipsoid. Whereas astronomically determined latitudes and longitudes are absolute—in the sense that every real-life point on the globe has a fixed astronomical latitude and longitude—ellipsoid-derived latitudes and longitudes are only absolute relative to a particular ellipsoid, which makes them relative in relation to the geoid. A change in ellipsoidal assumptions alters the ellipsoid-derived latitude and longitude of real-life points on the globe. (Of course, the astronomically determined latitude and longitude remain the same.)

At first sight, this seems to make it impossible to have precise position fixes. But with a little more thought, it is seen that this relativity of ellipsoid-derived latitudes and longitudes is irrelevant as long as the equipment used to derive a latitude and a longitude bases the calculations on the same ellipsoid as the map or chart (paper or electronic) on which the position is plotted. If the maps and charts are made to a particular set of assumptions and the position-fixing equipment operates on the same assumptions, the results will be precise fixes—in some cases, incredibly precise fixes: down to centimeter-level accuracy on a continental scale!

The rub comes if someone is navigating with satellite-based electronic navigation equipment that isn't operating on the same set of assumptions as those used to make a given map or chart. In this case, the bottom line is that a match is being attempted between two different ellipsoids. In the case of WGS 84

and Clarke 1866 (NAD 27), the resulting position error may be as high as 100 meters (328 ft.) in the United States; in the case of WGS 84 and the United Kingdom's Ordnance Survey (OS), it is also approximately 100 meters (328 ft.); for charts based on the 1950 European Datum (used in Europe), it may be up to 300 meters (985 ft.); and, in the case of WGS 84 and the Tokyo datum, used in much of eastern Asia, it may be as much as 900 meters (2,955 ft.).

Nautical Peculiarities

Finally, there are all those nautical surveys made without reference to any ellipsoid at all. Coastal surveys were traditionally made by setting up triangulation points on shore and continuing the land-based process of triangulation out to sea. Farther from shore, ships with high bridges and sometimes buoys

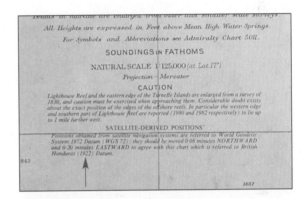

Two different datums used in charting Belize: the first Honduras 1922 (see the small print under "Satellite-Derived Positions") (top), and the second NAD 27 (see the small print under "Depths in Metres") (bottom). The latest edition of these charts uses WGS 84. The time between the tail end of the use of Honduras 1922 and the conversion to WGS 84 has been approximately fifteen years, in which time we have had three different datums.

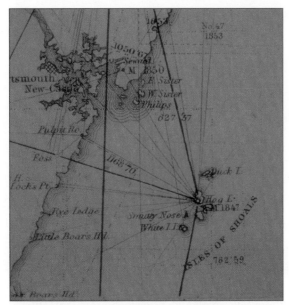

Tying the Isles of Shoals, off Portsmouth, New Hampshire, into the shoreside triangulation grid and datum.

on a short scope (so they would not move around) were used to provide fixed visual markers. Later, radar, Loran-C, and Decca extended the range of the triangulation process. These surveys were all tied into the shore-based ellipsoid and map datum (e.g., NAD 27 in North America). However, once the surveyors moved beyond the range of the shore-based triangulation system, there was no way to tie the surveys into any ellipsoid or shore-based datum. The necessarily precise astronomical and baseline measurements simply could not be made from the moving platform of a ship, resulting in potentially large errors. *The Mariner's Handbook*, published by the British Admiralty (publication NP 100), notes that *"many charted ocean dangers and shoals are from old sketch surveys and reports, often dating from the nineteenth century. Positions from such reports may be grossly in error; their probable positional error, if prior to the general introduction of radio time signals for shipping in the 1920s, is considered to be of the order of 10–20 miles, but may be greater"* (p. 23, 1999 ed.; emphasis added).

For transoceanic surveys, this inability to tie into a given ellipsoid or datum was immaterial because precise position-fixing was not necessary. Mariners navigating the oceans could not fix their position with any degree of precision using a sextant and other traditional means of celestial navigation.

Problems have always arisen, however, related to charts of remote islands, rocks, and other navigational features. Unable to establish a relationship to any el-

lipsoid or chart datum, the surveyors had to establish a local astronomically determined position, and then conduct a survey working away from that point using traditional methods of triangulation. Other than the fact that the astronomically determined starting points are often seriously in error (sometimes by miles: the British Admiralty says the worst discrepancy on its charts, which is in the South Pacific, is 7 miles), there are also surveying errors on the older charts (e.g., imprecisely measured angles between features or poorly calculated distances). These survey methods result in charts that have a local datum that is not compatible with and cannot be tied into any of the major datums: the charts are unreliable relative to all forms of celestial navigation, including satellite navigation. Nevertheless, prior to the satellite age, these surveys also were often adequate for mariners once a landfall was made because navigation was by traditional methods using bearings from identified points of land, changes in depth, and so on—all of which are unrelated to latitude and longitude.

With the advent of satellite-based navigation systems, mariners can precisely locate themselves any-

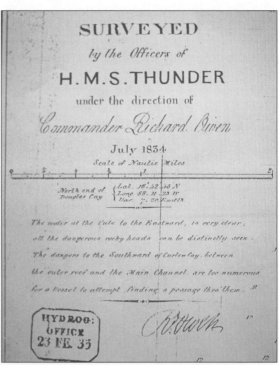

Early British Admiralty Belize surveys. These still form the basis of most soundings found on charts of the region. They were made to no particular datum and cannot be used with any form of electronic navigation. Note the hydrographic office date stamp in the lower left corner: that is 23 February 1835, not 1935!

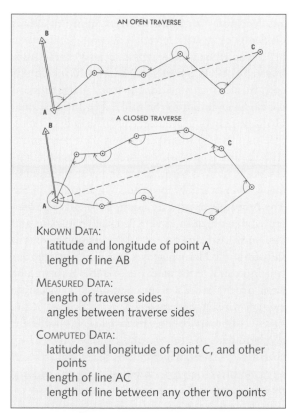

KNOWN DATA:
latitude and longitude of point A
length of line AB

MEASURED DATA:
length of traverse sides
angles between traverse sides

COMPUTED DATA:
latitude and longitude of point C, and other points
length of line AC
length of line between any other two points

Survey methodologies for remote islands, using an astronomically determined starting point, a measured baseline, and triangulation. The "closing of the loop" in the closed traverse allows the surveyors to test the accuracy of their survey (and make adjustments if the loop does not close). The open traverse is the least accurate survey method.

where in the world in terms of latitude and longitude. What few of them realize is that this position is with reference to a particular ellipsoid (for GPS, it is WGS 84), which may differ markedly from the underlying ellipsoid or datum of the chart they are using. Other than confusing the navigator and providing a false sense of confidence, it serves little purpose to know exactly where you are (latitude and longitude) relative to WGS 84 if your chart is based on an ellipsoid and datum that result in the lines of latitude and longitude running through substantially different real-world locations than those given by GPS.

In *The Mariner's Handbook*, the British Admiralty comments that "older surveys are often more accurate in relative terms than in absolute terms; that is, the soundings are positioned accurately in relation to each other, but as a whole may have absolute differences from modern datums such as WGS 84 Datum. In these cases, conventional navigation using charted features gives better results than modern tech-

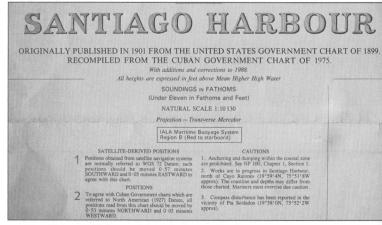

Chart of Santiago Harbor, Cuba. Note 1 indicates that satellite-derived positions based on WGS 72 (the forerunner of WGS 84) must be adjusted 0.57 minute southward (more than ½ a mile) to fit the chart. Note 2 tells us that to agree with the local Cuban charts (based on NAD 27) positions read from this chart must be moved 0.53 minute northward (from this, we can deduce that the difference between WGS 72 and NAD 27 in this area is 0.57 − 0.53 = 0.04 minute, which is about 73 m/80 yd.). It is not specified what datum has been used to produce the chart.

A recent chart of Thailand based on relatively modern surveys (1988) but using the Indian Datum of 1975 (see the small print at the bottom of the label).

niques such as GPS. Although a navigator may know his position relative to satellites to an accuracy of 10 meters, the shoals in which he may be navigating may only be known to an accuracy of 200 meters or worse" (*The Mariner's Handbook*, p. 21, 1999 ed.).

The half-mile difference between our actual and our plotted position we once experienced in Cuba is an example of the type of differences that can arise when satellite-based navigation equipment is operating on a different datum than the chart datum.

Neither the GPS nor the chart was "wrong"; in fact, the chart is a very good one. The two were simply referencing latitude and longitude to a different set of ellipsoidal assumptions.

Avoiding Reefs

This is where the GPS becomes potentially quite dangerous. Unless a GPS receiver is operating on the same datum as that underpinning the chart being used for navigation, the GPS fix may result in considerable navigational errors. If the GPS cannot be set to match the chart datum, or the lines of latitude and longitude on the chart cannot be shifted to match the GPS datum, the GPS must be treated as an unreliable navigational tool. (It is also important to remember that GPS is not infallible: the U.S. Department of Defense guarantees its level of accuracy only 95 percent of the time; the other 5 percent, it can be all over the place. We have occasionally gotten fixes with errors of more than a mile. Recent testing has also shown that the GPS signal can be relatively easily "jammed," and in fact you can buy jammers over the Internet for as little as $20, resulting in position errors of several miles. These are some of the reasons European countries have developed the eLoran system as a back-up for, and cross-check of, GPS, and

are developing their own GPS system, known as Galileo.)

Even when a GPS can be set to a chart datum other than WGS 84, there may be problems. In this case, the GPS is using a mathematical algorithm to convert one datum to the other. The International Hydrographic Organization (IHO) has a publication that outlines algorithms for making these conversions (IHO S-60). Unfortunately, these generalized, mathematically derived datum shifts sometimes introduce a new layer of errors into the navigational process. The British Admiralty, for example, found that when it used these algorithms with its charts of Croatia and the North African coast to add notes on the datum shift from the Hermanskogel and European datums (used to compile the charts) to WGS 84, the results were, in the words of one staffer, "not accurate enough for detailed navigation." Worldwide, the British Admiralty believes that there is not sufficient geodetic data to convert one third of its existing charts to WGS 84, which means that *when a GPS is set to a chart datum other than WGS 84, the resulting fixes frequently will be in error to a greater or lesser extent.* (Note that this has not stopped several commercial producers of electronic charts from making this conversion using the IHO algorithms. The British Admiralty will not convert a chart until it has enough

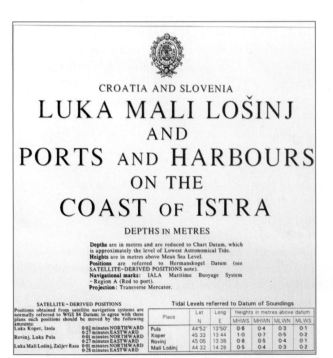

A recent chart of Croatia still based on the old Hermanskogel Datum (see the small print in the notes).

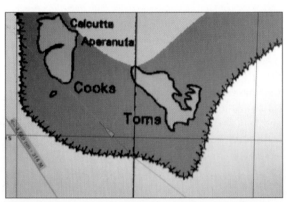

The GPS position, based on WGS 84, shows this boat sailing across a reef in the Cook Islands when the boat is actually SW of the reef.

CHART 1471—POSITIONS
Positions on this chart differ by varying amounts from those on adjoining chart 1471. Accordingly, positions should be transferred by bearing and distance and not by latitude and longitude.

A note on the Croatian chart indicating that GPS is an unreliable navigational tool.

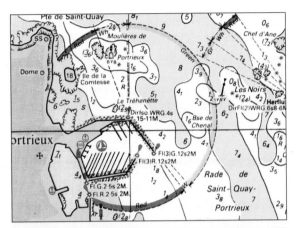

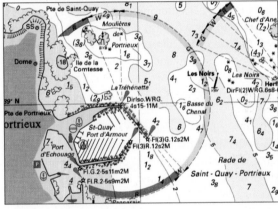

Old and inaccurate survey data can put a boat on a reef (see pages 24 and 51–52 for the loss of the Cork Clipper *in 2010).*

(Right) Two editions of the same chart. The horizontal datum has been changed from the European Datum (ED 1950) to WGS 84. Note how the latitude and longitude lines near the harbor mouth have shifted. If a GPS is set to the wrong datum and relied upon for navigation, the boat will hit the harbor wall! Note that this is a privately produced chart that uses a different color convention for water depths than government charts (see chapter 5). It covers an area in IALA Region A (see chapter 8), so the buoyage and associated symbology will not be familiar to U.S. readers.

locally determined information to justify the algorithm.)*

All North American maps and charts have been converted to a datum known as North American Datum of 1983 (NAD 83), which is consistent with WGS 84. These maps and charts are thus fully in sync with a GPS operating on the WGS 84 datum. Older charts may still be on NAD 27. Other cartographic and hydrographic offices have mostly completed the process of converting their maps and charts to WGS 84 where they have the necessary information to calculate the datum shifts. However, there are still many charts of outlying areas of the world that were developed around a locally determined astronomical point and datum and which are not related to any ellipsoid or major datum. Accurate conversion of these charts to WGS 84 cannot be done mathematically; a new

survey is required, which is expensive and, in many cases, unlikely to happen soon, given the conservative budgets of most hydrographic offices.

Therefore, for a considerable period of time, it is going to be essential for navigators to check the datum of every chart used, especially in the "third" world, and, when using a GPS, to ensure that it is operating on the chart datum. Remember that if the datum is not WGS 84–based, the GPS software may introduce an unknown degree of error in the datum-conversion process. Even if the chart is based on WGS 84, the GPS must be checked to ensure that it is also on WGS 84. It is only a matter of time before someone playing with the buttons on a GPS accidentally sets it to some obscure datum with a considerable offset, resulting in the boat running aground. Finally, even if the chart and GPS are on the

---

* *Because of these potential datum shift errors, a better practice with paper charts is to keep the GPS set to WGS 84 and apply the shift values quoted on the face of the chart (these will be printed somewhere under the title, and will be more accurate than the generalized datum shift algorithm in the GPS; if a shift is quoted, it can be used with confidence for that particular chart at the scale of that chart). Care needs to be taken to apply the shift the right way round. As far as I know, all electronic charts are based on WGS 84. However, many have been developed using the IHO algorithms; some incorporate quite substantial errors. I recently found one for a low-end chart-plotter that was almost ½ mile out with respect to WGS 84.*

same datum, there is no guarantee the charted features are in the right place, especially if the data is from older surveys in areas that could not be tied into a recognized datum.

In 2010 the *Cork Clipper*, a boat participating in an around-the-world race, ran aground on a remote Indonesian reef. The boat was a total loss. At the time of the accident the navigator was using a WGS 84–based electronic chart with the boat's GPS set to WGS 84. The plotted position showed the boat to be 0.6 mile from the reef but it still hit. A subsequent investigation found that the reef's charted position was based on a survey from the 1800s that placed it in the wrong place (for more on the loss of the *Cork Clipper*, see pages 51–52). Losing a boat is a painful way to learn about ellipsoids, chart datums, chart accuracy, and the limitations of satellite navigation.

Addendum: Map and Chart Projections

To transform survey data into a chart, the fundamental problem is how to accurately display (project) a spherical surface (the surface of the world) onto a flat piece of paper or computer or other screen. In practice, it cannot be done. To preserve one value (e.g., the correct relationship of length to breadth at any given point or the accurate depiction of angles), another must be sacrificed (in this case, consistent measurement of distance).

Chart Construction: Mercator Projections

Most coastal and inshore charts in other than high latitudes use a projection known as the *Mercator projection* or a modification of this, known as *transverse Mercator*. It is based on the idea of wrapping a cylinder around a globe, projecting the image of the globe onto the inner wall of the cylinder, and then cutting the cylinder up one side and laying the image out flat. (To be strictly accurate, a Mercator chart is obtained through mathematical formulas, and as such is a representation rather than a projection.) The net result is that instead of converging at the north and south poles, lines of longitude—those that run north and south between the poles, also known as *meridians*—become equally spaced (north to south) parallel lines. There is no convergence at the poles: the circumference of the world at the poles—which, in reality, is zero—becomes the same as that at the equator.

In real life, the farther north or south you go from the equator, the closer together are the lines of longitude as they move toward convergence at the

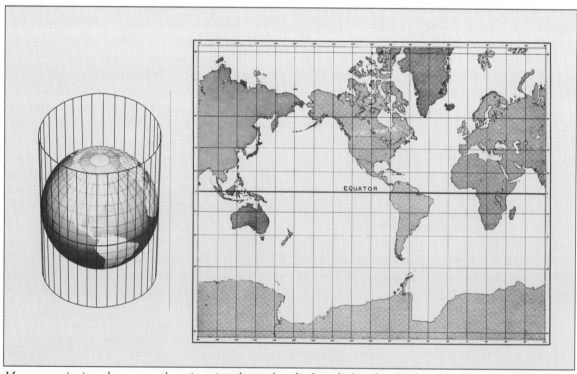

Mercator projection: the map, or chart, is projected onto the cylinder, which is then slit down one side and opened out. If the cylinder is centered on the equator, the farther the distance from the equator, the greater the distortion.

GPS Height Displays

GPS provides a three-dimensional position—that is, a vertical readout as well as the two-dimensional latitude and longitude readout. However, this vertical figure, particularly on cheaper and older GPS units, is often considerably in "error." Navigators are especially likely to notice this because a boat at sea is, by definition, at sea level (or, at least, fairly close to it), whereas the GPS may be giving the height of the vessel as plus 50 meters (160 ft.) or minus 100 meters (330 ft.), or whatever. Given the supposed incredible accuracy of a GPS, it is not unreasonable to wonder how the vertical readout can be so far off.

To understand this issue, we must distinguish among the three different surfaces referred to in this chapter: the ellipsoid, which is the reference point for all GPS fixes; the geoid, which is the sea-level surface of the world; and the topographical surface, which—when ashore—is almost always above that of the geoid (and is expressed in terms of feet or meters above sea level). The GPS provides height relative to the ellipsoid (referred to as *ellipsoidal height*); what we usually want to know is height relative to the geoid. However, because the geoid un-

dulates in a mathematically unpredictable fashion, there is no mathematical relationship between the ellipsoid and the geoid. In other words, the GPS cannot simply be programmed with an algorithm to convert heights relative to the ellipsoid into heights relative to the geoid. Global differences between the geoid and the WGS 84 ellipsoid range from as much as +78 meters (+257 ft.) in the region of Papua New Guinea to −103 meters (−340 ft.) in the Indian Ocean off India and Sri Lanka.

Some GPSs simply display height relative to the ellipsoid and leave it at that, which does not provide useful information for most of us. Other units, however, incorporate one of a series of computerized models of the geoid that have been developed by the National Geodetic Survey and the Defense Mapping Agency (DMA). With such a model, for any given position in the world, the GPS can apply the offset between the ellipsoid and the geoid as a correction to the measured height, and produce a vertical readout referenced to the geoid. Clearly, the accuracy of the resulting readout is directly related to the degree of sophistication and accuracy of the model (continues next page)

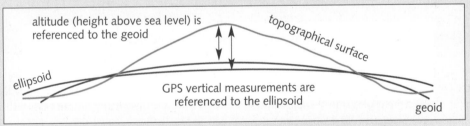

How the GPS three-dimensional height position is determined.

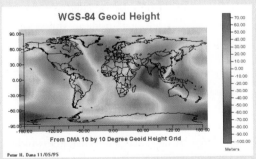

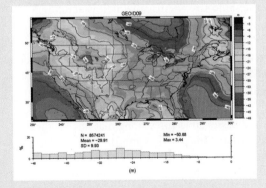

Chart of the global differences in ellipsoidal heights (WGS 84) and the geoid.

GPS Height Displays, *continued*

being used. More sophisticated models require more GPS memory. In general, the older and cheaper a GPS, the less adequate is the model of the geoid and the poorer is the fit between displayed altitudes and actual topographic altitude (discrepancies of 10–20 m/35–70 ft. are common).

In the United States, these geoid models can be downloaded from www.ngs.noaa.gov/geoid. The most recent and accurate (as of 2011) is Geoid09.

poles. This means that the distance on the ground covered by a degree of longitude steadily diminishes until it is reduced to zero at the poles. With a Mercator projection, however, the distance between the lines of longitude remains constant—in other words, the farther the distance from the equator, the greater the distortion on the chart.

Something similar is happening with lines of latitude (also known as *parallels*). In real life, all are equally spaced, with the result that the distance on the ground covered by a degree of latitude is the same at any point on the surface of the earth—with minor exceptions, because the earth is not perfectly spherical. With a Mercator projection, however, the farther north or south the distance is from the equator, the farther apart are the lines of latitude. At any given point on a Mercator projection, the distortion in the distance between the lines of latitude is equal to the distortion in the distance between the lines of longitude. Therefore, the chart preserves the correct relationship of length to breadth and the correct angular relationship between lines of latitude and longitude. However, it does so at the expense of losing any consistent measurement of distance—the farther from the equator, the greater is the distortion of distance relative to the equator. On a map of the world, using the equator as the midpoint, Greenland comes out the same size as Africa, which is actually fourteen times bigger.

The major advantage of a Mercator projection for sailors is that the lines of latitude and longitude intersect at right angles, making a convenient rectangular grid. Therefore, when drawn on the chart, a course that follows a constant bearing forms a straight line and passes all features along that line just as they are charted. This greatly simplifies route planning and tracking.

If a chart covers a relatively small area (confusingly known as a *large-scale chart*), the distortion of distance with a Mercator projection will be minimal (it is less than 2 percent on large-scale charts (1:80,000 and larger); however, where large areas are covered (*a small-scale chart*), it becomes significant. At a continental or hemispheric scale (e.g., a chart of the entire North Atlantic), the distortion is substantial.

Given that a degree of latitude covers more or less the same distance anywhere on the surface of the earth, latitude scales (those shown up the sides of a chart) are always used for measuring distances on small-scale Mercator charts. However, given that the Mercator projection causes the latitude scale to change with changes in latitude, *the part of the latitude scale alongside (i.e., east or west of) the points being measured is always used when measuring the distance between two points on a chart*. As noted, on large-scale charts (1:80,000 and higher) the scale distortion is minimal. These charts generally have a scale bar added at some point. This can be used for measuring distances anywhere on the chart (as can the latitude scale at any point).

Note that one minute of latitude is equal to 1 nautical mile (by definition), and 1 nautical mile is equal to approximately 2,000 yards. For those using imperial units, this greatly simplifies the arithmetic involved in any distance calculations. For example, one-tenth of 1 nautical mile (a *cable*) is 200 yards; one-hundredth (two decimal places) is 20 yards; and one-thousandth (three decimal places, commonly displayed on GPSs, although none are this accurate without significant corrections) is 2 yards.

Historically, minutes of latitude have always been divided into 60 seconds of latitude (i.e., not tenths), but since the advent of electronic navigation, it has become customary to use decimal minutes on electronic charts, small-scale paper charts, and many larger-scale charts. However, many older charts and some large-scale charts still have latitude scales subdivided into seconds (not tenths). When using electronic equipment to manually plot positions on paper charts, it is essential to ensure that the naviga-

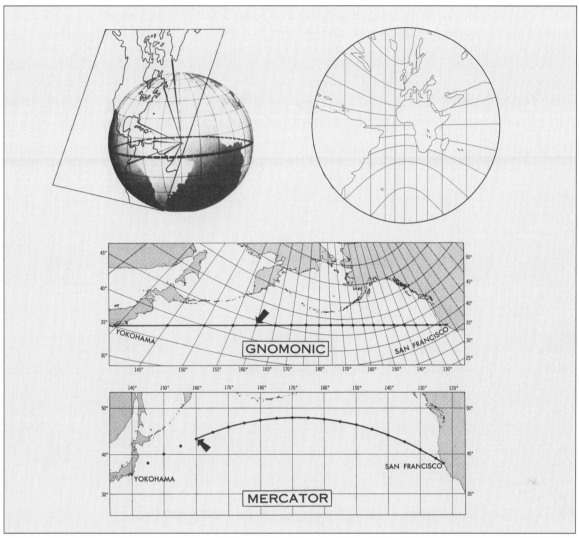

Gnomonic projection: the map, or chart, is projected onto a flat surface tangent to the surface of the globe.

tional electronics are programmed to the same units as are used on the chart.

Chart Construction: Gnomonic Projections

Coastal sailors are unlikely to see anything other than Mercator or transverse Mercator charts. However, these are not necessarily the best for ocean passages, not just because of scale distortions, but also because it is difficult to plot the shortest distance between two points. At first sight this seems a little absurd—after all, everybody knows the shortest distance between two points is a straight line. However, this is often not the case with a Mercator projection.

Because latitude and longitude lines form a grid on a Mercator chart with the lines intersecting one another at right angles, a straight line drawn on a Mer-

cator chart crosses all lines of longitude and latitude at a constant angle. However, if we think of a globe and connect a couple of points (e.g., Yokohama and San Francisco) by stretching a piece of string between them, the line formed by the string (the shortest distance between the two points) actually crosses the lines of latitude and longitude at changing angles, forming part of a *great circle*, which has its center at the center of the earth. If we record the points at which these lines are crossed and then plot those positions on the Mercator chart, a curved line is the result.

Therefore, for transoceanic planning purposes, a different type of chart is used. It employs something known as a *gnomonic projection*, which results in lines of longitude appearing as straight lines and lines of latitude appearing as curved lines. The benefit of this projection is that the shortest distance between two points is always a straight line. For navigational purposes, having drawn this line, the points at which the lines of latitude and longitude are crossed are transferred to a Mercator chart and then connected to determine a course to be steered, which gradually changes during the passage.

This changing course—the shortest distance between two points—is known as a *great-circle route*. The distance saved over the course described by drawing a straight line on a Mercator chart—known as a *rhumb-line course*—is insignificant on short passages but may be quite significant on longer passages, particularly east-west passages in higher latitudes; on north-south passages, the rhumb-line and great-circle routes are identical. However, the farther a course diverges from due north or due south and the longer the passage, the greater is the difference between the rhumb line and the great circle—and, therefore, the greater the benefit in using a gnomonic projection to calculate the great-circle route.

Horizontal Chart Accuracy

HOW ACCURATE IS THE MODERN CHART? This question must be a matter of fundamental concern for both paper and electronic chart users, since with GPS—especially differentially corrected GPS (DGPS) —we can unquestionably fix our boat positions with greater precision than was used to survey most of the details shown on our charts. This has been the case ever since the U.S. government turned off "selective availability" in 2000—the intentional degradation of the civilian GPS signal, with frequent 30-meter errors. What this means is that although we may have our GPS set to the correct chart datum (see chapter 1) and the position of our boat may be accurately plotted (either manually or electronically), the surrounding coastline and rocks may not be; it might look as if we are in clear water when we are about to hit the bricks! Before we are tempted to navigate narrow channels or sail close to any hazards, we need to know just how far out of position these charted bricks may be.

Unfortunately, this is surprisingly difficult to quantify because many variables are at work. Let's look at the key ones.

Survey Accuracy

No chart can be more accurate than the positioning accuracy of the surveys on which it is based. There is a significant amount of survey data still in use that was developed in the nineteenth and even the eighteenth centuries (e.g., parts of the Pacific Ocean and parts of the Caribbean). When these data were collected, there were no recognized standards for survey accuracy; therefore, the dependability of the survey results is largely a function of the skill and dedication of the surveying team. Both the horizontal accuracy (the position of one feature relative to another and the accuracy with which depth-soundings are placed on a chart) and the vertical accuracy (the depth-soundings themselves) are questionable—not to mention the changes that have taken place since these surveys were conducted: we came across one reef in the Bay Islands of Honduras that has grown vertically by 3.6 meters (12 feet) since it was last surveyed in the 1840s. (Coral can grow 5 m/16 ft. in a century.)

In the nineteenth century, various major hydrographic offices developed surveying standards that were then adopted by other hydrographic offices. The standards reflected both the practical limits of accuracy that could be achieved with the available surveying and depth-sounding equipment, and the fact

How safe is it to use electronic charts and navigation to cut things close? Our own boat, Nada, *hard aground on a rock ledge off the coast of Maine when we were trying to pick our way through a rock-strewn passage. It was a long wait for the tide to come back in!*

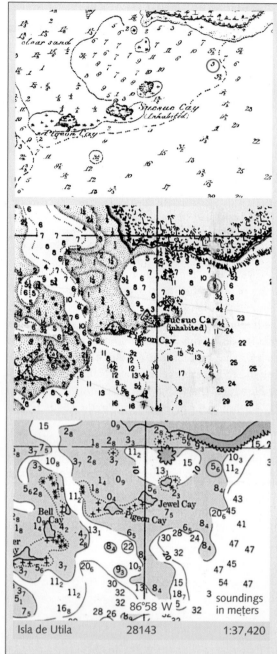

The same waters as shown on the original (1835) survey, a 1985 chart, and a 1996 chart. Note that although the later chart has been corrected in accordance with WGS 84 (through aerial photography), no new survey work has been done since 1835! All that has been changed is that fewer soundings are displayed, and they have been converted from fathoms and feet to meters. The sounding circled in red, which was originally charted at 3 fathoms (difficult to see) and is now shown as 5.6 meters is, in fact, an isolated coral head that now has less than 2 meters (6 ft.) over it because of coral growth over the past 175+ years.

The chart titles from the 1835 survey, the 1985 chart, and the 1996 chart. You have to read the small print to realize that there are no new soundings since 1835.

that it was not possible to navigate with pinpoint precision. Typical until recently (mid-1990s) was NOAA's general requirement that positioning accuracy for *coastal surveys* be within 1.5 mm at the scale at which the survey was being plotted. For example, if the survey scale was 1:20,000, the accuracy requirement was $1.5 \times 20,000 = 30,000$ mm = 30 meters (approximately 33 yd.). Prior to the satellite age, *the same level of accuracy could not be sustained offshore* because of the difficulty in tying into the coastal triangulation grid (see chapter 1). The charts compiled from a survey are generally made at half survey scale (e.g., a survey done at 1:20,000 is used to make a chart at 1:40,000), in which case the theoretical surveying error at chart scale becomes 0.75 mm times the scale of the chart (0.75 × 40,000 = 30,000 mm which is still 30 m).

In practice, errors may be significantly higher. Captain Nick Perugini, the former head of NOAA's Marine Chart Division, noted in the March 2001 issue of *Sea Technology* that "when NOAA survey crews and contractors obtain DGPS positions on prominent shoreline features and compare these positions to the chart, biases may be found that are on the order of 2 millimeters at the scale of the chart." This is for shoreside features. Larger biases can be expected offshore. In a letter written to me in 1996, the British Admiralty stated that most of its modern surveys have a positional accuracy of 5 to 20 meters, those done in the years after World War II are generally from 20 to 50 meters, and surveys from the early part of the twentieth century (pre–World War II) are from 50 to 500 meters to the "unknown."

The advent of electronic navigation, especially GPS, made all pre-1990s surveying standards obsolete. Hydrographic offices scrambled to catch up with this new technology, which led to a set of internationally recognized surveying standards that, in 1998, were adopted by the worldwide community of hydrographers under the auspices of the IHO. The standards were set out in *IHO Standards for Hydrographic Surveys* (IHO Special Publication No. 44, known as SP-44; this is now known as S-44, and is available online at www.iho-ohi.net).

S-44 sets minimum standards for the following four different categories of surveys:

1. **SPECIAL-ORDER SURVEYS**, which are associated with harbors and channels that have minimum under-keel clearances for the shipping that will be using the area, and in which the highest degree of accuracy is, therefore, paramount. In general, horizontal positioning accuracy must be within 2 meters (6.6 ft.) and depths in shallow water to within 0.25 meter (approximately 10 in.), with the allowable depth error increasing marginally with increased depth.

2. **FIRST-ORDER SURVEYS**, for less critical harbors, channels, and coastal areas with depths to 100

meters (330 ft.), which have not been surveyed to Special-Order standards. In general, horizontal-positioning accuracy must be within 5 meters (5.5 yd.), plus 5 percent of the water depth. In other words, in 6 meters (20 ft.) of water depth, positioning accuracy must be ±5.3 meters (5.8 yd.). Depths must be to within 0.5 meter (20 in.) in shallow water, with the allowable error increasing slowly with increased depth.

3. **SECOND-ORDER SURVEYS**, for areas with depths to 200 meters (660 ft.) that have not been surveyed to Special-Order or First-Order standards. In general, the allowable horizontal error is 20 meters (22 yd.) plus 5 percent of the water depth; the allowable sounding error is 1.0 meter (3.3 ft.) in shallow water, increasing with depth.

4. **THIRD-ORDER SURVEYS**, for offshore areas not covered by other surveys. In general, the allowable horizontal error is 150 meters (164 yd.) plus 5 percent of the water depth; the allowable sounding error is the same as for Second-Order surveys.

There are also minimum standards for surveying fixed and floating aids to navigation, and for how much of the bottom should be covered at what level of accuracy. On Special-Order surveys, the entire bottom must be surveyed with equipment that is capable of detecting any feature greater than 1 cubic meter in volume (not all such features are detected—there is a subtle difference between capability and actuality). For First-, Second-, and Third-Order surveys, surveyors run survey lines at ever-wider intervals. The lines are typically run so that, when plotted, they are 5 millimeters apart. For example, if the survey is conducted at 1:20,000, the survey lines will be 5 × 20,000 = 100,000 mm = 100 meters (110 yd.) apart. At a survey scale of 1:40,000, the lines will be 200 meters (220 yd.) apart. (Standard British Admiralty survey practice requires the officer in charge of the survey—the captain of a Royal Navy Survey ship—to examine the soundings along these lines and order the ship to run additional interlines between the standard lines, or even inter-interlines between these, to ensure all dangers have been found.)

In the past, much of the seabed between the lines remained unsurveyed. The British Admiralty notes: "Without sidescan sonar, on a scale of 1:75,000, a shoal one cable wide (200 yd.) rising close to the surface might not be found if it happened

Summary of Minimum Standards for Hydrographic Surveys

Order	Special	First	Second	Third
examples of typical areas	harbors, berthing areas, and associated critical channels with minimum underkeel clearances	harbors, harbor approach channels, recommended tracks, and some coastal areas with depths to 100 m	areas not described in Special Order and First Order, or areas up to 200 m in depth	offshore areas not described in Special Order, First Order, and Second Order
general horizontal accuracy (95% confidence level)	2 m	5 m + 5% of depth	20 m + 5% of depth	150 m + 5% of depth
accuracy of fixed aids to navigation and features significant to navigation	2 m	2 m	5 m	5 m
accuracy of natural coastline	10 m	20 m	20 m	20 m
accuracy of mean position of floating aids to navigation	10 m	10 m	20 m	20 m
accuracy of topographical features	10 m	20 m	20 m	20 m
depth accuracy for reduced depths (shallow water, 95% confidence level)*	A = 0.25 m B = 0.0075	A = 0.5 m B = 0.013	A = 1.0 m B = 0.023	same as Second Order
bottom features detected	features greater than 1 cubic meter	features greater than 2 cubic meters in depths to 40 m; 10% of depth beyond 40 m	same as First Order	not applicable
maximum spacing between survey lines	not applicable as 100% search compulsory	3 × average depth or 25 m, whichever is greater	3–4 × average depth or 200 m, whichever is greater	4 × average depth

*To calculate the error limits for depth accuracy, the values of A and B listed in the table have to be entered into the formula

$$\pm \sqrt{A^2 + (B \times D)^2},$$ where A = constant, B = depth-dependent error, D = depth

Adapted from tables in IHO Standards for Hydrographic Surveys, S-44.

to be between lines of soundings. In the same way, on a scale of 1:12,500, *rocks as large as supertankers*, if lying parallel with and between the lines of soundings, might exist undetected if they rose abruptly from an otherwise even bottom" (*Mariner's Handbook*, p. 25, 1999 ed.; emphasis added). Today, with the widespread use of sidescan sonar (SOund NAvigation And Ranging, see page 38), not much gets missed (since the 1970s, 100 percent bottom surveys have been the norm rather than the exception).

During the course of a survey, when a chart is compiled from survey data, the surveyor interpolates

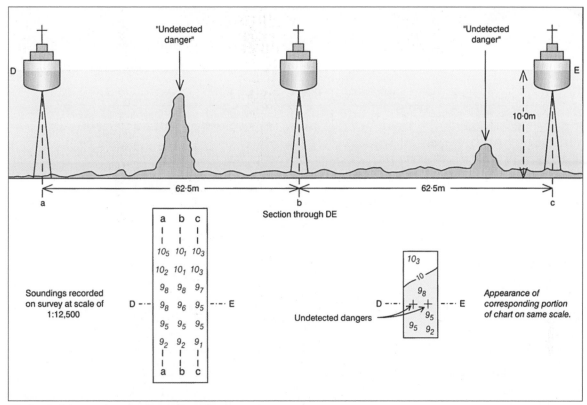

Undetected dangers between lines of soundings.

between survey lines to develop isobaths (lines of equal depth, also known as depth contours and depth curves). This may be of some significance for mariners; for example, on a circumnavigation of Cuba, we found an area with several long, shallow spits that ran out from the coastline between the survey lines (a recent survey). These spits were not picked up on the survey, due to its scale, and so were not shown on the chart.

Unlike previous standards, the S-44 standards are absolute in the sense that once a particular survey category has been chosen, the standards are unrelated to the scale at which the survey is conducted and plotted (e.g., horizontal positioning with a Special-Order survey must be within 2 m [2.2 yd.], regardless of the survey scale and how the data is recorded).

NOAA has adopted the First-Order standards for all its surveys, both inshore and offshore (see *NOAA Hydrographic Surveys Specifications and Deliverables*, published in June 2000, which can be downloaded from the NOAA website at www.nauticalcharts. noaa.gov). An "off-the-shelf" DGPS may still position a vessel with a higher degree of precision than that of these survey standards!

The National Imagery and Mapping Agency (NIMA, now known as the National Geospatial Intelligence Agency, NGA) has this to say about its levels of accuracy (which are likely to remain for many years): "The NIMA-specified accuracy for harbor, approach, and coastal charts is that features plotted on a chart will be within 1 mm (at chart scale) with respect to the preferred datum, at a 90 percent confidence level. For a large-scale chart of 1:15,000 scale, a 1 mm

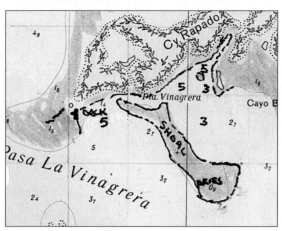

Hand-corrected chart to take account of a long, narrow shoal not on the chart.

Accuracy of Chart Information in Popular Cruising Destinations

Country	% adequately surveyed		% requiring resurvey		% never systematically surveyed	
	Depth <200m	Depth >200m	Depth <200m	Depth >200m	Depth <200m	Depth >200m
UK	49	0	22	0	29	100
Spain	96	40	4	10	0	50
Monaco (home of the IHO)	100	100	0	0	0	0
Croatia	30	0	39	13	22	87
Greece	35	10	55	60	10	30
Malta	1	0	99	100	0	0
Canada	30	15	10	10	30	25
USA	60	1	35	19	5	85
Bahamas	1	0	99	0	0	100
US Virgin Islands	0	0	10	5	90	95
UK Virgin Islands	60	70	40	0	0	30
Belize	15	0	85	0	0	100
Mexico	13	7	87	93	0	0
Australia	35	10	20	5	45	85
French Polynesia	17	11	38	2	45	87
Cook Islands	1	0	9	0	90	100
Fiji	5	15	70	0	25	85
Maldives	0	0	3	1	97	99

error equates to ±15 meters (16.2 yd.), which is the same order of magnitude as the absolute GPS error. For a smaller-scale chart of 1:80,000 scale, the chart error is 80 meters (86.4 yd.), which will become the limiting factor in position-plotting accuracy. The reverse can be true for large-scale (small-area) charts, such as a harbor plan inset at 1:5,000 scale. In this case, the navigator's plotting accuracy is limited by the absolute accuracy of GPS, rather than the chart; however, features on this chart should be accurate to ±5 meters."

Of course, adopting these standards and getting survey data that meets them, which requires new surveys to be conducted (the old data often cannot be "tweaked"), are two completely different assignments.

In recent years, most hydrographic offices have been under budgetary constraints at a time when there has been significant pressure to convert the existing paper charts to electronic versions. The result has been, in many cases, a reallocation of resources to the digitization program and a cutback in surveying, although in the United States a program of hydrographic subcontracting has led to an increase in surveying (since 1993, 35,000 square miles out of over 500,000 square miles have been surveyed with modern techniques; as of 2011, the area on the "critical" list for re-survey totaled 22,000 square miles with estimates that it will take up to 40 years to resurvey all the waters). One way or another, it will be many years before even the inshore areas of the world are resurveyed to contemporary standards; some areas may never get surveyed. The first to be covered will be priority areas for commercial shipping, especially given the ever-increasing draft of ships and the reduced "under-keel" clearances in many ports and shipping lanes; these areas are often not of much interest to recreational boaters (the areas of primary interest to recreational boaters will be quite low on the priority list).

Another IHO publication, *Status of Hydrographic Surveys Worldwide* (formerly IHO S-55; now C-55, and also available online at www.iho-ohi.net), takes a broad look at the quality of worldwide hydrographic survey data from the perspective of contemporary accuracy requirements. It is a sobering document that shows we have a long way to go before this data is considered adequate. As of 2011, a somewhat random sampling (see table) of a number of favorite cruising destinations around the world includes sometimes surprising, and often shocking, accuracy information.

Data Storage, Retrieval, and Output

Until the development of electronic databases, the standard method of preserving survey data was in a written format; as the survey progressed, the findings were plotted onto a chart of the area. Various corrections were made to the data (e.g., correcting soundings for tide changes) until a final version of the plot was derived. This was known as a *smooth sheet*, which was submitted to the hydrographic office for approval, after which it became the official record of the survey and represented its limit of accuracy.

This raises some interesting issues. The finest

line that can be drawn is approximately 0.1 mm wide, but such a thin line is difficult to see; therefore, it is not recommended—or even forbidden—for drawing features such as coastlines and other critical objects. As a result, various hydrographic offices (including the British Admiralty and the Italians) have adopted 0.2 mm as the finest line to be used on a chart. (NOAA uses 0.1 mm lines for depth curves and shoreside contour lines; 0.15 mm lines for man-made shoreline; and heavier line weights for natural shoreline and other features.)

Let's say a hydrographer decides to plot the smooth sheet at a scale of 1:20,000 (i.e., 1 mm or 1 in. on the smooth sheet represents 20,000 mm or in. on the ground). At 1:20,000, a line that is 0.2 mm wide represents $20,000 \times 0.2 = 4,000$ mm on the ground, which is 4 meters (4.4 yd.). Even if the survey is accurate to within centimeters, this plotting accuracy has now become the limiting condition in the accuracy of the final product. If the smooth sheet is plotted at 1:50,000, the plotting accuracy is ± 10 meters (11 yd.). If the pencil used to plot the data isn't sharp and draws a line 0.5 mm wide, the plotting accuracy at 1:50,000 changes to 25 meters (27 yd.)! NOAA's current plotting standards (and those of the NGA and other hydrographic offices and some private chart-makers) require a positional accuracy of 1 mm or better at chart scale.

In the past, paper was used for smooth sheets. Paper is notorious for being somewhat unstable: in a humid environment, it absorbs moisture and stretches, although not uniformly; in a dry environment, it dries out and shrinks, again not uniformly. These changes have the potential to add more errors to the stored data. To combat this, hydrographic offices often used cloth-backed paper, which is dimensionally more stable. Eventually, paper was replaced

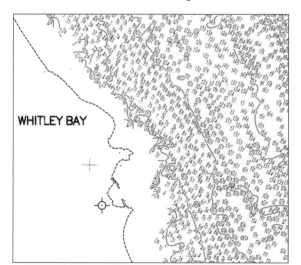

An example of a cloth-backed smooth sheet.

A modern paper-chart compiler at work: the work is all done electronically.

The charted position of buoys should always be considered approximate as ice and other natural forces can move them off station.

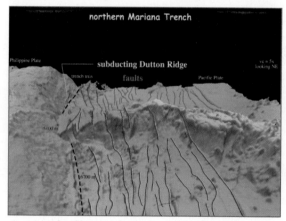

An example of bottom data collected from the deepest waters in the world and processed using the latest surveying and data-processing techniques.

by plastic, notably Mylar (beginning in the 1960s), which is much more dimensionally stable.

To compile a chart for sale to the public, a cartographer would use (*and often still does*) the smooth sheets, along with shoreside surveys of landmasses (usually the responsibility of another government department) and other sources of information (the information on a NOAA chart comes from as many as sixty different sources). It's a fascinating process to watch. First, the hydrographic office must determine the area to be covered by the chart and the physical size of the chart, which determines its scale. Next, the cartographer collects the most up-to-date and largest scale (most detailed) maps and smooth sheets available, reduces them to the same scale as the chart, and produces them on sheets of Mylar. These are then raster-scanned (described later in this chapter) if the

chart is to be compiled electronically (as most now are). The process of composition takes place as the cartographer uses his or her accumulated experience—refined through the collective experience and traditions of the hydrographic office and regulated by its standards—to create the chart.

Quite often, the most recent and accurate surveys of an area do not have adequate detail but the older surveys do, especially for soundings in shallow water, which used to be of interest to commercial and navy ships when their draft was relatively shallow. Therefore, those areas were often thoroughly surveyed in the past, but are no longer of interest and have low priority on the resurvey list. Nevertheless, they are clearly of great interest to recreational boaters. The cartographer may well use the recent surveys to establish the boundaries of landmasses and other details, extracting additional data from older surveys to fill in missing information (see chapter 3 for more details on sounding selection).

Due to surveying errors, the older surveys may not line up (register) properly with the new surveys. I have watched a British Admiralty cartographer place the Mylar with an old survey of the Virgin Islands beneath the one containing the chart under development, slide the top Mylar around until a best fit is achieved, and add details from the old chart to the new one. (If the chart is being compiled electronically, the same methodology is used with the raster scans by manipulating the on-screen images.) For example, if soundings are being added to a bay, the top Mylar may be slid around until the headlands on the chart under development more or less match those on the old survey; moving to the next bay around the coastline, the cartographer repeats this exercise. Clearly, such methods introduce a degree of uncertainty in addition to the original (unknown) surveying errors.

The cartographer also has some discretion in the placement of labels and other details, which varies from one hydrographic office to another. If, for example, a sounding ends up overlapping an aid to navigation, a NOAA chart compiler may displace the sounding a little to make the chart easier to read. The NOAA website notes: "When attempting to show two or more significant features very close together on a chart, the chart-maker may displace one feature slightly for best presentation. For example, a sounding may be displaced slightly in order to show a buoy in its published position." Where the NOAA chartmaker may move the sounding, the British Admiralty compiler will, if necessary, move the buoy, on the basis that the position of floating aids is not fully reliable. Or, if a channel is so narrow that it is difficult to draw, the NOAA cartographer may widen it to improve clarity (e.g., in the event that a channel or channel buoys or markers plot at less than 0.5 mm in width, it is NOAA policy to plot them at 0.5 mm), whereas the British Admiralty compiler will never widen it, and will most likely simply close it up if it is too tight to draw clearly.* NOAA's *Nautical Chart Manual*—its internal instructions to its cartographers—notes that the "ultimate decision regarding depiction of the various features appearing on nautical charts must rest on the professional judgment of the cartographer" (pp. 1–12). After all the science, there is quite an art to creating charts, the best of which are works of art in their own right.

When the chart is finished, until recently it has always been output to a series of sheets of Mylar, one for each color that will be used in the printing process. These sheets are used to make negatives from which the printing plates are made. The printing itself uses a process known as *offset lithography*. Given that each color has to be printed from a different plate, if the plates are not perfectly lined up (registered), further inaccuracies will creep in. Once the chart is printed, the quality of paper used will affect its stability, just as with paper-based smooth sheets.

This long-established process is still used but is slowly being superseded by storage of survey data in electronic databases, which can be maintained electronically at any scale up to and including a theoretical 1:1 relationship with the surface of the earth. The level of accuracy with which the data has been surveyed can be preserved in the database without further errors being introduced. When it's time to use the data, it can be electronically scaled down to whatever scale is appropriate for the chart being created. This chart can either be used in an electronic format or output to paper, printing directly from the electronic file. In this way, many of the errors formerly introduced by data storage, retrieval, and printing processes are eliminated; however, the errors inherent in the original survey are, of course, still present. (The OceanGrafix "Print-on-Demand" charts in the USA, which now outsell traditional paper charts by 2:1 in spite of a 20% price premium, are a partial expression of this process in as much as the paper chart is printed directly from an electronic file. However, the electronic files are still mostly created from raster scans of the smooth sheets with the raster scans then processed using traditional cartographic techniques, introducing the potential to corrupt the accuracy of the source data as described above.)

WEND and the "Navigation Surface"

In the early days of electronic charting, before many charts had been made, and before a realization of how hard it can be to make them had sunk in, and while the "visionaries" held sway, the IHO developed the concept of a worldwide vector-based (see below) electronic database, known as the Worldwide Electronic Navigational Chart Database, or WEND. It was envisioned that all hydrographic offices would use the same processes to create electronic databases, and that all would do this for their own waters, with the WEND combining these databases into a unified database of the whole world, maintained at the level of accuracy of the survey data within it. Reality has severely diluted the vision. Apart from anything else, there has only been slow production of new survey data in electronic format, and a slow development of electronic charts from existing data. The northern Europeans were the first to try to create a regional database (a Regional Electronic Chart Coordinating Centre, or RENC) from their digitized chart data. They soon discovered that there were significant variations in electronic chart implementation at the various hydrographic offices, with numerous "data gaps" at the margins of national waters, inconsistent contour lines, different methodologies applied to charts at different scales, and so on. There were other issues related to money, copyright, and the encryption needed to protect copyright (NOAA, for example, releases all its data for general use without payment of royalties, and so is not concerned about encryption, whereas almost all other hydrographic offices and private label providers license their products and charge royalties, which requires encryption in order to prevent unlicensed use). In furtherance of the WEND concept, the IHO developed an encryption standard (S-63), but in practical terms the RENC approach

---

* *The British Admiralty works on the principle that the navigator must use a chart of sufficiently large scale to ensure safety. If a channel is very narrow at the scale of the chart, a larger-scale chart needs to be used. If a larger-scale chart is not available, the passage has probably not been surveyed at a sufficiently large scale to allow safe navigation. In such a situation it is important for the navigator to be aware that an inadequately surveyed channel is being explored, requiring appropriate caution.*

and WEND seem to be largely dead in the water. In the meantime, the British Admiralty has forged ahead with its own International Centre for Electronic Navigational Charts (IC-ENC), which is a worldwide source of electronic charts with cooperation from numerous other hydrographic offices, but which falls well short of the original WEND vision.

In 2000, NOAA helped to fund the Center for Coastal and Ocean Mapping (CCOM) at the University of New Hampshire in the United States. The CCOM has defined something it calls the "navigation surface," broadly corresponding to the WEND, which is an electronic image of the surface of the sea bottom based on all the available information and, as such, with new survey data, potentially accurate to the centimeter level. NOAA and the CCOM recognized that the combination of modern multibeam echo-sounder (MBES) and sidescan sonar (SSS) survey techniques are capable of greatly accelerating the creation of highly accurate bottom data to populate this "navigation surface." (MBES is used to measure depths while SSS is used to ensure that no bottom features are overlooked; the hydrographer ensures that the SSS data is integrated into the bottom plot.) However, the technology results in a near overwhelming mass of data causing traditional cartographic processing techniques to become a bottleneck in terms of integrating and using the data.

To overcome the bottleneck, the CCOM has developed a set of algorithms, the Combined Uncertainty and Bathymetric Estimator (CUBE), which provide an automated mechanism to process and store multibeam echo-sounder data at the level of accuracy at which it is collected. CUBE has been accepted by NOAA, various other hydrographic offices, and almost every hydrographic software developer, and similar software has been developed elsewhere. It reduces data processing times by a factor of 30 to 70, which will help to rapidly increase the amount of high-quality data in the navigation surface database. Various other algorithms assist in reducing this data to an appropriate level and out-

putting it for charts at different scales, which is a much more complicated process than it seems at first sight. For example, when using the data for chart-making, the mass of data in the database has to be reduced to a level at which it is legible for a given chart scale ("decluttering"), but in the process the key navigational information (such as least depths) appropriate for that scale needs to be retained, resulting in what is known as a "shoal-biased sounding set." This requires complex prioritization algorithms in the decluttering process.

Unfortunately, the efficiency of multibeam echo-sounder mapping decreases as water depths decrease (the shallower the water, the narrower the beam projected onto the bottom, and the closer the survey lines have to be run). NOAA and other hydrographic offices have been using laser-based airborne LIDAR (Light Detection and Ranging) technologies to define shorelines and chart shallow depths. (LIDAR emits two laser beams at different frequencies, one of which bounces off the surface of the water while the other penetrates to the bottom, and then measures the differences in the timing of the return beams to calculate depths.) However, there are significant issues with this technology which the CCOM is investigating and attempting to resolve. NOAA and CCOM, and other hydrographic offices, are also investigating another new technology, phase differencing bathymetric sonar (PDBS), which looks promising in terms of providing accurate data in shallow water more than twice as fast as multibeam echosounding.

One way or another, if the broad array of new surveying techniques is integrated with data processing software such as CUBE, and additional shoal-biased output software, the addition of new survey data to charting products can be speeded up, with a very high level of accuracy maintained at all chart scales. This should significantly accelerate the development of something that approximates the WEND concept. The U.S. policy of releasing its data for free over the Internet will make this highly accurate data accessible to a wide user base, at least in U.S. waters.* Having

---

*The U.S. model of giving charts away for free over the Internet (it is the only hydrographic office in the world to do this) now results in several million electronic charts being downloaded from NOAA's website every month. However, one of the ironic side effects in recent years has been to make up-to-date official charts of many parts of the world less accessible to the cruising community, particularly for U.S. sailors. There was a time when NIMA (now the NGA) had a worldwide suite of paper charts based on data from other hydrographic offices for non-U.S. waters. But because the U.S. does not copyright its data, many countries terminated their reciprocal agreements. About the same time, the IHO decreed that if a country produces an English-language chart of its own waters, other IHO members are not allowed to make or publish their own chart without permission, which NGA will not seek. As a result, in 2005 the NGA ceased production of its international charts. Today, the British Admiralty is the only official hydrographic office with a worldwide suite of charts, both paper and electronic, for sale to the general public, and these are expensive. However, the private sector has stepped in to fill the gap left by NIMA/NGA, producing excellent worldwide cartography from all available sources.

The author comparing raster and vector charts on a passage down the Intracoastal Waterway (ICW) on the U.S. east coast.

said this, as absurd as it seems it should be noted that as of 2011 NOAA, and most other hydrographic offices, *were still transferring digital data to smooth sheets and producing charts from these smooth sheets instead of creating charts directly from the digital data!*

Raster and Vector

Now for some "wrinkles" that apply specifically to electronic charts, the details of which the user need not remember *but the gist of which should always raise a cautionary flag when using these charts.*

Generally speaking, there are two types of electronic chart—raster and vector—although with ever-improving software, the lines between them have blurred to some extent and will blur considerably more in the near future (e.g., raster charts from NV Chart that have vector-based data running in the background—see below).

A typical *raster scan* is an electronic "photograph" of a paper chart or Mylar. The original is broken down into rows and columns of tiny squares (picture elements, or *pixels*), each of which is referenced by its row and column number (a bitmap). Each pixel is assigned a color that the computer stores, along with its row and column location. To re-create the image electronically, the computer simply re-creates all the colored blocks in the same relationship to one another as in the original. As such, the raster image

is an exact copy of the paper chart or Mylar from which it is scanned. In order to make it useful for electronic charting purposes, geographic references are added during the scanning process, making it possible to overlay such things as a boat's GPS position, and also to add later corrections by replacing blocks of the chart with new blocks. Note that because of the "photographic" nature of the image, other than zooming in and out, the individual features on the chart cannot be manipulated in any way.

A *vector plot* is quite different. To date, most have begun with a raster image derived from a paper chart or the Mylars for a paper chart on which a geo-referencing system is superimposed (this is likely to be a latitude and longitude grid based on the WGS 84 datum). All the features on the raster image are then traced (either by line-following software or by hand) and assigned a set of geographical coordinates, which are stored, along with a table that lists the attributes of that feature.* For example, when a depth contour is traced, the computer stores the coordinates for the point at which every change of direction occurs, and the attribute table records the depth and any other pertinent data. A buoy would have its precise location stored with the attribute table recording such things as its shape, color, number, and so on. (Much survey data collected in recent years is already stored in this format. Theoretically the vectorizing-from-raster process can be eliminated, but to date typically it has not been—see above.)

---

* For the purposes of this book, both here, and in what follows, I have provided an oversimplified picture of raster and vector charts. The British Admiralty, for example, in its current raster chart production starts from a combination of electronic databases, "hard copy" (smooth sheets, etc.) digitized on a vector basis, and raster scans to produce the image from which the final raster chart image is "burned." The raster images are already geo-referenced before they are used to produce vector charts.

The Limits of Accuracy

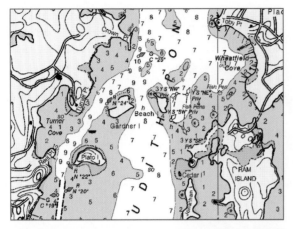

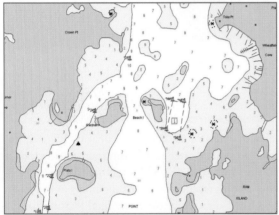

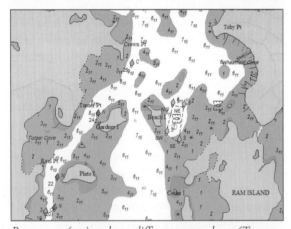

Raster scan (top) and two different vector charts (Transas and NIMA/NGA) of the same area. Note the differing symbologies on the vector charts.

In use, the navigation software reads this data to locate points on the chart. For depth contours and other lines, these points are connected with lines. For buoys and other precisely located features, an appropriate symbol is placed on the chart, together with associated information derived from the attribute table (e.g., buoy name and/or number).

Because the data, such as that for a buoy, is stored as a point, or a series of points, with an attached attribute file, unlike a raster file it can be recreated in different ways. For example, with a click of the mouse you can choose to use IHO or NOAA symbology and the display characteristics of aids to navigations will change accordingly. Similarly, for intertidal and other colored areas on a chart, the lines will be recreated by connecting a series of dots to create an enclosed area (known as a *polygon*) and then the navigation software can determine the color. You can often choose between different color schemes (e.g., British Admiralty, NOAA, and others), and have options for nighttime, twilight, and daytime colors and intensity. Depending on the way in which the data is stored in the vectorizing process, you may be able to choose the depth above or below which a specific color is used, customizing this for your draft (as opposed to it being fixed, as it is on all paper and raster charts). Depths can be displayed in fathoms, feet, or meters, and other units similarly adjusted. The data is stored in "layers" that can be turned on and off, enabling a chart to be displayed in different ways for different uses (for example, turning off labels to declutter the chart). The chart projection can be changed from Mercator to gnomonic or something else. And so on.

Given that display characteristics are governed by the display software, the same electronic vector-based chart data from one hydrographic office or supplier will appear a little differently (and sometimes quite differently!) on electronic charting systems from different manufacturers; however, if the software manufacturer does a good job, the chart will not look very different from a paper chart.

Unfortunately, vector charts derived from paper charts or raster scans potentially introduce new errors and inaccuracies over and above those found on the raster scans. There can be outright errors and omissions introduced by the necessary human operators who either do, or control, the vectorizing process (over the years, I have found quite a number of these errors). The process itself can introduce additional errors of as much as 0.5 mm at the scale of the chart (i.e., if the chart being vectorized is at a scale of 1:20,000, the vectorizing error may represent as much as $20,000 \times 0.5 = 10,000$ mm $= 10$ m). This is because of the somewhat "coarse" nature of the resolution of the raster images often being vectorized.

Let's say, for example, that the dot depicting the

location of a lighthouse is four to six pixels wide in the raster image. The vector operator can click on this dot at any point and still be within the limit of accuracy with respect to the original paper chart or Mylar from which the raster image was derived. But if the click is made at one edge of the dot, when the dot is re-created at four to six pixels on the vector chart, it could, in effect, be displaced by two to three pixels. Enlarging the raster image at the time of vectorizing minimizes the errors because the exact placement of original lines and features can be more closely replicated. For example, if the image is zoomed enough when tracing lines, it is possible to stay within the width of the displayed lines.

During the vectorizing process, the operator has to make numerous judgment calls. For example, soundings on a paper chart or Mylar, and the corresponding raster image, do not have a precise location. In fact, the spot that a sounding represents is assumed to be at the "center of gravity of the set of figures" printed on the chart (*Chart Specifications of the IHO*, Publication S-4). To add these soundings to a vector chart, the operator judges the center of gravity of the sounding on the raster image, and clicks on it to establish the precise sounding location for the vector chart. There is ample room for error (if you compare vector charts to the source paper chart, you will frequently see numerous soundings in a slightly different position), with the result depending on the skill and attention of the operator. There are also numerous small cartographic conventions on charts that convey important information (such as using italic or upright typeface for a sounding, or the size of the font, or even the width of the line with which the sounding is printed—see the second half of this book), which may get overlooked in the vectorizing process, especially if the person doing the vectorizing is not a trained cartographer (many are not). The quality-control process is of paramount importance with respect to vectorized charts.

These kinds of raster-to-vector issues do not occur if newer survey data collected and stored in a vector format is directly outputted to a vector chart. However, as noted above, for years we have had the ironic situation where new survey data that is collected and stored in a vector format has been used to create smooth sheets from which raster charts are produced (introducing cartographic errors in addition to the modifications the cartographer makes to the positioning of the data in order to improve the clarity of the chart), and then the raster images have been vec-

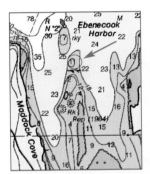
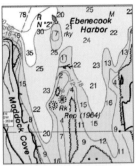
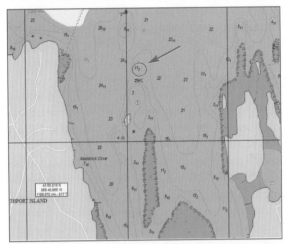
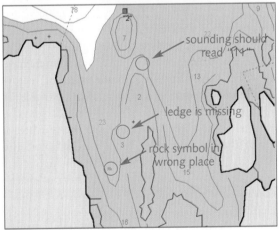

A paper chart (top left) and its raster scan (top right). The two are indistinguishable. Below are two vector charts of the same area. Note that on the middle chart the soundings are often in slightly different positions and may be different as a result of conversions to meters and back to feet. On the lower chart a number of important features are incorrect or missing.

torized once again to create vector-based data. *The positional integrity of the vector-based data from which the raster chart began is compromised and may be lost!* Various hydrographic offices have been struggling to reverse this framework in a manner that makes the vector chart the primary product, created directly from the vector data, with the raster chart a derivative of this, but at the time of writing (2011) this goal has not been achieved.

This anomalous situation has arisen because producing raster charts from the existing paper charts and Mylars is inherently a much faster and cheaper process than creating vector charts. So the major hydrographic offices focused first on creating a complete suite of raster charts for their waters and only secondarily produced vector-based charts. The long-term goal of the IHO and national hydrographic offices is to have all survey data and charts in the vector format, but this is still years away.

The vector charts that have been produced so far by official hydrographic offices concentrate on major ports and shipping lanes. As of 2011, NOAA had vector charts of all major U.S. ports and an increasing number of coastal charts connecting these, with a goal of having a complete suite of vector charts for U.S. waters by 2014, but, as noted above, these vector charts have largely been derived by digitizing raster charts, and there are numerous errors, omissions, and inconsistencies between them. Worldwide, as of 2011 the British Admiralty had 10,900 vector charts in its portfolio (many of them sourced from other hydrographic offices), covering 2,700 ports. A number of private-sector chart manufacturers have produced "unofficial" worldwide suites of vector-based charts from paper and raster charts. Notable are the charts from Transas, which emerged from the Russian hydrographic office in 1990 after the breakup of the Soviet Union. It had access to all the Russian charts and hydrographic data which it has expanded into its worldwide TX 97 suite of charts. C-Map also has a worldwide suite with its CM93/3 charts. Private label vector charts vary in quality. Many are extremely good, but all suffer from the accuracy degradation inherent in vectorizing from raster.

A German company, NV Charts, is producing an interesting raster/vector blend, or "hybrid." Data is collected and stored in a vector database, from which raster charts are produced (both paper and electronic), but with the database running in the background of the electronic raster charts and geo-referenced to the raster image. Clicking on a feature on the chart pulls up the information in the attribute file, just as it would with a vector chart. The goal is to combine the improved looks and readability of most raster charts with the "intelligence" of vector charts (see also the addendum, Raster versus Vector).

Much modern electronic charting software can handle both raster and vector, and will move more-or-less seamlessly between the two, often choosing vector-based charts when they are available and only using raster when they are not.

Resolution Issues

There are significant issues with both raster and vector charts created by the limitations of the display devices used in electronic charting systems. To understand these, let's look first at raster charts.

As we have seen, in order to make a raster chart, blocks of color on a paper chart have to be broken down into individual pixels (squares) of color that are subsequently displayed on a computer screen. The number of squares (pixels) into which the chart being copied is divided is expressed in terms of pixels per inch or dots per inch (dpi). In the hydrographic world, the British Admiralty scans at 1,016 dpi and NOAA at 762 dpi. Why these funny numbers? Partly, it is historical accident: NOAA's first drum scanner scanned at 762 dpi!

The resulting files are huge—many megabytes (mb) per chart—and would overwhelm many electronic navigation devices, resulting in extremely slow refresh rates and other problems. As a result, the source raster files are always output to the end user at a much lower resolution. In the case of NOAA, this is 254 dpi, and in the case of the British Admiralty, 127 dpi. If you convert 254 dpi to mm, you get 0.1 mm, which is the thinnest line NOAA permits, and if you convert 127 dpi to mm, you get 0.2 mm, which is the thinnest line the British Admiralty permits. It would seem that with these resolutions you can approximate the resolution (and clarity) of a paper chart, but this is, in fact, not the case.

Let's consider a boundary between two blocks of color which falls one third the way across a pixel. To accurately reflect this boundary, and produce a crisp electronic reproduction, you would need pixels one third the width of the original pixel, which also means one third the height, so now you have nine pixels in place of one and are back to very large files. There are various techniques (notably "anti-aliasing") that can be used to sharpen images with relatively low pixel counts (the British Admiralty does this), but nevertheless raster charts simply do not have the definition of the original paper charts. To overcome this, research has shown that chart details need to be shown about 1.5 times larger than on a paper chart. In other words, to be legible raster charts need to be displayed at a larger scale than the original paper chart. This violates one of the cardinal rules of navigation, which is to not use a chart at a larger scale than it has been compiled (we will investigate the reason for this rule in a moment).

Displaying the Image

Regardless of whether the chart has been reduced to a resolution of 254 or 127 dpi, what happens when we display this electronic file on our chart-plotter, laptop, desktop computer, tablet computer, or "smart" phone? The display screen is also divided into individual pixels of widely varying size. Typically, the smaller the screen on a device (e.g., a phone) the smaller the display pixels (i.e., the higher the dpi). There are two reasons for this:

If large pixels were used on a small screen, you would be unable to display much information;

Devices with small screens are used very close up, so a high image resolution is necessary to produce clear images.

For example, as of 2011 an iPod Nano, with a diagonal screen dimension of 1.54", had a resolution of 220 dpi; an iPad with a screen size of 9.7" had a resolution of 132 dpi; and a MacBook Pro, with a screen size of 15.4", had a resolution of 128 dpi. These resolutions are representative of similar categories of devices from a broad range of manufacturers. There are very few devices on the market with screen sizes over 12" that have a resolution above 150 dpi, and most are well below this, with some below 100 dpi. This is a situation that has not fundamentally changed in the past decade even with the introduction of "high definition" (HD) devices (my recently bought 23" HD monitor has a screen resolution of 96 dpi). Screen resolutions have, in fact, inched up some, but not increased dramatically (as long ago as 1993 the British Admiralty surveyed screen technology and decided that 0.2 mm pixels—127 dpi—was about as good as it was likely to get, hence their choice of this pixel size, which turns out to have been a remarkably good bet).

To make the numbers easy, let's assume a screen resolution of ±100 dpi. If you make the conversion from inches to millimeters, this equates to a pixel side length of ±0.25 mm and a pixel area of $0.25 \times 0.25 = 0.0625$ mm². This compares to $0.1 \times 0.1 = 0.01$ mm² for a pixel based on 254 dpi (NOAA), and

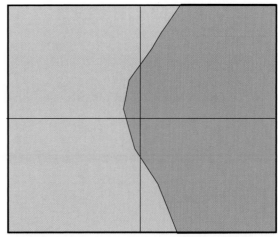

The effect of reducing the pixel size when scanning a chart. If this is a single pixel, the two colors must be averaged, but if the pixel side length is halved, resulting in four pixels, the individual blocks of color are "captured" but the pixel file size is four times as big.

$0.2 \times 0.2 = 0.04$ mm² for a pixel based on 127 dpi (British Admiralty). If one pixel on the screen is used to display one pixel in the electronic file, and the electronic file is based on 127 dpi, the resulting image will be somewhat larger than the original paper chart (each 0.04 mm² pixel has been enlarged to 0.0625 mm²: the image will be a little more than half as big again). If the electronic file is based on 254 dpi, the resulting image will now be more than six times as large as the original paper chart (the pixels have been blown up from an area of 0.01 mm² to 0.0625 mm²). In other words, given most current display screen technology, any electronic chart file output above 127 dpi will result in an image that is considerably enlarged compared to the equivalent paper chart.

Now we get into a minefield. In practice, some (but not many) electronic charting systems "recognize" the scale of the original paper chart and display the electronic chart at a similar scale (usually with some degree of enlargement to enhance clarity, as noted above). The ability to maintain display scale is, in fact, a legal requirement for high-end equipment. Let's consider the implications of this for a paper chart output at 254 dpi. Each pixel is enlarged more than six times. To keep the displayed image more or less the same size and scale as the paper chart, five of every six pixels in the electronic file must be omitted from the display. If the paper chart is output at 127 dpi, the file pixels are blown up just over 1.5 times; therefore, only one in three file pixels needs to be omitted to keep the scale the same. The chart-

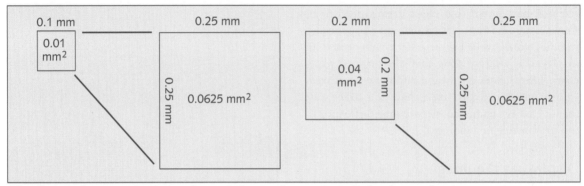

The effective enlargement that occurs when a pixel scanned at one size is displayed at another size.

display software "decides" what to drop. It looks at all the pixels in the electronic file that have to be fitted into a single pixel on the screen, and either "averages" the colors or—if one color is predominant—uses the predominant color. Something similar happens any time the "zoom-out" function on a raster electronic chart system is used to display a larger chart area at a smaller scale. Because a larger area of the paper chart is being looked at, there are many more pixels in the electronic file than can be displayed on the screen. The display software must drop pixels from the electronic file, sometimes as many as 95 percent of them. One result is that letters (e.g., labels) and numbers (e.g., soundings) become increasingly difficult to read.

When zooming in with a raster chart, a smaller area of the original paper chart is displayed electronically. The same number of pixels is on the display screen as there always was, at the same physical size as before. However, they are being applied to a smaller area of the paper chart and, therefore, to a smaller electronic file—more of the available pixels in the electronic file get used. If the file is based on 254 dpi and the display pixel size is 0.0625 mm², it is possible to zoom in until the displayed image is 6.25 times larger than the original before running out of pixels in the electronic file. However, if the file is based on 127 dpi, the pixels will run out when we have zoomed to just over 1.5 times the paper chart size. If we zoom in beyond this point, there will be—in effect—blank pixels on the screen, with nothing left in the electronic file to fill them. The display software fills them; again, it has to decide how to do this. If you keep zooming in, the software has more and more blanks to fill, which it does by mimicking the color of adjacent pixels. This causes the display image to separate into blocks of color (each block now seen is the data from one pixel extended to cover many adjacent pixels), ultimately becoming illegible again.

Clearly, this electronic expansion and contraction process has the potential to introduce distortions and errors. With expensive high-end equipment (e.g., the ECDISs found on ships; see chapter 4), there are rigorous built-in controls; however, when it comes to the type of equipment commonly found in the recreational market, it is up to the manufacturer to set the standards (in practice there are few controls).

Overzooming

With raster charts, the best display image (clearest, most detailed, with crisp lettering and numbering) is created when there is a 1:1 relationship between the pixels in the electronic file and those on the screen. If we assume a screen pixel of 0.0625 mm² and the electronic file is based on 127 dpi, the displayed image will be something over 1.5 times the size of the original; if the electronic file is based on 254 dpi, it will be 6.25 times larger. Let's assume the original chart was at a scale of 1:24,000. It is now being displayed at a scale of 1:15,360 (127 dpi file) or 1:3,840 (254 dpi file). For the end user, symbols and text that typically are small and cramped are now larger and farther apart, making it easier to read the chart.

The end user may like the clarity of this display, but in reality it can be dangerous. The survey standards and plotting accuracy applied to the original chart (1:24,000) will not be rigorous enough for the larger-scale version. For example, at 1:24,000, the chart compiler's allowable plotting accuracy is 1 mm which equates to ±24 meters on the ground, on top of the survey errors, which—even at contemporary standards—may be another 5 meters or more. In other words, even with up-to-date surveys, the charted position of features can be 30 meters out of place; with older surveys, these positions may be considerably farther off. In comparison, for an original chart drawn at a scale of 1:3,840, the chart compiler's plotting error is ±3.8 meters. The underlying survey work will likely have been done to Special-Order standards (even if it is still technically designated as a First-Order survey); therefore, the total displayed positioning error is likely to be less than 5 meters.

Using a 1:24,000 chart displayed at chart scale, no sane navigator would be tempted to try a passage through a channel, a reef entry, or between rocks that was shown as 1 mm wide on the chart (24 m in the real world); on the enlarged version, the same channel is 6.25 mm wide and might look passable. However, because the large-scale chart has been created by zooming in on a smaller-scale chart, *all the inherent errors in the smaller-scale chart are still present*, as opposed to the lesser errors that would be expected at this larger scale. *The only thing that has changed is the navigator's perception.* There is a distinct possibility that if this passage is attempted, the boat will run aground. In fact, the passage may not even exist in the first place. If it is an apparent passage between a couple of rocks, there may be dozens of rocks; however, at 1:24,000, the cartographer had room to show only a couple, and that is what is on the chart.

Most electronic charting software includes mechanisms to warn of overzooming. However, almost none of this software includes a setup procedure that requires the operator to input the screen size and resolution, and as a result the software typically assumes the image is being displayed at its compilation (paper chart) scale when there is a 1:1 relationship between file pixels and display pixels. As we have seen, with many NOAA products this often results in the display being 625% overscale! Changing the screen resolution on most display devices also has the effect of zooming in or out on the displayed image, but so far as the display software is concerned there has been no change in display scale.

Because of the potential overzooming problems when raster chart files are displayed, the British Admiralty developed the Hydrographic Chart Raster Format (HCRF) for its ARCS (raster) charts, and retains tight control over how its files are used by electronic chart software producers and other end users. These controls are designed to ensure that a chart will be displayed to the navigator at the scale the chart compiler intended and that it will retain the integrity of the image. HCRF has now been adopted into the performance standards governing the legally acceptable format for raster charts used by the world's shipping industry (more on this in

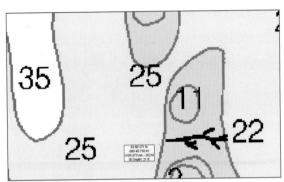

Overzooming a raster chart. Letters, numbers, and symbols are larger than on a paper chart.

chapter 4). Several national hydrographic offices now produce HCRF versions of their national charts. NOAA raster charts, on the other hand, do not use HCRF; in addition, the U.S. government is much less controlling in how chart files get used, so the charts frequently end up overzoomed. Private producers of raster charts commonly also exercise limited control regarding overzooming and other display issues. (There are some interesting philosophical issues underlying the different technologies, formats, and processes adopted by the British Admiralty and NOAA. They have been hotly debated over the years, but are not germane to this book.)

Related, but different, issues arise with vector charts. Once again, because of the relatively low resolution of most display screens, in order to get an easy-to-read image, an electronic chart needs to be displayed at a larger scale than the equivalent paper chart. The industry seems to have settled on a zoom level of around 1.7:1 as being appropriate. Beyond that, as with raster charts, the display software typically does not "know" at what scale the image is being displayed, and so overzooming is commonplace.

With a raster chart, there is a sense of when you are overzooming since the letters, symbols, and numbers are all displayed larger than normal. Eventually, the image starts to break down as the electronic file runs out of pixels and the software begins to fill in the blanks. With vector charts, the image itself may provide little evidence of overzooming, because whatever the scale, the software re-creates the various points and lines at the same size and width; fills in the colors; and often adds the labels, numbers, and so on at the same prescribed font size (i.e., the same font size, regardless of scale). However, with increased zooming, curved lines start to break down into a series of points connected by straight lines, and soundings become increasingly widely spaced, but that may be

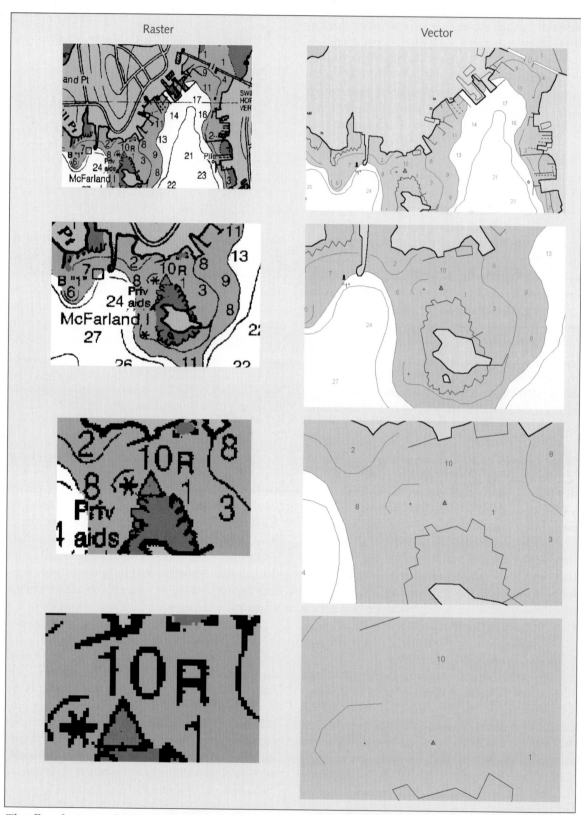

The effect of progressively overzooming raster and vector charts in terms of making what is a questionable channel seem less questionable. Note how it becomes clear the raster chart has been overzoomed whereas on the vector chart the channel appears to get wider, the rocks smaller, and the overzooming is by no means so obvious.

about it for clues. Unless the user is specifically warned via a message box, or the software includes provisions to prevent overzooming, it is easy to use a chart at a scale for which it was not designed.

The fact that at each new zoom level vector software re-creates symbols at a constant display size introduces another danger. Using the example of a chart at 1:24,000 with a couple of rocks that indicate a rock-strewn area, with raster, the displayed image increases in size with zooming. Although the distance between the rocks on the display increases with the zoom level, it does so *proportionately*. With vector, regardless of the zoom level, the rocks are displayed at the same size, which *disproportionately* increases the distance between them—reinforcing the impression that there may be a clear channel where there is none. Consider another example—a wreck symbol. At 1:24,000, this almost certainly covers a greater area than the wreck itself. However, at some point when zooming in with a vector chart, the symbol (if it is re-created at the same size at each zoom level) will cover less area than that occupied by the wreck. Anyone using this overzoomed chart to navigate a track that runs close to the symbol will hit the wreck.

Zooming in on a chart, whether raster or vector, violates one of the immutable rules of navigation: *A chart should never be used at a scale larger than that at which it was compiled.* This rule is routinely violated by users of electronic charts and in fact, given the state of current display technology, has to be violated to make the charts legible.

High-end electronic charting systems do "understand" the relationship between screen size, pixel count, and chart scale, and will warn the user if a chart is being used grossly over scale (overzoomed). These generally limit zooming to a maximum of two times the scale of the chart from which the electronic chart was made. Most recreational systems have neither the warning nor the limit, or very inadequate warnings—the zoom function must be used with discretion and a clear understanding of its limits and dangers. Remember that just because a system seems to suggest a particular passage can be made does not mean it is safe, sensible, or even possible.

Mix and Match

Here's another obscure wrinkle similar to that of overzooming that can produce an unwarranted degree of overconfidence in the accuracy of a vector chart, but for which the software may give no warning.

Let's say we digitize a paper chart that has a scale of 1:100,000 and, therefore, a chart compiler's plotting accuracy of 1 mm × 100,000 = 100,000 mm = 100 meters. Once the chart is vectorized and is in an electronic database, the data can be applied to an electronic chart at any scale. It might appear in a chart that is effectively displayed at 1:20,000, which—in its paper version—would have a plotting accuracy of 20 meters. However, we have incorporated data that was originally only plotted to within 100 meters. In other words, the electronic chart will give us a false sense of security regarding its accuracy.

High-end vector-based equipment filters out such things, and in fact by clicking on a sounding

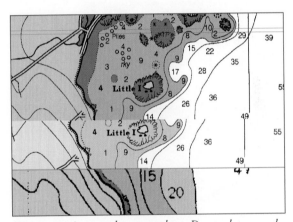

First-generation seamless raster chart. Due to datum and other inconsistencies between the two charts being quilted together, Little Island got included twice! The error in matching the charts, and the differences in scale of the two source charts, are immediately obvious. The source chart for the upper part of the image is at 1:20,000; that for the lower part 1:40,000.

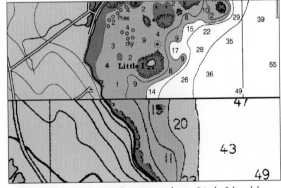

Second-generation seamless raster chart. Little Island has been corrected. The seam between the two charts is still clearly visible, warning the end user that the two parts of this electronic image have been surveyed and compiled to different standards of accuracy.

you can often pull up the *metadata*, which is background information that should include such things as the date of the survey and its level of accuracy, but for the low-end equipment and electronic charting systems often found in the recreational marketplace, there is no such filtering or metadata, and in fact these electronic charts are often compiled from paper charts derived from survey data collected at different scales. Most modern paper charts have a source diagram (see page 49) that shows the user not only the age and origins of the survey data used for that chart, but also the scale of the various surveys. High-end electronic charts are *required* to have the same

data included in the metadata and readily accessible, but low-end products may not have it. Even if present, it will not generally be displayed—the user has to look for it—as opposed to a paper chart, where it is clearly printed on the chart. (It will also be on a raster chart, but probably not on the part visible on the screen—it is necessary to scroll around to find it.)

Warning and cautionary notes are similar. These often crop up on paper charts, referring the user to a more detailed explanatory note somewhere else on the paper chart. On a raster chart, the user will still see the first note, but may have trouble finding the second, explanatory, note. On a vector chart, both notes may

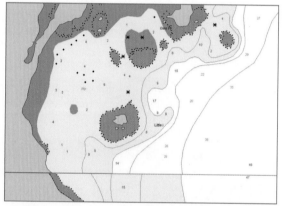

Vector chart of Little Island. Note that the discontinuities in the source chart are still visible (see page 47), but the resizing of the soundings no longer warns that the sparse data was collected at different scales and levels of accuracy.

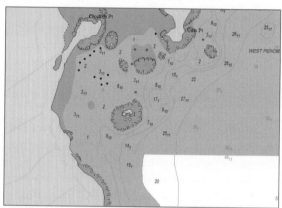

Another vector chart of Little Island with even fewer clues warning that the source data was collected at different scales and different levels of accuracy.

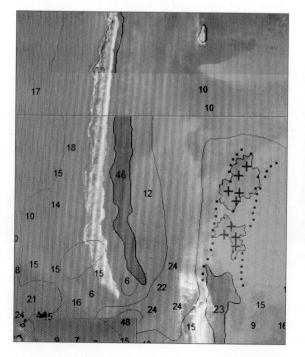

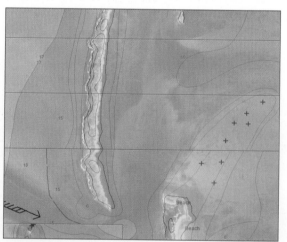

First generation (2004) vector chart (left) with overlaid aerial photography. The chart reveals discontinuities in the underlying surveys. A raster image would have revealed that the lower half was surveyed at a much smaller, and inherently less accurate, scale. A corrected (2007) chart (above) based on new surveys.

be missing or buried in the metadata in a manner where the user fails to see them at all.

Chart Updates

In some areas hydrographic data rarely changes from natural causes, notably areas with stable, rocky terrains (for example, the U.S. northeast, and much of the Scottish coastline). In others, it changes constantly (for example, many of the popular inlets from the Atlantic Ocean into the Intracoastal Waterway—ICW— on the U.S. east coast change from year to year, and even week to week). Occasionally, there are dramatic happenings in the natural world, such as the reported 8-foot lateral shift in Japan's landmass caused by the 2011 earthquake, not to mention all the shoreline changes wrought by the subsequent tsunami; hurricanes regularly reconfigure

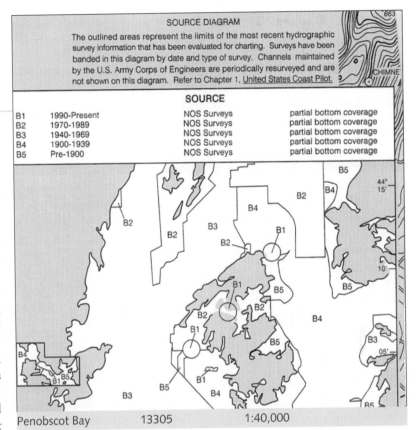

Paper-chart source diagram.

popular cruising grounds in the Caribbean. And then there are all kinds of manmade alterations such as dredging, shoreline construction, and so on. Hydrographic offices log and store these changes, maintaining an aggregate file for each chart in their databases. Traditionally, these changes have been incorporated into each new edition of a paper chart when it is published, but these new editions have typically been years apart and sometimes decades apart (out of a suite of 1,019 charts, NOAA issues around 100 new editions each year).

Between chart editions, diligent mariners have kept charts updated via *Notices to Mariners* (NTMs in the U.S.; NMs in the U.K.), which are issued on a regular basis by the hydrographic offices. In the U.S., NTMs come from two sources, the nine U.S. Coast Guard districts, which issue *Local Notices to Mariners* (LNMs) on a weekly basis, and the U.S. NGA, which issues NTMs covering issues primarily of interest to (deep-draft) shipping. The LNMs include such things as sunken vessels, buoy changes, obstructions, changes in channel markers, and missing or inoperable aids to navigation, and cover changes of interest to recreational sailors (including over 95% of the information

in NTMs). In the UK, the British Admiralty issues NMs for its entire suite of worldwide charts. Prior to the Internet age, NTMs and NMs (and equivalent products from other hydrographic offices) were published in print form, typically weekly. Today, they are put on hydrographic office websites (at http://ocsdata.ncd.noaa.gov/ntm/Terms.aspx for NOAA and http://www.ukho.gov.uk/ProductsandServices/MartimeSafety/Pages/NMPublic.aspx for the British Admiralty), although the British Admiralty still maintains a paper edition.

Even with Internet availability, it's a major chore tracking NTMs and updating paper charts, and as a result almost no recreational sailors do it (I have to confess, I have rarely done it myself). However, it should obviously be done periodically, especially for coastal charts, and especially in areas subject to change (either natural or human). You can log onto the relevant hydrographic office website with the chart number and edition number to download the updates. If yours is an out-of-date edition, it should be replaced with the latest edition, and then that should be corrected. Each chart correction gives the number and edition of the affected chart, with instructions to add, delete, change, or relocate a feature, which is identified by its position. Officially, corrections are made in magenta, but a blue or black pen is fine (don't use red as it cannot be seen in dim, or red, nighttime lighting). Note that OceanGrafix Print-on-Demand charts in the United States (available since 2000) are automatically updated to the day of printing.

In theory, it should be easy to update electronic charts by downloading corrections from the Internet. Raster charts are corrected by downloading "patches"—replacement files for specific areas of the chart. Vector charts are corrected at the level of individual features and attribute tables. In practice, this works for high-end products (and is a legal requirement on ships; the various standards for ECDIS require the hydrographic offices to supply weekly updates for their raster and vector chart products) but is rarely the case for the products found in the recreational marketplace, although this is slowly changing. For example, NV Charts has an excellent Internet-based free monthly update service for its paper and electronic charts of the Baltic and Sweden's west coast, and C-Map's MAX Pro cartography was the first recreational vector cartography to offer users regular worldwide updates. For the large number of users with digital charts contained on cartridges, typically the only available update mechanism is to buy a new cartridge.

For regular updates to be possible, the chart and software provider needs to track notices to mariners and other sources of changes in chart data, which requires a significant infrastructure, and needs a mechanism to supply updates to its users. Once again, this is a reality for high-end products, but is extremely unevenly implemented in the recreational marketplace (ranging from regular comprehensive updates to nothing at all; several leading providers in the recreational marketplace only update their products once or twice a year). The ability to regularly, comprehensively, and economically update electronic charts should be one of the critical features in making the decision between competing products (see below for more thoughts on this).

User Beware

For many different reasons, the user of any chart should not be lulled into a false sense of security about its accuracy. As noted in chapter 1, before GPS there was always a degree of uncertainty about a boat's position. This led navigators to be cautious and

to give a wide berth to hazards depicted on a chart; in general, the techniques used to position hazards on a chart were more accurate than the navigational tools available to a mariner. Since the advent of GPS, this situation has turned around: the equipment with which we navigate now has a positioning accuracy considerably greater than that underlying the charts we use (including electronic charts, which are still largely based on paper charts and old survey data).

Electronic charts especially have to be used with caution. The combination of the ability to overzoom them and the fact that the boat's position is displayed in real time electronically on the chart with an incredible degree of precision (eliminating the traditional uncertainty inherent in plotting on paper) can lead to dangerous overconfidence on the part of a navigator. There is a disturbing tendency with many mariners to treat an electronic chart display as if it were radar. For example, if a boat is shown in center channel (on a chart that is often grossly overzoomed), it is presumed that it must be in center channel. But whereas radar gets its images from the real world and, therefore, provides an accurate display of a boat's position relative to its physical surroundings, *the electronic chart gets its "image" from the cartographer's interpretation of the surveyor's information, with all the inherent errors described previously*. The combination of GPS and electronic charts tempts navigators to run closer to hazards and to attempt trickier channels than they would have done in the past, with potentially unpleasant results.

In general, the absolute accuracy of the "average" harbor, approach, or coastal paper chart is generally not less than 1 mm with respect to the chart datum; that is, the charted positions of features should almost always be within 1 mm of where they would be if the chart were completely accurate. In other words, most of the time the cumulative errors will not exceed 1 mm × chart scale. For a 1:40,000 chart, this is 40,000 mm = 40 meters (44 yd.). For vector-based electronic charts, especially many developed for the recreational market, *it should be assumed that the accuracy is 1.5 mm at the original scale of the chart* (e.g., 60 m/66 yd. at 1:40,000 scale) *until such time as these charts are produced directly from the vector database* (after which the accuracy will be a function of the accuracy of the database). *This level of error will remain regardless of the extent to which the chart is zoomed in.* But having said this, it needs to be recognized that many specific bits of data on both paper and electronic charts were derived from older and/or

(Above and right) The Cork Clipper on an Indonesian reef which was charted out of position with fewer clues on the electronic chart (below) in use than on the paper chart. The latest generation electronic chart of the same reef provides no clues regarding the charting errors.

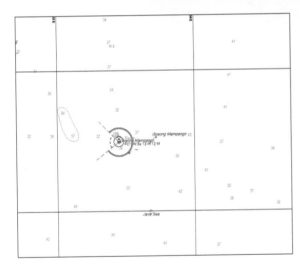

The extinguished light and missing radar reflector on the reef.

less accurate surveys than the norm; as a result, they fall outside these parameters (sometimes by a wide margin), as will *almost all charts of areas beyond the immediate coastal belt.*

The loss of the *Cork Clipper* on an Indonesian reef in 2010 is instructive. The reef is charted with a light and radar reflector ("Fl.5s 12M (exting) Racon (D)"). The navigator was primarily using raster electronic charts (updated less than 2 weeks previously) and radar, with the latest edition paper charts ready as a backup. The light was not visible (which is not surprising given that the chart showed it as extinguished)

and the radar was not picking up anything (subsequent investigation found the Racon device was destroyed). At one display scale the electronic chart has the notation "POSITIONS (see Note)." The note, if pulled up, contains a report from 1992 that the reef is 0.9 mile

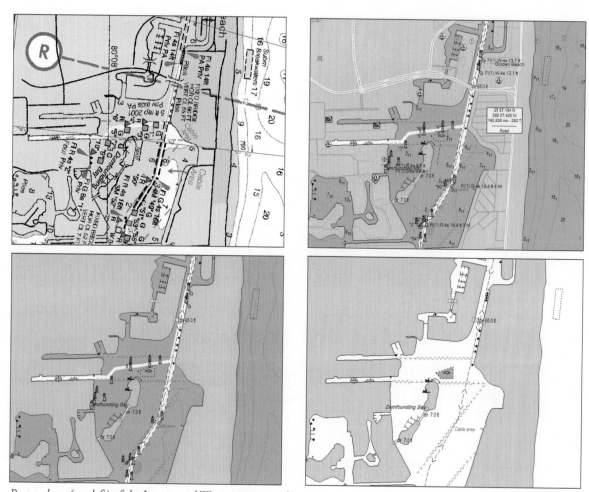

Raster chart (top left) of the Intracoastal Waterway approaching Miami. A vector chart of the same area (top right and lower two images) with more and more "layers" of information progressively turned off to declutter the image, making the chart easier to read but with the danger of turning off important information.

farther east than charted. (Given that the boat's position was shown as 0.6 mile east of the reef when it struck the *west* side, the report is accurate.) The warning clues are more obvious on the paper chart, but this was not in direct use at the time. The charts, both electronic and paper, reveal that they are based on survey data from 1880 and 1901, providing another important clue regarding potential inaccuracies.

In the loss of the *Clipper*, the electronic chart used had a combination of charting errors, carried over from the paper chart, with less obvious warnings than the paper chart regarding the potential inaccuracy of the data. Interestingly, on a latest generation (2010) vector chart that I have, the light is not shown as extinguished, the cautionary notes are absent, and the reef is still in the wrong position. This electronic chart provides *no warning clues at all* for

the navigator. To avoid unpleasant accidents, it is essential to have a thorough grasp of, and a healthy respect for, the limits of chart accuracy and the tools you are using!

Addendum: Raster versus Vector

The fundamental difference between raster and vector charts arises from the ability to vary the way in which the data in the vector file is displayed, whereas the display characteristics of the raster file are fixed. Some of the more significant consequences of this are:

Many users of traditional paper charts prefer the familiar images created by raster charts. What is more, many raster charts are easier to read because they have been compiled by professional cartographers who understand the needs of the users as op-

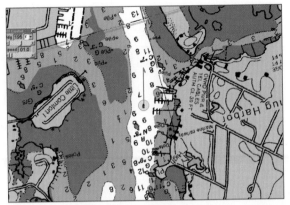

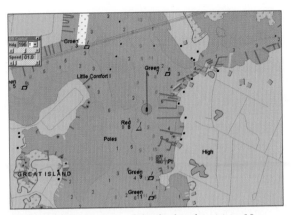

The instantaneous display of a boat's position can lead to overconfidence in the accuracy of the displayed position. Note that these two electronic charts are shown "course up," rather than "north up" (which is how a paper chart is constructed). With the raster image (left), the labels and soundings remain north up and so are upside down. With the vector image (right), they are reoriented: this is one of the strengths of this technology.

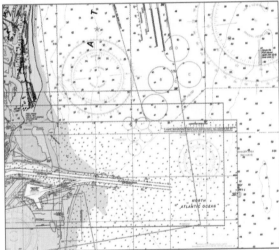

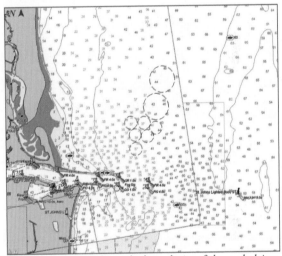

Raster (left) and vector (right) images of the same area. Note that the raster image shows the boundaries of the underlying surveys far more clearly. On the vector chart different colors have been selected to highlight changes in depth soundings—this is not possible on a raster chart.

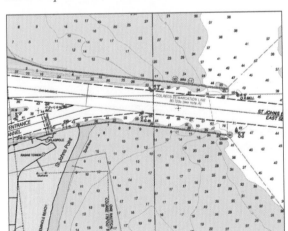

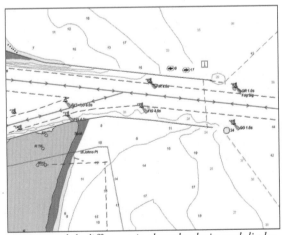

Progressively zooming in on the raster and vector charts reveals numerous subtle differences in the technologies and display characteristics.

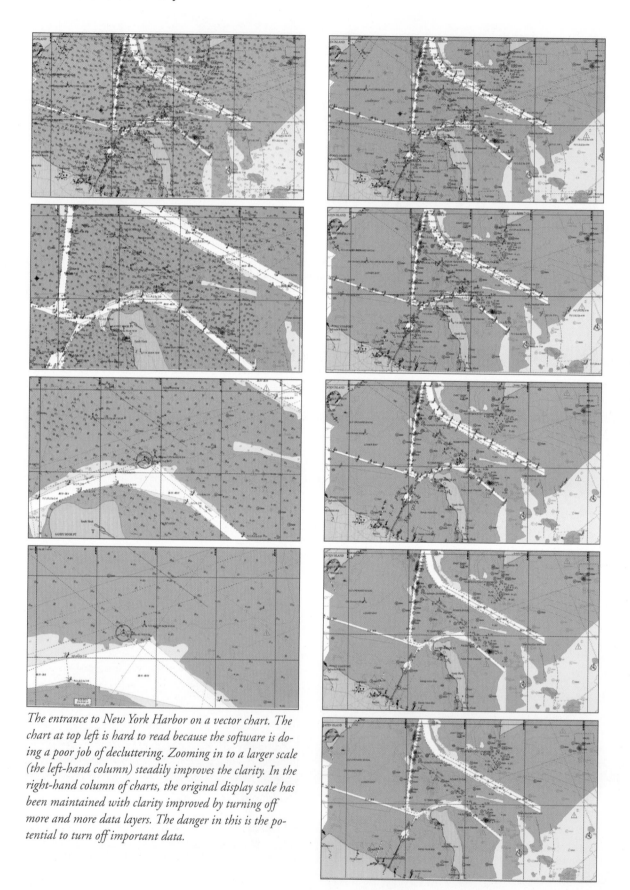

The entrance to New York Harbor on a vector chart. The chart at top left is hard to read because the software is doing a poor job of decluttering. Zooming in to a larger scale (the left-hand column) steadily improves the clarity. In the right-hand column of charts, the original display scale has been maintained with clarity improved by turning off more and more data layers. The danger in this is the potential to turn off important data.

posed to digitized and compiled by people with less cartographic training.

As you zoom in and out on a raster chart, the images get larger or smaller until they are illegible. This has the benefit of emphasizing that the chart is being used at an inappropriate scale. On the other hand, the resizing that takes place on a vector chart can make soundings and labels easier to read. However, if the vector chart does not have effective decluttering software, at some point when zooming out the resized soundings and labels will begin to overlap each other and become illegible.

The vector software can decide whether or not to display something, whereas the raster chart always has to include everything in the file. In practical terms, with vector, only the data necessary for the navigational task at hand needs to be displayed, which can greatly simplify displays and improve navigational awareness, but this is also a potentially dangerous tool in as much as the *user may turn off information layers that would be better left on. In general, vector requires an operator who is better educated in the use of the product than is needed for raster.*

With vector, soundings and other data can be displayed in whatever units you want—e.g., fathoms, feet, or meters.

The vector data can be programmed to emphasize critical features (e.g., limiting depths), customized to the characteristics of a given boat (e.g., draft), and to provide warnings and alarms (e.g., if a given depth contour is crossed), which is not possible with raster charts, although the NV Charts "hybrid" raster/vector approach described on page 42 will have these capabilities with a raster display.

In anything other than "north up" mode, the soundings, labels, and other text on a raster chart are displayed the "wrong" way up, whereas regardless of chart orientation they are displayed the "right" way up on a vector chart.

With higher-end vector charts, clicking on any feature (e.g., a depth sounding) will bring up the metadata, enabling the user to gauge the accuracy, whereas this cannot be done with raster (although once again the NV Charts "hybrid" raster/vector approach will have these capabilities with a raster display).

A vector chart provides information for only those features on the screen, whereas a raster chart often provides additional information. For example, if a lighthouse is off the screen but its light is within range of what is on the screen, the vector chart will show no data related to it, whereas the raster image

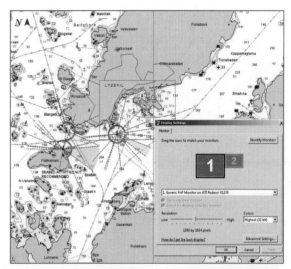

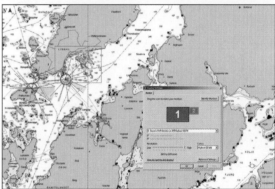

Changing the screen resolution will change the scale of a displayed chart. Many electronic chart software packages will not recognize this, but some will.

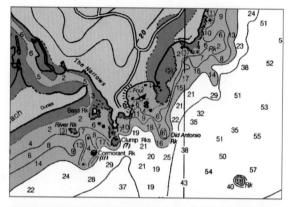

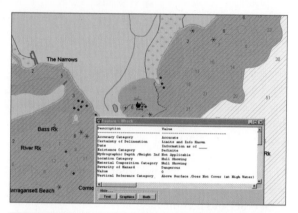

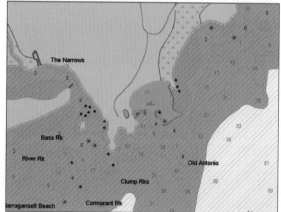

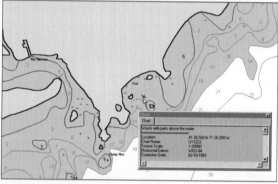

Two different versions of the metadata associated with the wreck in the center of the chart.

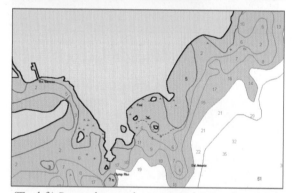

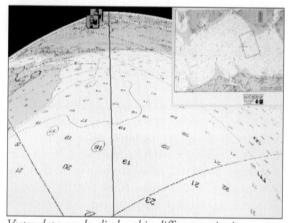

(Top left) Raster chart with overzoomed vector chart (middle). The overzooming is indicated by the cross-hatching. Many vector charts do not show overzooming (bottom).

Vector data can be displayed in different projections.

will show the range circle associated with the light, alerting the chart user to its presence. Given the small screens used for electronic charting, relative to the size of paper charts, and the fact that the electronic chart is almost always overscale, which further reduces the area covered on a given screen, loss of "peripheral vision" with electronic charting is quite significant, so this feature of raster can be very useful.

Vector data is stored independent of any specific chart projection (this is provided by the display software). As such, the data can be displayed with different projections for different purposes (e.g., Mercator for general-purpose navigation; gnomonic for great circle planning; and various other ingenious projections for helping the navigator process the chart information and to provide improved "peripheral vision").

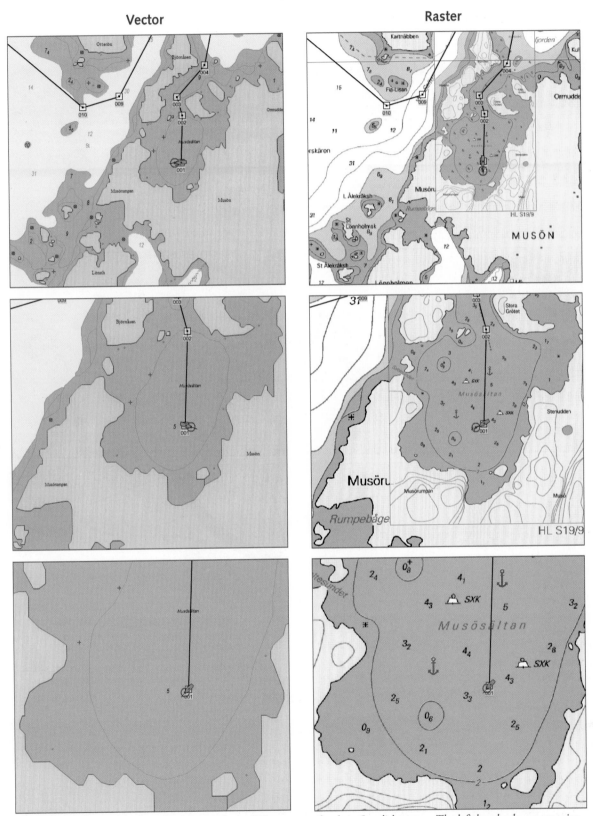

A comparison of vector and raster cartography at different zoom levels in Swedish waters. The left-hand column contains vector charts based on official cartography. The right-hand column contains raster charts based on private cartography (NV Charts).

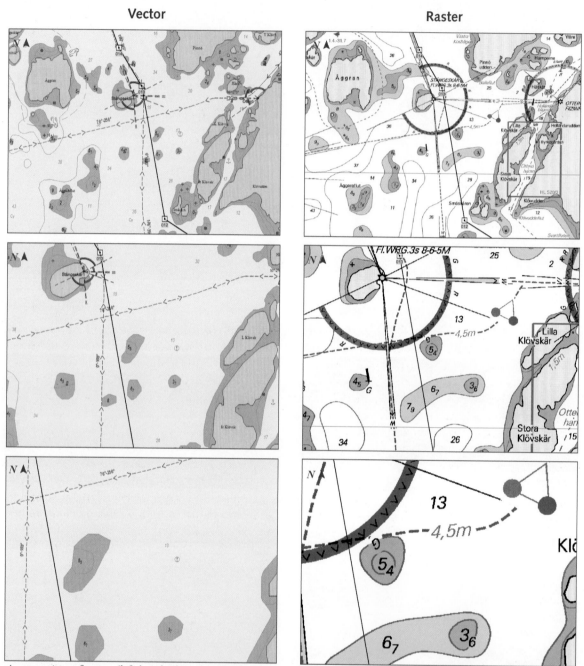

A comparison of vector (left-hand column) and raster (right-hand column) cartography for the light (top two charts). When zooming in, the existence of the light, which is now off the chart, has been lost on the vector chart but still shows on the raster chart.

Vertical Chart Accuracy

3

IN CHAPTERS 1 AND 2, we looked at factors affecting the horizontal accuracy of charts, in terms of both datum issues and the accuracy with which the details on a chart are displayed. Of those details, arguably the most important are the soundings. We need to investigate the extent to which the soundings can be trusted; that is, how accurate are the vertical measurements? There are two components to this question: a technical component concerning vertical datums and, less complicated, an accuracy component concerning survey techniques and standards. Let's look at accuracy first.

Sounding Accuracy

Until about 1940, soundings in shallow water were made with a graduated pole and in deeper water with a lead line—a weight on the end of a length of line marked at measured intervals. The accuracy of these soundings, particularly those in deeper water, greatly depends on the skill of the operator. Later, in rock-strewn areas, lead-line techniques were supplemented with wire-drag technology, which consists of a buoyed wire towed at a set depth to establish minimum clearances.

Charts based on lead-line surveys—which still form the basis of the majority of soundings in hydrographic databases (approximately 50 percent of the soundings currently displayed on U.S. charts)—are especially fallible. Even if the soundings are highly accurate, a single lead-line sounding samples the seabed over an area of only a few square inches or centimeters; the next sounding may not be taken for some distance. The Cunard liner *Queen Elizabeth II* hit an uncharted rock off Block Island (on the east coast of the U.S.) in August 1992 in an area that had last been surveyed in 1939.

In *The Mariner's Handbook*, the British Admiralty cites the example of the Muirfield Seamount, "which lies on the route from Cape of Good Hope to Selat Sunda, 75 miles southwest of Cocos Islands. Its existence was not suspected until 1973 when MV *Muirfield* reported having struck an 'obstruction' and sustained considerable damage to her keel. At the time, she was . . . in charted depths of over 5,000 meters." A subsequent survey by HMAS *Moresby* in 1983 found a least depth of 18 meters over the seamount, "the summit being level and about half a mile in extent rising sharply on all sides from deep water" (p. 23, 1999 ed.). Note that it was ten years before the survey took place!

In 2005, the U.S. nuclear submarine USS *San Francisco*, sailing through the Caroline Islands at a depth of 525 feet in waters charted at over 7,000 feet, slammed into a similar seamount at 25 knots, caving in the bow, killing one crew member, and injuring everyone else on board (see next page). Interestingly, the paper version of the electronic chart in use at the time had a notation that some features could be off by as much as three miles. For some time the crew had been logging depths that were more than 1,000 feet less than the charted depth, and the area was gradually shoaling. Instead of checking with the three other charts of this area on board, which showed an area of "muddy" water potentially revealing the seamount, they assumed that they had a misreading fathometer. There are several lessons here for mariners!

Since the 1930s, numerous types of acoustic devices have been used to collect soundings, notably single-beam and multibeam echo-sounders. These

Damage done to the bow of the USS San Francisco *after hitting an uncharted seamount.*

Using echo-sounders and sidescan sonar to collect soundings and seabed information.

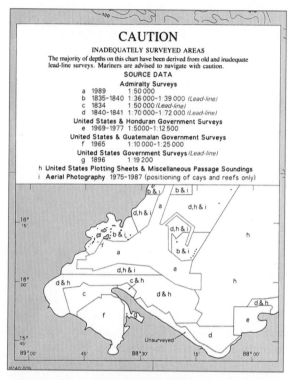

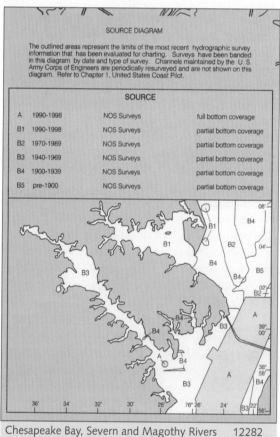

A couple of source diagrams. One notes the bottom coverage and one doesn't.

measure the time it takes for a sound signal (a "ping") to bounce off the bottom and return to the transmitter. The time is converted to depth. A promising new technology for shallow water (which is the hardest to survey for a number of reasons) is phase-differencing bathymetric sonar. Since the early 1970s echo-sounders have been supplemented by sidescan sonar, which doesn't measure depths but helps to reveal bottom features which might otherwise get overlooked. In recent years, we have had laser-based optical devices (LIDAR—Light Detection and Ranging) that can be used from aircraft to define shorelines and chart relatively shallow depths with clear water. The majority of hydrographic information, however, still requires the use of a ship to put a transducer into the water, and the speed of sound through water limits the speed at which a survey can progress.

Echo-sounders and more recent technologies inherently have a higher degree of accuracy than lead-line surveys; nevertheless, potential errors can still be introduced by factors affecting the speed with which sound travels through the water or the heaving, rolling, and pitching of a vessel. This not only raises and lowers an echo-sounder's transducer relative to the seabed, but also causes the transmitted beam to vary from the vertical so that the part of the bottom actually being scanned is offset from the intended part. On a modern survey vessel, elaborate procedures remove any errors that might be introduced; with older surveys, the quality of the data is more questionable.

As noted in chapter 2, the IHO has a set of survey standards (IHO S-44) that prescribes accuracy rules for different order surveys, ranging from those for Special-Order surveys (the most rigorous) to those for Third-Order surveys (the least rigorous). The standards vary from an allowable error in shallow water of ±0.25 meter (10 in.) to ±1.0 meter (3.3 ft.), with the allowable error increasing with depth. Modern survey data can be expected to comply with one or another of these standards, most likely with the more rigorous standards (if not Special-Order, then at least First-Order; i.e., ±0.5 m/20 in. in shallow water), but only a small proportion of soundings in existing databases have been surveyed to these standards.

The result is that the soundings on a chart almost certainly come from a variety of different sources with a variable degree of reliability. Almost all modern paper charts have a source diagram, except large-scale charts, such as harbor charts, which are compiled from a single survey. A source diagram is included on most NOAA charts published after November 1992 (see chapters 5 and 8). It gives the origin, date, and scale of much of the survey data used to compile the chart. On large-scale charts compiled from a single source, this information is provided in an "Authorities" note on the chart. However, for certain areas, notably the Intracoastal Waterway (ICW) in the United States, where the data have come from another source (in this case, the Corps of Engineers), there may still be little source data. Electronic charts may have similar source data (although many in the recreational marketplace do not), but even when present the operator frequently has to search for it (see chapter 2). Using any chart when sailing in questionable waters (minimum depths or doubtful clearances over underwater hazards), the operator should automatically check this metadata, exercising additional caution if it indicates any question about the reliability of the soundings or if it is not present.

Vertical Datums

Collecting data is only the first part of the sounding process. The data must be reduced to some common *plane of reference*. This is easily understood if you think of data collected in tidal waters over a period of hours, when the state of the tide is constantly varying. To make sense of the data, this tidal effect must be discounted; that is, all the soundings must be reduced to a common *vertical datum* (not to be confused with the horizontal datum, such as WGS 84, used to determine horizontal relationships). This raises at least three questions: What datum, how is it established, and how can the data be reduced to it?

Fundamentally, tides respond to astronomical forces, primarily the influence of the moon (with a secondary influence from the sun). When looking for a basis for a vertical datum, we can define two situations in which the influence of the moon is at its greatest (full and new moon) and at its least (midway between full and new). The former produces unusually high high tides and low low tides, known as *spring tides*; the latter produces unusually low high tides and unusually high low tides, known as *neap tides*. For both scenarios, the actual highs and lows vary from month to month, and from year to year over a nineteen-year astronomical cycle, with some more extreme than others. We can either average the highs and lows at spring tides or use the highest spring tide and the lowest spring tide likely, or even the highest and lowest spring tides ever recorded. We can also define an average high tide (average of all high tides including springs, neaps, and others) and low tide, and an average mean sea level (MSL): all highs and lows averaged out. This still does not exhaust the choices: in many parts of the world with two daily tides (the norm), one has a higher high and a lower low than the other, creating a large number of possible permutations.

One of these options has to be selected as the datum (sometimes called the *Chart Datum* or *Sounding Datum*) for displaying soundings and drying heights (the height above the low-water level, at low tide, of areas that are covered at high water). The idea is to show the "least depth of water found in any place under 'normal' meteorological conditions." The chart datum "shall be a plane so low that the tide will not frequently fall below it" (IHO S-4). Unfortunately, at one time or another, almost everything described above has been used as a datum for different purposes on charts; even today, different hydro-

The Limits of Accuracy

graphic offices use different vertical datums, the six most common of which are as follows:

1. **LOWEST ASTRONOMICAL TIDE (LAT).** This is a theoretical calculation based on the influence of the heavenly bodies on the tides over a nineteen-year astronomical cycle. It calculates the lowest likely low-water level. As a result, it tends to be lower than even low-water spring tides; in fact, the water level will almost never be lower than the LAT, and mostly will be higher. In other words, it is a conservative datum: there will almost always be more water depth than is shown on the charts. It is the default datum of the IHO, and is recommended for use on the basis that it "is the only Chart Datum with worldwide application, and has the additional merit of removing all negative values from tide tables. It is recommended that this is adopted as a long-term objective, to be considered when opportunity for change arises" (IHO S-4). It was devised by the

British Admiralty and is now used by the BA and many other hydrographic offices but not by NOAA and NOS/OCS. Interestingly, on March 19, 2011, when the moon was at the closest point to the earth (known as the *lunar perigee*) in its latest nineteen-year cycle, it caused tides a little below even LAT, resulting in a number of groundings on the UK's south coast.

2. **LOWEST NORMAL TIDE (LNT),** which is today synonymous with LOWER LOW WATER LARGE TIDE (LLWLT). This is the average of the lowest low water levels recorded in each of the nineteen years in the previous astronomical cycle. As such, although not as conservative as LAT, it is a conservative datum—*the low water level will almost never be below it.* This datum is used by the Canadian hydrographic office. (Note that on older charts, LNT can refer to a variety of low water datums.)

3. **LOW-WATER ORDINARY SPRINGS (LWOS) AND MEAN LOW WATER SPRINGS (MLWS).** These are averages of the low water associated with spring tides. As such, they are less conservative than LAT and LLWLT but more conservative than the following datums. At low tide during spring tides, it is not unusual for the actual water depth to be less than the charted depth. The German hydrographic office uses MLWS, resulting in differences with British Admiralty and French charts (which both use LAT) of up to half a meter (20")

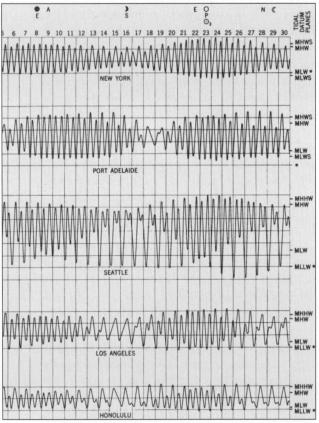

Daily tidal variations for various places around the world. The springs and neaps show up clearly. Note also those places with a semidiurnal tide (twice daily) in which one low tide is lower than the other.

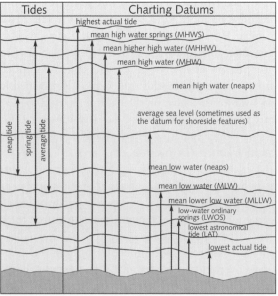

Various states of the tide that can form the basis for a vertical datum.

in some German waters (the German charts show more water).

4. **MEAN LOWER LOW WATER (MLLW).** This is often used in areas with two daily tides where one is lower than the other. It is an average (mean) of the lower of the low tides. As such, *at low tide, the actual water level is often lower than the charted depth*, sometimes by more than a meter (3 feet or more), notably at low-water spring tides. MLLW is used extensively by NOAA and NOS/OCS. Many NOAA charts have a table that includes an Extreme Low Water column. This represents the lowest recorded tide level and gives some idea of how much less water there may be at low water springs than is shown on the charts.

5. **MEAN LOW WATER (MLW).** An average of the low tides, this is sometimes used in areas where there is no significant difference between tides. Again, the actual water level is often lower than the charted depth, notably at low-water spring tides.

6. **MEAN SEA LEVEL (MSL).** The least conservative of the five datums, this is used in areas where there is no appreciable tidal range (less than about 0.3 m/1 ft.).

What about the height of objects and landmasses above sea level? For these, it is not acceptable to use a low-water datum. Take, for example, the clearance under a bridge. If we use the low-water datum to calculate this height, most often the clearance will be overstated—in other words, the actual clearance will be less than the charted clearance, with potentially catastrophic results. As a result, some type of high-water datum must be used for these clearances. IHO S-4 recommends that "the datum above which clearances are given shall be a high-water level, preferably Mean High Water Springs (MHWS) where the tide is appreciable. In areas where the tide is not appreciable, it shall be Mean Sea Level (MSL)."

NOAA and NOS mostly use Mean High Water (MHW) as the high-water datum, as opposed to Mean Higher High Water (MHHW) or MHWS, even in areas where the low-water datum is MLLW. In this case, the high-water datum is not as conservative in terms of high water as the low-water datum is in terms of low water. *High tides are sometimes higher than the high-water datum. At these times, bridge and other clearances are less than the charted clearance.* Most other hydrographic offices now use MHWS as a high-water datum, which is more conservative. The Canadian hydrographic office uses Higher High Water Large Tide (HHWLT), which is

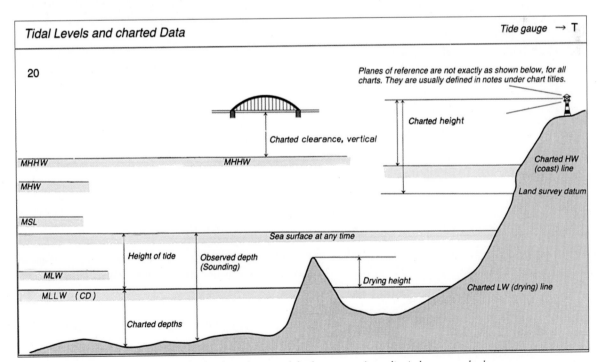

Examples of different states of the tide that have been used for low-water (sounding) datums—also known as Chart Datum (CD)—and also high-water datums.

The Placement of Soundings on a Chart

Most charts are compiled from surveys that were conducted at a larger scale (generally at least twice as large) as the scale of the resulting chart. During a survey, soundings are recorded in a more or less continuous stream so that there is a high density on the resulting smooth sheet or electronic equivalent. These are thinned out by the surveyor. Even so, the cartographer typically has many more soundings available than will fit on the chart, and most will have to be omitted to keep the chart uncluttered. With the following goals (more or less in order of priority) in mind, the cartographer decides which soundings to use:

- highlight shoal areas and least depths over rocks, pinnacles, domes, and ridges

- highlight the least depths in channels (which then become the controlling depths)

- highlight critical soundings, which are generally the shallowest *seaward* soundings (i.e., they may not be the shallowest soundings over a shoal, but they will be the shallowest ones in proximity to a channel or other potential navigation route)

- show deeps—local deformations in the bottom producing soundings significantly deeper than their surroundings

- add supportive soundings that further define the shape of the bottom, depth curves, and changes in slope

- add fill soundings on larger areas of level bottoms that otherwise do not have many soundings

Although the main concern of shoreside mapping is an accurate depiction of topography, the primary goal in chart-making is to contribute to safe navigation. As a result, the overriding concern is to highlight potential dangers and to show potential navigation routes, even at the expense of strict topographical accuracy. If there is an isolated shoal or rock to seaward of a larger shoal, the seaward limit of the larger shoal is usually extended on the chart to encompass the isolated shoal, even though there may be relatively deep water between the two. Similarly, in an area of numerous shoals with intervening channels of deeper water, the deeper water is often not shown.

In other words, the boundary of a shoal is often drawn to encompass all depths that might prove hazardous to navigation rather than to accurately depict the bottom. Similarly, if there is a reef or bar, the shallowest sounding is always given, but not necessarily the deeper soundings. From the perspective of a small-boat sailor, it is often possible to sail in areas that appear on the chart as unnavigable. This is increasingly the case as the draft of merchant and navy vessels increases and hydrographic offices show less interest in inshore details.

The smaller the scale of a chart, the less the detail that can be included and the more the generalization that has to occur. Because of the primary concern to show shoals and hazards, these features are retained, while deeper-water soundings are left out for lack of space on the chart. The curves representing the seaward limit of shoal water get displaced to seaward to encompass any isolated shoal areas. The result is that as scales are reduced, charts become increasingly less useful for inshore navigation, which is the primary interest of recreational sailors. *For safe exploration of coastal waters and to get the most out of the experience, it is essential to use the largest scale charts available.*

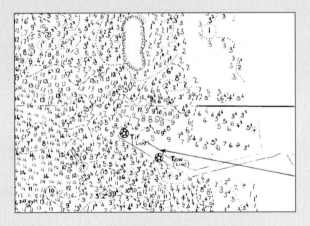

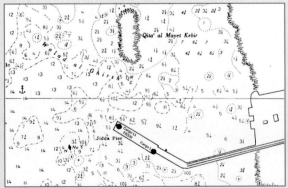

Going from a smooth sheet (top) *to a chart* (bottom), *showing the choice of soundings made by the chart compiler.*

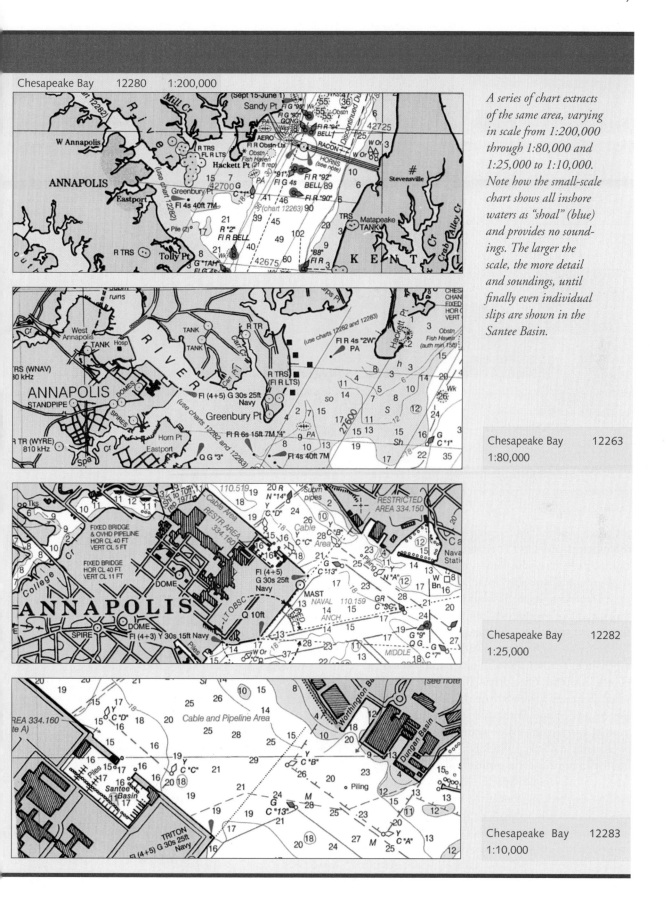

Chesapeake Bay   12280   1:200,000

Chesapeake Bay   12263
1:80,000

Chesapeake Bay   12282
1:25,000

Chesapeake Bay   12283
1:10,000

A series of chart extracts of the same area, varying in scale from 1:200,000 through 1:80,000 and 1:25,000 to 1:10,000. Note how the small-scale chart shows all inshore waters as "shoal" (blue) and provides no soundings. The larger the scale, the more detail and soundings, until finally even individual slips are shown in the Santee Basin.

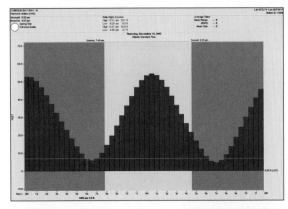

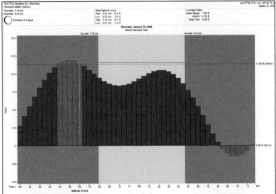

(Top) Tide table for the Bay of Fundy based on LNT. Even at low water springs there is more water than charted. (Bottom) Tide table for Seattle based on MLLW. At every low water springs there is less water than charted.

the average of the highest tides recorded in each of the nineteen years in the previous astronomical cycle, and as such is quite conservative—clearances will almost never be less than what is charted.

Sometimes the high-water datum is used to define the line of contact between the land and the sea, that is, the shoreline (coastline), also known as the *Shoreline Plane of Reference* (SPOR). Unfortunately, at other times it is not, and a third vertical plane of reference is brought into play! This is especially likely when shoreside surveys are used to define the shoreline because shoreside surveyors frequently use some kind of average or MSL to define the boundary between land and water. Work is under way in various countries to produce a uniform plane of reference (e.g., the National Spatial Reference System—NSRS—in the U.S.), but it will be some time before this is consistently applied.

The high-water datum or SPOR is important when determining the height of lights, notably lighthouses, if they are used to calculate a boat's distance

from the coast (see chapter 8). In practice, the height of these lights may be referenced to either the chart's high-water datum or to MSL. Regardless of the plane of reference for lights, shoreside contour lines and spot heights (e.g., the tops of hills and mountains) may well be referenced to MSL and not the high-water datum. However, landmarks for which specific heights are given (e.g., buildings, monuments, antennas, radio towers) may be referenced to the high-water datum.

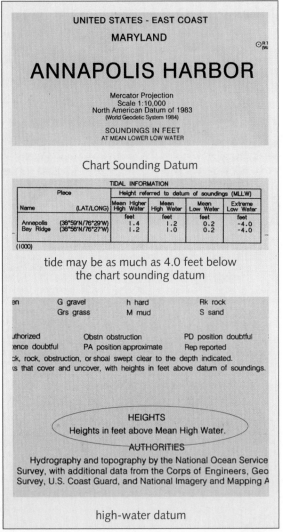

The low-water (sounding) datum is always displayed beneath the chart title (in this case, "Soundings in Feet at Mean Lower Low Water"), very often with a table giving abbreviated tide information, which will give a sense of how far below the chart sounding datum (if at all) the tide may fall (in this case, as much as 4.0 ft.). The high-water datum may be anywhere on the chart, generally in the form of a small, inconspicuous note.

This is all rather confusing. In the worst case, three different vertical datums will be used on a single chart, as follows:

1. The Chart Sounding Datum, generally LAT, LLWLT, MLWS, or MLLW, to which all soundings are referenced.

2. The high-water datum, typically MHWS (MHW for NOAA; HHWLT for the Canadians), to which all bridge heights are referenced, and sometimes the height of lighthouses and landmarks for which heights are given.

3. MSL, which may be used as the reference for shoreside contours and spot heights and, in areas without much tide, for the SPOR and possibly the high-water datum.

At the least, there will be two vertical datums, one for the soundings (the Chart Sounding Datum) and one for the coastline and all heights above the high-water datum.

Much of the time, the chart user doesn't need to know the vertical datums in use. However, *any time the under-keel or above-mast clearance is likely to be tight, this information, along with accurate tidal information, becomes critical. At such times, it is essential to know the datum in use and whether the actual water depth or overhead clearances are likely to be less than charted (not uncommon at low water springs, with depths sometimes being a meter or more [several feet] less, and clearances at high water springs also being off by several feet).* Regardless of the datum, the prudent navigator will want to allow for several additional feet with power-line clearances, notably with high-voltage cables, because of the arcing that is possible, particularly in damp weather. European sailors, who are accustomed to soundings based on the conservative LAT, need to be particularly watchful when boating in U.S. waters where soundings are based on the significantly less conservative MLLW.

The low-water datum in use on a paper chart is easy to find—it is always prominently displayed under the chart title, along with the horizontal datum and similar information. The other vertical datums, frequently shown in a small note at any point on the chart, may not be as easy to locate. On vector-based electronic charts, it is typical for

I wonder if this was a day on which the low tide fell below the charted depths!

none of this data to be displayed, but it should be somewhere in the metadata file; on raster charts, you have to scroll around to find it.

Where electronic charts are compiled from charts based on different datums, the depth contour lines will not meet directly, resulting in something known as *datum jump*. This occurs, for example, in areas of the North Sea where British Admiralty and French data based on LAT meets up with German data based on MLWS. The navigator will be moving between areas in which the charted depths under the keel can change by up to 0.5m/20". On raster charts this will be visible in terms of the datum jump, but on vector charts it may not be visible.

As more hydrographic offices convert to LAT for the low-water datum, there will be a period in which the user is likely to have charts with a mix of datums. More significantly, the tide tables may be based on a different vertical datum than the chart in

The result of a collision with an overhead power line.

use. For example, you might have a new set of tide tables based on LAT and an older chart based on MLLW. When the tide tables are used in conjunction with the chart, you will get an overly optimistic view of depths, sometimes to a significant extent (1 m or more/several feet). It is important to read the fine print on the chart and the tide tables to ensure that the vertical datums match—and to build in an appropriate allowance if they don't.

Technical Wrinkles

The LAT and MLLW and other vertical datums vary over time, so the specific level used for the vertical plane of reference must be tied to a particular point in history. In practice, it is referenced to an "epoch" of nineteen years.* The appropriate datum is derived by continuously collecting data for many years at numerous "stations" and then averaging the numbers for each station over the specified nineteen-year period. From this information, tidal benchmarks are established at various points around the coast (as well as the Great Lakes in the U.S.). In the United States, when I wrote the first edition of this book NOAA was using the 1960–78 epoch, but this has now been updated to the 1983–2001 epoch. Given that water levels are rising at an average of 2.02 mm per year in many areas, this results in minor, but potentially significant changes in depths, as is shown in the accom-

panying table of the datum differences (around 0.4 ft./0.1 m) for the entrance to Chesapeake Bay.

When a survey is conducted, the surveyors essentially have to calibrate their instruments to these tidal benchmarks, and then remove all tidal and other influences that create a deviation from them. This can be a complex task; for greatest accuracy during the survey, tide data has to be collected continuously at the reference stations so the necessary corrections can be input. Of course, the data must be adjusted for the fact that the survey is invariably conducted at a location removed to a greater or lesser extent from the tide station. Under current NOAA standards, "the allowable contribution of the error for tides and water levels to the total survey (error) budget falls between 0.20 meter (8 in.) and 0.45 meter (18 in.), depending on the complexity of the tides." In many cases, the survey will include measures to detect and eliminate even these errors. However, there are also many parts of the world in which accurate tide data is simply not available, in which case the conversion of soundings to the chart's vertical datum is a bit of a crude affair.

This methodology for adjusting depths to a chart's vertical datum is changing. With differential GPS, using additional shoreside stations together with commercially available correction services, it is possible to measure vertically with a GPS to centimeter-level accuracy. However, this measurement is to the WGS 84 ellipsoid, not the geoid (see chapter 1). Some geoid/ellipsoid offset models that have been developed are also now approaching centimeter-level accuracy in parts of the world (see, for example, the U.S. Geoid09, which can be downloaded from www.ngs.noaa.gov/GEOID). Let's say we have a boat that, at a given moment in time, knows its vertical position in relation to the ellipsoid, plus the depth of the water. The geoid, by definition, represents mean sea level (MSL). The difference between the boat's vertical position in relation to the ellipsoid and the geoid/ellipsoid offset is a measure of the boat's vertical distance from MSL. By applying this difference to the measured depth, the sounding can be corrected to MSL. At this point, we get into a complication because prevailing winds, currents, and other effects can cause the real-world MSL at a given location (as measured through averaged tide readings over a nineteen-year epoch—see above) to differ

Datum Differences Over Time

EPOCH DATUM CHECK

Station:	8638863		
Name:	Chesapeake Bay Bridge Tunnel, VA		
Control:			
Units:	Feet		
Epoch:	1983–2001	1960–1978	Difference
MHHW:	28.18	27.83	0.35
MHW:	27.95	27.60	0.35
MSL:	26.69	26.33	0.36
MLW:	25.40	25.00	0.40
MLLW:	25.27	24.88	0.39

* The tidal epoch is based on the period generally reckoned to constitute a full cycle for the various astronomic influences on the tides. The longest cycle to which the tide is subject is due to a slow change in the declination of the moon, which covers 18.6 years.

from the idealized geoid MSL by up to two meters. A further, locally based correction has to be applied to the geoid MSL. There are then algorithms available to convert the resulting MSL to whatever vertical datum is to be used on a chart (e.g., LAT, MLLW, etc.; in the U.S., these conversion algorithms can be downloaded from http://vdatum.noaa.gov/). The end result is a sounding corrected to a chart's vertical datum without having to track the state of the tide at the time the sounding is taken (averaged tidal information is still needed to determine the offset from geoid MSL).

The next generation of GPS satellites, the first of which was launched in 2010 with the rest due to be launched before 2020, have an additional signal (L5) output at a different frequency to the existing L1 and L2 signals. Measuring the phase differences between the L1, L2, and L5 signals will remove ionospheric refraction errors, which are the principal positioning errors in existing non-military GPSs, resulting in centimeter-level horizontal and vertical positioning accuracy with respect to the WGS 84 ellipsoid. This is truly remarkable technology, which, once it becomes widely adopted, will transform the processes of hydrographic surveying and should greatly accelerate the production of accurate soundings (for more on this, see chapter 4).

Factors Affecting the Accuracy of Charted Soundings

It is obvious that the degree of accuracy with which soundings have been taken to date varies to an extent that is impossible to quantify. Beyond this, the complexity of reducing these soundings to any particular datum needs to be appreciated because where there is complexity, there is room for error. Older soundings are not likely to have been reduced with the same degree of accuracy as newer soundings—the necessary technical sophistication simply wasn't available. As impressively accurate as most charts may be, where the water beneath the keel is limited, it still behooves a mariner to treat soundings with considerable caution.

Even if the soundings are precisely measured and accurately reduced to chart datum, a number of circumstances can result in the water depth (or bridge clearances) being less than the charted depth (or charted clearance), sometimes substantially (maybe more than 1 m/several feet), including the following:

1. **CHOSEN LOW-WATER DATUM.** As noted, some datums are more conservative than others. Except for LAT and LLWLT, the water at low-water spring tides will typically be less than charted depths. Similarly, the water at high tide regularly may be higher than the high-water datum, reducing charted overhead clearances. This will continue to be the case, even with soundings accurately derived from vertical DGPS readings, because it is a function of the chosen chart datum and not the accuracy with which the soundings have been measured.

2. **WIND-DRIVEN TIDES.** In many areas, the wind significantly affects water levels, either increasing or decreasing them. For example, a consistent north wind blowing down the Chesapeake Bay may drop water levels in some of the rivers and creeks by 1 meter or more (several ft.). The combination of high winds and changes in barometric pressure (discussed in item 4 of this list) can produce major storm surges—the most dramatic are associated with hurricanes and typhoons. In 1953, a storm surge of 3 meters (10 ft.) inundated large areas of The Netherlands and the east coast of England; in 1982, a negative surge in the Thames estuary dropped the tide by as much as 2.25 meters (7.4 ft.); in 2005, the 7–9 m

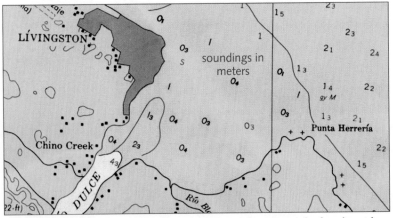

The bar at the mouth of the Rio Dulce in Guatemala. Despite the fact that tides are extremely modest in this region, at high tide with an onshore wind, a boat with a 1.8-meter draft (6 ft.) can enter without hitting bottom.

Hurricane Katrina makes landfall over New Orleans in 2005.

Shrimp boats piled up by Katrina's tidal surge.

Flood waters inundating New Orleans after the levees were breached.

rise considerably. Depths in the mouth of the Amazon, for example, may vary by 18 meters (60 ft.). An interesting combination of this scenario and wind-driven effects occurs with the bar across the mouth of the Rio Dulce in Guatemala, where an onshore wind tends to build all day and then fade overnight. For those restricted by draft, the best time to cross is when a high tide occurs in mid- to late afternoon, with a strong onshore wind and a powerful freshwater outflow. Together, these conditions substantially raise the water level.

4. **BAROMETRIC PRESSURE.** Persistent extremes of high or low pressure can influence water levels: high pressure lowers levels and low pressure raises them (a 34-millibar change in barometric pressure results in a 0.3 m/1 ft. change in sea level; this is one of the reasons for storm surges in hurricanes).

5. **EPOCHAL INFLUENCES.** In the United States, the current epoch used to determine chart sounding datums is 1983–2001, which is also

The aftermath of the 2011 Japanese earthquake and tsunami.

(24–30 ft.) storm surge associated with hurricane Katrina overwhelmed the levees protecting New Orleans and flooded 80% of the city.

3. **FRESHWATER INFLUENCES.** These are particularly relevant in tidal rivers and at their mouths. After periods of heavy rainfall, water levels may

Large breaking waves inundate a popular Thailand anchorage during the 2007 tsunami.

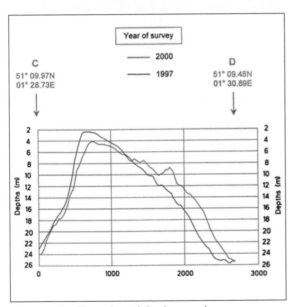

An example of how charted depths may change over time—in this case, by as much as 4 m in just 3 years.

used by several other hydrographic offices. The midpoint, which is approximately the date around which readings are averaged, is 1992. Since then, global warming and other factors have continued to raise sea levels worldwide by some small, but measurable, amount. In the Great Lakes, the tide datum has to be adjusted every twenty-five to thirty years to take into account movement of the earth's crust.

6. **TIME.** Soundings are most likely to be correct at the time of the survey. Storms and other natural phenomena (such as wildfires that damage vegetation, allowing silt to enter rivers), large floods, human influences on hydrography (construction of jetties, etc.), and in fact just about any activity subsequent to a survey can alter the seabed.

As always, the message is a cautionary one: *Do not accept chart sounding and height data at face value when sailing in restricted waters!*

4

Regulations and Revolution

WHEN THE FIRST EDITION of this book was written (in 2001) it was reasonable to assume that the majority of its readers would be paper chart users. This is no longer the case. If we have not already passed the point at which the majority of boaters and sailors are using electronic charting as their primary, and in many cases, their only, source of charts and other navigational data, then I am sure we soon will.

The loss of the Titanic *in 1912 prompted the first Safety of Life at Sea (SOLAS) convention and treaty.*

Electronic charting is a fast-moving field in which the private sector tends to set the pace. This results in a mass of exciting new ideas and data that raise all kinds of issues about reliability and the quality of the data. In this chapter I will explore these issues, beginning with a review of the principal regulations and standards that currently set the framework for electronic charting. Then I will move on to explore emerging developments and their implications. Unfortunately, to get to the exciting stuff we first have to plow through a sea of acronyms.

The Legislative Framework

The loss of the *Titanic* in 1912 prompted the first Safety of Life at Sea (SOLAS) convention, but it took the formation of the United Nations (UN) in 1945 to establish a structure for legally binding international standards. The UN set up the International Maritime Organization (IMO) to develop a comprehensive regulatory framework for shipping. The International Regulations for Preventing Collisions at Sea (COLREGS) were issued in 1972, and the SOLAS Convention in 1974. Chapter V of SOLAS governs navigation safety-related issues, including a requirement for ships to carry up-to-date charts (often referred to as "chart-carriage" requirements).

The International Hydrographic Organization (IHO) began developing standards for electronic charts and associated display devices as early as the 1980s. A standard protocol for exchanging vector chart information (S-57: *Transfer Standard for Digital Hydrographic Data*) was issued in 1992. This does what its name implies: it creates a uniform structure for transferring digital hydrographic data. The data still has to be compiled into an electronic chart, which takes additional software. An electronic chart that uses S-57 as its digital data standard and which *is issued by a national hydrographic office* is known as an Electronic Navigational Chart (ENC). (A vector chart compliant with S-57 but which is not issued by a national hydrographic office does not qualify as an ENC.)

IMO resolution A.817 (19), defining standards for Electronic Chart Display and Information Systems (ECDIS), was first issued in 1995, then revised in 2006. This specifies minimum characteristics for electronic chart navigation equipment on commercial shipping. The IMO asked the International Electrotechnical Commission (IEC) to develop a mechanism for testing ECDIS for compliance with Resolution A.817(19), resulting in IEC standard 61174 governing "type approval" for ECDIS. Another IHO standard, S-52: *Specifications for Chart Content and Display Aspects of ECDIS*, regulates display characteristics on an ECDIS. S-52 contains a definition of the colors to be used for electronic charts in ECDIS, and a library of electronic chart symbols. The combination of these standards ensures that every ECDIS—developed by commercial companies in the private sector—produces more or less the same end product from the same electronic chart database.

An IHO standard for raster charts (S-61) was issued in 1999. This recognizes two formats, the Admiralty Raster Chart Service (ARCS) format used by the British Admiralty, and the BSB File Format developed by MapTech in conjunction with NOAA in the United States. Both are used by various other hydrographic offices. A raster chart that complies with S-61 and which *is issued by a national hydrographic office* is known as a Raster Navigational Chart (RNC). (A raster chart compliant with S-61 but which is not issued by a national hydrographic office does not qualify as an RNC.)

Taken as a whole, these standards (A.817 [19], IEC 61174, S-57, S-52, and S-61) address a host of important issues that ensure that:

- overscale data displays are not used in electronic charts;
- charts cannot be overzoomed;
- electronic charts have at least all of the information of an equivalent paper chart and that it is at least as accurate;
- electronic charts are easy to update through an electronic version of *Notices to Mariners*;

Modern electronic navigation equipment being tested by electronics expert Ben Ellison.

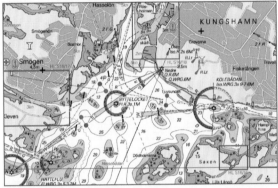

Although privately produced electronic charts, such as this one of the west coast of Sweden from NV Charts, are not recognized as acceptable to meet legally regulated "chart carriage" requirements, many are superior to charts from the official hydrographic offices.

the display system can be seen both in daylight and at night.

With these pieces in hand, SOLAS Chapter V was amended in 2002 to accept a "type-approved" ECDIS, running ENCs displayed according to S-52, as a legal alternative to paper charts so long as there is some kind of a back-up, which can be another ECDIS. (There is no longer a legal requirement for ships to carry paper charts.) Where ENC coverage is not available, RNCs, running on an ECDIS (at which point the ECDIS is operating in a Raster Chart Display System [RCDS] mode), can be used as a legal alternative, but when operating in RCDS mode there must be a certain number of paper charts also available for use. Approved electronic chart displays are being phased in as a legal requirement on new ships from 2012, and on older ships in the years up to 2018.

Circa 2000, the development of standards controlling the official electronic charting world was more-or-less frozen in order to give the hydrographic offices time to catch up and to digitize their charts, and also to provide stability, as any significant changes to the standards would require making changes to the ECDIS already at sea. In the succeeding decade there were only limited amendments to the IMO, IEC, and IHO ECDIS-related standards. However a new *Universal Hydrographic Data Model*,

known as S-100, has been developed by the IHO and published in 2010. S-100, which will eventually replace S-57, is based on the European ISO 19000 series of geographic information standards (GIS) which are widely used in both Europe and North America for shoreside digital mapping and other applications. The future ENC product specification, numbered S-101, is being derived from S-100. What we should see is a worldwide convergence of hydrographic and shoreside GIS digital mapping standards in both the public and private sectors.

The Private Sector

During the years it took the national hydrographic offices to develop their standards through the IHO, the private sector went ahead and digitized thousands of charts in both raster and vector format using a range of available and proprietary formats (for example, Arc/INFO, AutoDesk DXF/DWG, and IntergraphDGN). Subsequently, we have seen a considerable convergence with the official standards (it is, for example, now common to see recreational products that comply with S-57 and S-61), but even so to be considered an ENC or RNC, and to be a legally acceptable alternative to paper charts, *an electronic chart has to be issued by a national hydrographic office.*

Regardless of the quality of privately produced products, and regardless of their compliance with S-57 and S-61, even when these products are running on a type-approved ECDIS (and many do), without that official stamp of approval they are not a legal substitute for paper charts (and in fact, regardless of type approval, the ECDIS is no longer considered to be an ECDIS, and it has to alert the user to the fact that the electronic chart in use is not an approved chart). While it is taking a long time for the national hydrographic offices to complete worldwide vector (ENC) coverage, the private sector has had much of the world covered for some time. What is more, the official ENCs are plagued by differences in the chart development practices of the national hydrographic offices, whereas the private-label charts are consistent with one another, and often also contain additional useful features. We have the ironic situation where it is not unusual for ships to carry ECDIS-compliant ENCs for legal reasons but to navigate with private-label charts (notably Transas TX97 and C-Map CM93/3; NV Chart reports that the U.S. Coast Guard navigates with its charts in Bahamian waters).

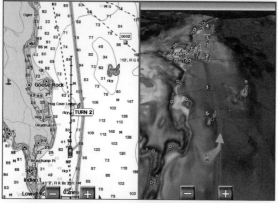

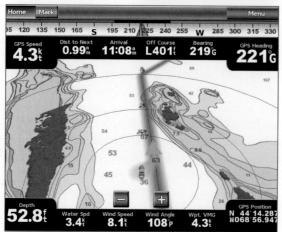

Examples of 3-D and other recently developed display technologies from Furuno and Garmin.

The recreational world does not have to comply with the "chart-carriage" requirements applied to commercial shipping and does not care about such things as "type approval." In any case, type-approved ECDIS equipment is prohibitively expensive, and often physically too large. A considerable array of alternative equipment is available to display a wide range of electronic charting products, sometimes with more features than ECDIS. All such systems fall under the general framework of Electronic Charting Systems (ECS). This covers everything from low-end chartplotters to systems with equivalent functionality to a full-blown ECDIS. With ever-increasing computing power, the functional differences between ECDIS and many ECS have steadily diminished. An alternative, less rigorous standard to the ECDIS standards was developed by the Radio Technical Commission for Maritime Services (RTCM), and titled *Recommended Minimum Standards for Electronic Chart Systems* (ECS). It was first released in 1994. Version 5.0 (RTCM10900.5) was issued in 2011. In 2010 it became embodied in an international standard—IEC62376. This covers the operational and performance requirements for ECS, and methods of testing and required test results. It defines three categories of equipment—A, B, and C—with A being tested to the most rigorous standards that are designed to provide a back-up to ECDIS, and C to the least.

In 2000 the International Organization for Standards (ISO) stepped into the ECS arena. In 2003 it released ISO19379: *Ships and Marine Technology—ECS Databases—Content, Quality, Updating, and Testing.* Where the RTCM/IEC standard focuses on equipment, the ISO standard focuses on requirements and test methods for the production of an ECS database. "It addresses the elements of the database relevant to safety of navigation including content, quality and updating (and) provides guidance on production and testing of an ECS Database." As such, the RTCM/IEC and ISO standards are more-or-less complementary. Given the somewhat anarchic way in which the private sector has evolved, checking for compliance with IEC62376 and ISO19379 is a useful way of checking an ECS for adherence to internationally accepted minimum standards.

Added Value

The various standards described above create a framework applicable to both the official and private sectors covering production and display of electronic

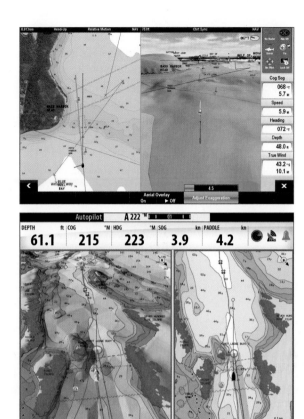

Innovative displays from Raymarine and Simrod.

charts. In recent years we have seen an explosion of "value-added" products thrown into the mix, primarily from the private sector. This includes such things as tides and currents, blended aerial photography, sea-level photography (e.g., harbor and marina entrances), information from cruising guides, detailed marina charts, a Google Earth overlay, and so on. More recently, a lot of work has gone into 3-D displays of bathymetry, and we have seen the ability for software to plot a safe path between two points without straying into areas that fall below a minimum depth.

The larger private sector chart providers are also adding a significant amount of hydrographic and other data to their charts that is not sourced from national hydrographic offices, producing a blend of official and private data. In several areas of the world, 100% privately produced charting products are vastly superior to the official products. The Bahamas is a good example; the paper and digital Explorer Charts—www.explorercharts.com—and those from NV Charts—www.nv-navigator.com—have set the standard for everyone else. In the software world, we have a mass of "apps" that provide additional functionality and enable various electronic charting and related products to be run on tablet PCs, smartphones, and other handheld devices. This is especially the case in the United States where the fact that NOAA is providing ENC and RNC data for free gives software developers the opportunity to create applications without the cost and burden of providing the data needed to make the software relevant.

Within the official hydrographic world interesting parallel developments have been taking place, exemplified by the activities of the Center for Coastal and Ocean Mapping (CCOM) at the University of New Hampshire. In chapter 3 I mentioned CCOM's work to enable massive amounts of accurate multibeam echo-sounder data to be rapidly processed and added to electronic databases (which, in the case of NOAA, then becomes freely available to the general public via the Internet). Concurrent with this "CUBE" (Combined Uncertainty and Bathymetric Estimator) project, the CCOM has been working to define "The Chart of the Future"—"a marine decision support system that takes full advantage of existing and emerging technologies in order to maximize safety and efficiency in routine marine responsibilities."

The Chart of the Future integrates bathymetric and tide models with real-time tide, current, and weather data. It includes ship details such as draft and speed over the ground. It is then capable of displaying chart data in such a way as to predict under-keel clearances at the boat's current position, and at projected positions and arrival times along its intended track. In this, depth soundings change to reflect the state of the tide and real-world conditions at the anticipated time of arrival at a given geographic location. In effect, the conventional, static, two-dimensional chart is being expanded to include a dynamic vertical dimension (e.g., a changing tide value, based on a tide model, is applied to soundings and depth contours) and a time dimension (providing real-time adjustments to the tide model), resulting in 4-D cartography. In addition to depths, time-varying information being investigated includes such things as currents, sea ice, and weather. The CCOM is researching mechanisms to use the increasingly widely available AIS system for transmitting data to and from shore stations and between ships, including the use of satellite-based AIS communications (AIS—Automatic Identification System—is already being used in this manner in a number of major ports around the world).

Given the limited capacity of humans to absorb and process information, modern technology can present navigators with an overwhelming mass of data to the point of being confusing rather than helpful. The CCOM and others are investigating the ways that humans process information and researching mechanisms to distill data down to only what is essential for the task at hand. They are also looking at innovative ways to display the data that will help navigators make safe decisions. For example, research has identified three perceptual channels in the primary visual cortex of the brain: the color channel, the texture and form channel, and the motion channel. Using separate channels to display different kinds of information can make the information more accessible. On a weather chart this might be color for temperature, texture for pressure, and moving "streaklets" for wind direction and speed. Similarly, a 3-D graphics display which uses color to highlight all depths that are less than a boat's draft can often distinguish safe and unsafe water with greater clarity in a format that is easier to use than a mass of detailed soundings. One of the challenges lies in creating software that selects appropriate data from vector-based files and then displays this in a manner and at a scale that enhances the navigational experience without adding any additional risks.

In 2007 the CCOM decided to demonstrate some of these concepts by developing a digital version of one of NOAA's *Coast Pilots* with other data sources built in. The result was the GeoCoastPilot—a digital and interactive version of the written *Coast Pilot*. Among other features, the Coast Pilot is linked to a 3-D map environment such that with the click of a mouse the mariner can pull up a 2-D or 3-D chart, or see, in 2-D or 3-D, a pictorial representation of any feature in a geospatial context (i.e., as seen from the boat or some other reference point). This latter feature requires a multirama—a collection of photos of a landmark or other feature taken from multiple vantage points—situated inside a simplified 3-D representation of a port or some other feature.

An outgrowth of this work is exploring mechanisms to apply the GeoCoastPilot concept to "spatially aware" handheld devices enabling you, for example, to point your smartphone at a lighthouse and have it identify the lighthouse, or else have features identified on a simplified chart running on the phone. (Spatially aware phones have a built-in GPS, compass, inclinometer, and accelerometer, so they "know" where they are, the direction they are pointing and at what angle, and if they are going up or

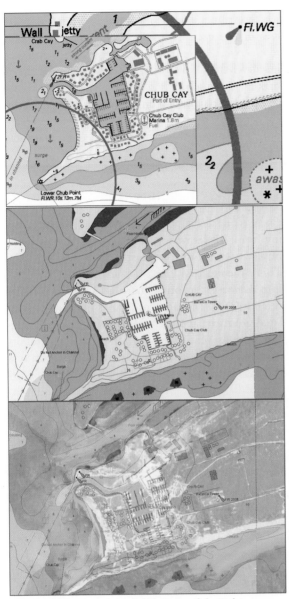

Raster and vector private label charts of the Bahamas from NV Charts. These, along with charts from Explorer Charts, are vastly superior to charts from official hydrographic offices. The lower chart includes a georeferenced aerial photography overlay.

Experimental chart products from the CCOM: (Top) An illustration from the GeoCoast Pilot; (Middle) A combination of different technologies for displaying depth; (Bottom) A display of the 2010 oil spill in the Gulf of Mexico using color texture and moving arrows to highlight information.

down and at what speed.) The CCOM 2010 *Annual Report* notes: "The task of matching chart features to real-world objects is fundamental to navigation in confined waterways and is known to be cognitively difficult, which means that it must necessarily draw attention from other potentially critical tasks. It seems likely that a spatially aware handheld navigation aid may substantially reduce the difficulty of the task and free cognitive resources that may be critical

in an emergency." Initial studies comparing the use of a spatially aware handheld device versus a conventional display show a 10% increase in identification speed and a *50% reduction in errors.*

The IMO has coined the term "e-Navigation" to cover these kinds of developments. The International Association of Lighthouse Authorities (IALA) is heading up the development work, with participation from the IHO. E-navigation is defined as "the

(Top) User-generated content (UCG)—the buoys—added to a Navionics Chart. (Bottom) Electronic chart displayed on an iPad.

harmonized collection, integration, exchange, presentation, and analysis of maritime information onboard and ashore by electronic means to enhance berth-to-berth navigation and related services, for safety and security at sea and protection of the marine environment." As mentioned above, in 2006 the IHO began working on its next generation digital data standard, S-100, which is intended to support a wide variety of digital data sources—including new applications that go beyond traditional hydrography—and to be integrated into the broader geospatial community and web-based services (which S-57 is not). Information about S-100 (as with other IHO documents) can be downloaded from http://www.iho.int. Long before S-100 is completed, we can expect the private sector to be implementing many of these new technologies.

One of the desirable side effects of these various technological developments will be an increasing ability to download chart updates in near real time, which is something the navigational community increasingly expects in this digital age. In a recent email to me, Nick Perugini, who manages NOAA's Internet inquiry system, notes that, "in the old days of chartmaking it was understood by the customer that charts could be inaccurate and untimely so far as updates are concerned, but since GPS and the Internet expectations have changed—customers expect accurate and timely updates."

The "Wiki" Revolution

There is one development in particular that is emerging from this ferment of activity that has profound implications for the future of charts and navigation. This is the incorporation of "user-generated content" into databases, enabling chart users to add Point of Interest (POI) data and corrections to charts and related products, and to share this with other navigators. Various websites are providing a structure for organizing the data gathering and dissemination in a process now known as "crowdsourcing" (defined by Wikipedia as "the act of outsourcing tasks, traditionally performed by an employee or contractor, to an undefined, large group of people or community [a crowd], through an open call").

Crowdsourcing represents a radical departure from traditional chart-making processes, which, until the 1980s, were more-or-less the exclusive preserve of national hydrographic offices. In recent decades, the private sector has moved into the hydrographic arena, significantly expanding the information available to mariners and adding products of interest to the recreational marketplace, but without radically changing the model for creating and delivering navigational information. Now the entire user base itself can be pulled into the process, massively expanding the rate at which new data is generated, and the range of information available to the navigator, with almost instant availability via the Internet. As opposed to being something that is simply displayed for the end user, the navigational database is becoming interactive. The Wiki revolution is catching up with the navigational world.

Just as with Wikipedia (the online encyclopedia), interactive navigational websites (such as ActiveCaptain—www.activecaptain.com—launched in 2007) allow members to add and edit navigational features and comments, give detailed descriptions and reviews of marinas and anchorages, include passage notes, and provide a host of additional miscel-

Choosing an Electronic Chart System

Commercial shipping must use type-approved ECDIS. For the rest of us, there is a near-bewildering choice of ECS devices and software. The following are some thoughts on how to choose between them:

PC versus chartplotter. There was a time when the software, and many of the charts, running on dedicated chartplotters had limited functionality and display characteristics—if you wanted a "full-function" ECS, it had to be PC-based. However, the performance and versatility of plotters has steadily improved over the years, narrowing the gap. PC-based systems almost all run on Windows, which, with many systems, periodically crashes (over the years, we've had numerous crashes, sometimes at extremely inopportune moments), whereas plotters are more-or-less bulletproof. PCs (and other computers, e.g., Macs) are also far more vulnerable to damage. Plotters use less power, which is important on many recreational boats. The argument in favor of plotters and against PCs strengthens all the time.

The ease of use of the system. This is very subjective and changes constantly. The best way to find a system that suits you is to go to a large marine chandlery and experiment with the various systems on display.

The quality of the cartography for a given area. In some parts of the world almost all providers are using the same base cartography, notably in the United States because it is provided free by NOAA. In other parts of the world, there are major differences in the quality of the cartography, especially if the best cartography comes from private sources (e.g., the Bahamas and many developing areas). The quality of the cartography for a given provider can also change significantly over time. For example, the ownership of Nobeltec has changed several times in recent years, resulting in a change in cartography providers (from Transas to C-Map, with further changes in the offing). Garmin has shifted from Transas to developing its own cartography. And so on. Sometimes this results in improved cartography, and sometimes not. Particularly for those venturing into poorly charted regions, it is important to check with Internet chat sites and other sources for the best cartography at any given time.

Update services and cost. These vary enormously from being almost nonexistent, or expensive if they do exist (e.g., you have to buy a new cartridge at full price or with little discount), to being regularly available in a cost-effective fashion. This is also an area where technology is evolving quite rapidly, changing what is offered. If your primary sailing area is geologically stable with little manmade alteration of the shoreline, updates will be less important than if you are in an area with regular changes in the bottom and/or a lot of human alterations.

Radar overlay, particularly when navigating restricted waters in poor visibility or difficult conditions. The radar imports real-world data to overlay on the mathematically constructed picture of the world that is created by the charting system. The latest broadband radars have a phenomenal ability to pick up even small features (such as lobster-trap buoys) at close range, but are not as good as traditional radar at longer ranges.

Added value. This becomes ever more important and is a constantly moving target. Once again, it is best to check close to purchase time. Integrated tides and currents are particularly useful, as is geo-referenced aerial photography, especially if it can be overlaid on a chart as a "see-through" screen (it can, for example, display all the docks as you come into a marina; we have also sailed extensively in the Bahamas through areas charted as impassible using overlaid aerial photography to identify deeper water). Embedded links to other products (such as cruising guides) can pull up a wealth of useful information. 3-D displays for bathymetry are moving from the realms of a gimmick to a useful situational awareness tool. ActiveCaptain and similar user-generated content overlays are a specific form of added value that has enormous potential.

Integration with NMEA 2000. NMEA 2000, which superseded NMEA 0183, is now the dominant navigational communications protocol. It is expanding into engine controls, tank monitoring, onboard power distribution, and other areas. A charting system integrated with NMEA 2000 creates the potential for all kinds of useful information to be exchanged and displayed, and also creates a platform for increasingly powerful diagnostic and troubleshooting tools.

Cost. I have put this at the bottom of the list. It is obviously important, but should be the least important consideration. How much is your boat worth? The price of good cartography is typically a lot less than insurance deductibles in the event of an accident!

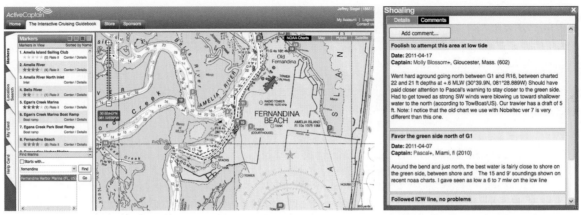

Two examples of UGC found on the ActiveCaptain website. We are only beginning to tap the potential of "crowd sourcing" for expanding navigational information.

lanea deemed of interest to fellow navigators (such as lock and bridge opening times, fuel prices, and so on). With some sites this information remains on the website's server, but with others whenever an Internet connection is available the latest updates can be downloaded and cached on a personal computer and other platforms (e.g., iPhone and iPad, Android, etc.). At the time of writing, an ActiveCaptain layer and data were being added to several of the better-known navigational software packages (e.g., MaxSea Time Zero, Furuno, Rose Point's Coastal Explorer, Nobeltec, and others).

Clearly, this ability of anyone to add data to navigational products on a near real-time basis has enormous potential benefits but also carries substantial risks as the traditional quality-control processes get tossed overboard. Given differential GPS, users can consistently generate accurate horizontal positioning information (much of the time to within 2 meters), but given the complexities of reducing vertical measurements (depths and heights) to chart datums (see chapter 3), especially in tidal waters, user-generated soundings and similar data will be far less reliable. As such, managing the data stream to create useful and trustworthy outputs for the mariner is a significant issue. Websites such as ActiveCaptain are leading the way in establishing a framework for organizing the data and enrolling the user community to police its accuracy. (ActiveCaptain differentiates "facts," for which it has a verification process, from "opinions" for which there is no verification process; it also limits the categories of information posted to its website to those that it deems significant to cruising sailors.) Various electronic chart providers are explor-

ing their own mechanisms to manage the information flow. Navionics was one of the first, adding a User Generated Content (UGC) layer, which can be turned on or off by the navigator, to its vector chart products. When appropriate, user-generated data which passes Navionics' internal validation processes becomes part of its central chart database.

Arguably, some of the most useful information that could come out of this process is accurate and timely sounding data. However, this requires a mechanism that does not now exist to readily adjust soundings to the chart sounding datum, although various organizations in Europe and the United States are refining a capability to take geo-referenced sounding data from any boat and post-process it into relatively accurate data that is referenced to the chart sounding datum. This is then fed back to the users (see, for example, www.olex.no, http://argus.service.com).

As noted in chapter 3, the combination of DGPS, additional shore stations, commercial GPS correction services, accurate geoid models, data to convert geoid mean sea level (MSL) to local mean sea level, and algorithms to convert mean sea level to other chart datums is beginning to be used by professional hydrographers to generate accurate sounding data without having to go through traditional tide calculations. The technology today is very expensive and the equipment relatively cumbersome. But the next generation of GPS satellites with the L5 signal (see chapter 3) will, at some point in the not-too-distant future (probably beginning around 2014), put centimeter-level vertical accuracy (with respect to the WGS 84 ellipsoid) in the hands of consumers. The much-delayed European Galileo system will feature the same signals, while the Russians are upgrading their GLONASS system (and the Chinese are also up to something). Reduction of soundings derived in this fashion to MSL, and conversion to chart datum, is then a matter of applying the correct offsets and algorithms. In the United States and its associated territories (Puerto Rico, the Virgin Islands, Guam, American Samoa, and the northern Marianas) much of the software is already available for free on the Internet, although this is not the case elsewhere. It is not unreasonable to think that in years to come the navigational user community may be able to generate and transmit accurate sounding data in near real time, which will break open the last bastion of the national hydrographic offices and unleash a flood of high-quality hydrographic data, particularly in those areas of interest to recreational sailors rather than hydrographic offices.

These things will not happen overnight—it has taken GPS 30 years to become the cheap, accurate, and ubiquitous horizontal positioning tool we now all take for granted, and there are a number of technical and software challenges that need to be over-come to make the ability to collect accurate sounding data a day-to-day reality for recreational sailors. Nevertheless we can see the writing on the wall. Given the accelerating pace of development, we can expect to see this kind of technology filtering down to the consumer level within a decade.

The Chart of the Future

It is impossible to predict with any degree of certainty where technology will take us in the next few years and decades. However, one thing is certain: the two-dimensional chart delivered by hydrographic offices, which has been a relatively static component of navigational practices for several hundred years, will, for many navigators, at some point become a thing of the past. Paper charts, many of which are works of art, will eventually be relegated to wall hangings, although this will likely take longer than most visionaries assume. (The demise of paper charts has been predicted for decades, but they stubbornly hang on, and in fact both NOAA and the British Admiralty have introduced new paper chart products in recent

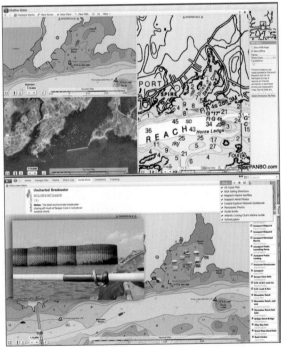

For many years there has been a massive breakwater at Eastport, Maine (U.S.), which has never been shown on official charts. UGC provides an opportunity for this kind of information to be added to electronic charts by the user base.

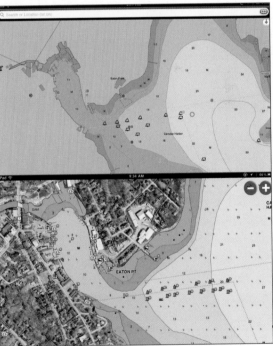

(Top) A recent edition of the official chart of Camden, Maine (U.S.), incorrectly positions the harbor-entrance buoys. These have been correctly positioned (bottom) in the lower chart using UGC. There's also a Google Earth overlay.

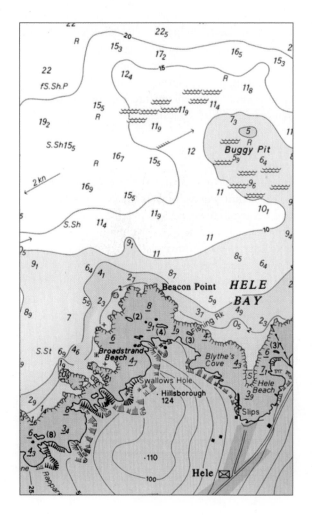

years.) The replacement for paper charts will integrate and organize vastly more information in a wide range of innovative fashions, with this data increasingly provided by the user community in an interactive fashion. Hopefully, the end result will aid rather than confuse the navigator, improving the safety of navigation!

Regardless of what emerges, traditional symbology will still be with us for a long time to come as a mechanism to organize and display a significant portion of the most critical navigational data. This is what is covered in the second half of this book.

A taste of things to come. On this British Admiralty chart of Ilfracombe in SW England, look for: overfalls and tide rips (≈≈≈), a flood stream arrow (feathers on one side), an ebb stream arrow (no feathers), metric soundings (italicized), drying heights (underlined), out of position heights (in parentheses), heights above high-water datum (vertical numbers) including spot heights ashore but with land contours italicized, the rocky foreshore symbol, a submerged rock symbol (✳), and rock awash at the low-water datum (✳), cliffs along the coastline, and a pipeline, with the direction of flow out to sea.

Plans on the Coast of Somerset and Devon 1:12,500	BA 1160

Part 2

Symbology

5

Introduction to *INT-1*

A CHART, WHETHER PAPER OR ELECTRONIC, is a magical product that creates an accurate three-dimensional picture of the surface of a sphere in a two-dimensional format (a flat piece of paper or a computer screen). The skills and techniques that make this possible have evolved over at least 2,500 years, and continue to evolve. The modern chart, however, can be traced back to the sixteenth-century Dutch cartographer, Gerhard Mercator, who developed the chart projection named after him (see page 24). His projection is still the basis for most chart production today.

Gerhard Mercator was one of several people attempting to synthesize the mass of new information about the world coming out of the Age of Exploration, itself sparked by Columbus's voyages to the Americas. Subsequent journeys to the ends of the earth by other adventurers resulted in and were supported by a wave of private chart-making. Given the increasing interest of the European powers in building worldwide empires—and the cost of developing the accurate hydrographic data needed to do it—private chart-making inevitably would give way to governmental control. Arguably, the British Admiralty, formed in 1795, is the most famous of the resulting "official" hydrographic offices.

Whether private or public, to compile a chart and present the necessary information in a condensed yet intelligible format, numerous conventions have to be adopted about how to display it. Over the course of several hundred years, private and public chart-makers struggled with this issue, coming up with a variety of ever-evolving responses. By the end of the nineteenth century, all major powers had a first-class hydrographic office, many of which were producing charts for much of the world (all had worldwide interests and aspirations) and none of which were using the same conventions. This resulted, for example, in the Germans, French, Dutch, and British all producing charts of the English Channel, each chart using different conventions to display the same information.

Mercator's Atlas, which really put him on the map!

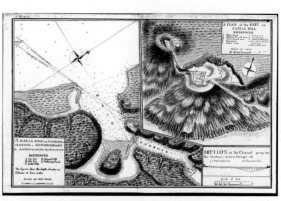

An old chart of the English Channel, illustrating symbology different from that used today.

Standardization

As early as 1884, a Mr. Knorr of the U.S. Hydrographic Office published a pamphlet in which he pointed out that tremendous economies could be achieved, freeing up resources for chart improvements, if hydrographic offices would share data and adopt the same conventions. The idea fell on deaf ears at the time. It was repeated at an International Congress of Navigation held in St. Petersburg, Russia, in 1908, and taken up by M. J. Renaud, a French hydrographer, at an International Maritime Conference in 1912, also held in St. Petersburg. World War I temporarily halted the discussion, which was revived by Renaud in 1918. He won the support of the British Admiralty, resulting in the first truly international hydrographic conference in London in 1919. This led to the formation of the International Hydrographic Bureau (IHB) in 1921, which subsequently morphed into the IHO (the IHB continues to exist as the bureaucratic infrastructure of the IHO). The IHO currently includes in its membership all the major hydrographic offices from around the world, and is recognized as the worldwide governing body under the auspices of the United Nations. The IHB-IHO, from its inception, has been headquartered in Monaco.

Today, the objectives of the IHO are to

- coordinate the activities of national hydrographic offices
- produce the greatest possible uniformity in nautical charts and documents
- promote reliable and efficient methods of carrying out hydrographic surveys
- develop the sciences of hydrography and oceanography

Although the goal of producing uniformity in charts was there from the beginning, its realization has taken time. It wasn't until 1967 that the concept of a worldwide series of international charts was formally adopted, resulting in the establishment of the Commission on the International Chart, Small Scale (CICSS) (a small-scale chart covers a large area in little detail; a large-scale chart covers a small area in great detail). The CICSS devised two series of charts covering the entire world, one at a scale of 1:10,000,000 (nineteen charts) and the other at a scale of 1:3,500,000 (sixty charts).

In 1972, the IHO resolved to apply the international-chart concept to larger scales. This resulted in the formation of the North Sea International Chart Commission (NSICC), which produced a scheme of unified charts covering northwest Europe and the northeast Atlantic. Of greater significance is that the work of the commission resulted in a detailed set of chart specifications, which created the opportunity for international standardization for medium- and large-scale charts. This led to the formation, in 1977, of the Charts Specifications Committee (CSC), which became the Chart Standardization Committee (CSC). Its principal work was completed and adopted by IHO members worldwide in 1982, almost a hundred years after the publication of Mr. Knorr's pamphlet.

The CSC continues to exist as a mechanism for reviewing possible chart-specification changes. Proposed amendments go to the CSC for discussion; if approved by the committee, they are submitted to the IHB, which sends them to all IHO members for comment. In the absence of objections, the changes are adopted after three months. In this way, the international hydrographic community now adheres to a common set of standards that must be used on charts that will receive the IHO "INT" (International Chart) designation, and that are increasingly used in national charts that do not fall within the INT framework (e.g., the French adopted these standards for all new charts in 1985).

How Standardized Are We?

This history emphasizes how recent the international standardization has been and that, technically, it still only applies to charts with the INT designation, although most hydrographic organizations are using the standardized conventions for all new chart production. The process of actually converting charts is extremely time-consuming, and is usually implemented only when a new edition of an existing chart or a completely new chart is produced. New editions of some charts are produced on a regular basis, but others may go decades between new editions. As a result, even among the major hydrographic offices, not all charts have been converted. Even when converted, many older charts are still in use—especially by recreational users—that predate standardized conventions.

For paper charts, the INT standards are spelled out in IHO Publication S-4, *Regulations of the IHO for International (INT) Charts and Chart Specifications of the IHO* (available from the IHO at www.iho-ohi.net/iho_pubs/IHO_downloads.htm). IHO S-4, in turn, forms the basis of various national publica-

17. SYMBOLOGY USED ON AUSTRALIA NAVIGATIONAL CHARTS

1. The following symbology is used in Australian Navigational charts and generally has not been adopted into the International Hydrographic Orginisation INT 1 (symbols and abbreviations) publication:

INT 1 Reference	Description	Symbol
D 17b	Helicopter Landing Site	
J 21	Approximate Rock Reef	
J 21	Rock Symbol	
J 22	Approximate Coral Reef	
J 22	Areas Considered to be Coral Reef	
J 22	Areas of possible shoaling	
J 22	Coral Pinnacle	★
L 17	Moored Storage Tanker	
M	Preferred Route	
M 28.2	Two-way Route direction arrow	
U 3	Visitors Mooring	
N 22	Limit of Marine Protected Area	
N	Ship Reporting System	

2. The following symbology is used in Australian Navigational charts and has been adopted into the International Hydrographic Orginisation INT 1 (symbols and abbreviations) publication:

E 26.1, L 5.1	Wind Turbine	
E 26.2, L 5.2	Wind Farm	
L 24	Underwater turbine	Turbine
M 17	Archipelagic Sea Lane	ASL (see Note)
N 22	Particularly Sensitive Sea Area	PSSA (see GBRMP Note)
N 22	Great Barrier Reef Marine Park High Restriction Areas	MR (see GBRMP Note)
N 22	Environmentally Sensitive Sea Area	GBRMP (see Note)
N 22	Environmentally Sensitive Sea Area	ESSA (see Note)
N	Designated Shipping Area	DSA (see Note)
S 17.1, S 17.2	Automatic Identification System Aid to Navigation (Fixed, Floating)	

A recent symbology update from the Australian hydrographic office.

S-4 notes: "It is likely that . . . there will be national requirements, reflecting a country's needs or preferences, to introduce minor variations into the specifications. . . . The intention is to permit some variations between the charting practices of IHO member offices where they would not mislead a navigator, while striving for complete uniformity where essentials are concerned. The depiction of topographic relief is in the first category, as opposed to the definition and use of a submerged rock symbol, which is in the second." NOAA's *Nautical Chart Manual* states explicitly that "some IHO recommendations, such as metrication and pictorial landmark symbols, have met with user resistance [in the U.S.] and will not be included in the specifications for new [U.S.] charts until sometime in the future." There is also a handful of private paper chart-makers worldwide (the most notable of which are Stanfords Charts and Imray, Laurie, Norie and Wilson, both in the U.K.; and NV Charts in Germany) that use their own, somewhat different, conventions.

IMO and IHO standards for electronic charts and display symbology are spelled out in publications A.817 (19), S-57, S-52, and SP-61 described in chapter 4. However, in the world of electronic chart-making, there is still a certain degree of anarchy concerning symbology on vector charts (because it is an electronic "photo" of a paper chart, a raster chart always looks like the original paper chart). Whereas in the world of paper chart-making, the official hydrographic offices have a near monopoly and control is easier, in the electronic world, private companies and the ever-changing technology are setting the pace and the hydrographic offices are scrambling to catch up and assert their leadership and control.

For the recreational user, almost all electronic charts have been produced outside of any official

tions, such as NOAA's Chart No. 1, the British Admiralty's Chart 5011: Symbols and Abbreviations Used on Admiralty Charts, the French Symboles et Abreviations Figurant sur les Cartes Marines Francaises, and the German Karte 1.

In addition to the internationally agreed-upon standards, these latter publications include minor additions and variations used on national charts. IHO

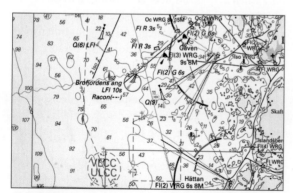

(Left) Official chart of Swedish waters, using buoy and other conventions that are somewhat different from U.S. charts.

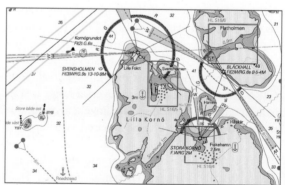

(Right) Private label (NV Charts) chart of Sweden using its own variation on international charting conventions.

framework so far. In the early days of chart-plotters, the equipment had extremely limited memory and computing capabilities; therefore, a rigorous simplification of charts to minimize hardware requirements (which required simple vector-based charts) was needed. The resulting electronic charts didn't look much like traditional paper charts, with symbology varying from one company to another.

As time goes on, however, the ever-increasing computing power of hardware and the decreasing cost of memory—combined with the move toward standardization in both the hydrographic offices and the commercial sector—are resulting in fewer differences in the display characteristics of vector charts. The electronic chart library of symbols endorsed by the IHO (S-52, appendix 2, "Colour and Symbol Specifications for ECDIS") will mostly be immediately familiar to the user of a traditional paper chart, and will be increasingly used for all vector-based chart production. Therefore, in the following discussion, I do not specifically address electronic chart symbols.

INT-1: Organization and Utility

In terms of presenting the symbols, the IHO, in conjunction with the German Hydrographic Office, has produced something known as *INT-1*. In this book, I am using both the U.S. version of *INT-1*, called *Chart No. 1*, and also the British Admiralty's version, called *Chart 5011*. These mimic the system of organization and categorization in *INT-1*. My publisher (International Marine) and I have somewhat rearranged *Chart No. 1* to "internationalize" it, significantly expanding it with explanatory notes. We have used the international symbols from Chart 5011 because the colors are more representative of international use. Throughout, we have added illustrative examples from real charts to test your knowledge.

Although I recommend reading this book in its entirety in conjunction with a chart to gain familiarity with symbology (a good winter project), most readers will occasionally want an explanation of an unfamiliar symbol in a hurry. It is difficult to devise an effective

structure or index that allows you to go from an image on a chart to an image in a book. To facilitate rapid identification of any given symbol, it helps to understand the structure of *INT-1*. First, the contents page is divided into the following five main sections:

GENERAL (see pages 100–116): background data found on any chart (e.g., datums)

TOPOGRAPHY (see pages 117–143): generally speaking, shoreside features, including surface terrain, man-made features, and port installations

HYDROGRAPHY (see pages 144–192): seaward features, including depths, hazards, the nature of the seabed, tides and currents, and offshore installation

AIDS AND SERVICES (see pages 193–240): includes lights, buoys, fog signals, and radar reflectors

INDEXES (see pages 242–266)

This seems like a good arrangement: if you want to look up a symbol related to seaward features, for example, you initially go to HYDROGRAPHY—until you realize that these divisions do not actually occur in *INT-1* itself! We have put them in for you. Each of the five principal divisions is then subdivided into a number of sections. A capital letter is assigned to each section, from A to X. The following structure results:

GENERAL

A   Chart Number, Title, and Marginal Notes

B   Positions, Distances, Directions, Compasses

TOPOGRAPHY

C   Natural Features

D   Cultural Features

E   Landmarks

F   Ports

G   Topographic Terms

| DIRBOYA1 | FOGSIG01 | LIGHTS01 | LIGHTS82 | LIGHT503 | MAGVAR51 | NORTHAR1 | OBSTRN02 |

Sample electronic chart symbols from the IHO's approved library.

Symbology

HYDROGRAPHY

H Tides, Currents

I Depths

J Nature of the Seabed

K Rocks, Wrecks, Obstructions

L Offshore Installations

M Tracks, Routes

N Areas, Limits

O Hydrographic Terms

AIDS AND SERVICES

P Lights

Q Buoys, Beacons

R Fog Signals

S Radar, Radio, Electronic Position-Fixing Systems

T Services

U Small-Craft Facilities

INDEXES - (reprinted in this edition as a single *INT-1* index)

V Index of Abbreviations

W International Abbreviations

X List of Descriptors

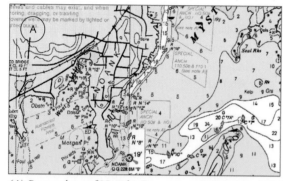

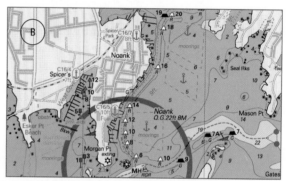

(A) Raster chart of Noank, Connecticut (U.S.), from NOAA. It is identical to its paper chart version. (B) Raster chart of Noank from NV Charts, a private chart manufacturer. It is identical to its paper chart version but different in a number of respects from the NOAA chart.

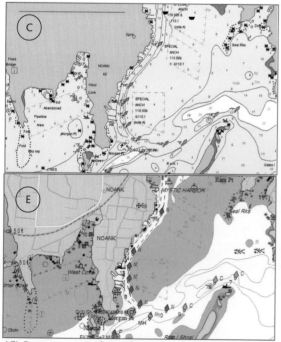

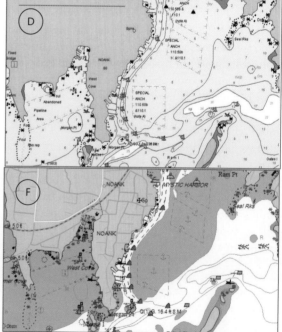

(C) Passport vector chart of Noank using its version of NOAA symbology. (D) Passport vector chart of Noank using its version of ECDIS symbology. (E) MaxPro vector chart of Noank using its version of NOAA symbology. (F) Max Pro vector chart of Noank using its default symbology.

Most of the categorization is self-evident, although the alphabetical groupings are somewhat arbitrary. For example, churches, temples, and mosques —which are clearly "cultural" features in some sense (section D)—are considered landmarks (section E). The greater problem is that the overall structure is not user-friendly inasmuch as rapid symbol identification depends on a working knowledge of the alphabetic structure: Every chart user should become familiar with this structure.

To facilitate symbol searches, we added the section headings to the page margins. As you leaf through the book, you can quickly find the relevant division and then look for the appropriate alphabetical section within that division.

Within each alphabetical section (e.g., "K Rocks, Wrecks, Obstructions"), the entries are numbered consecutively and divided into subgroups (e.g., "General," "Rocks," "Wrecks," "Obstructions"). However, these subgroups are not especially helpful in finding any particular symbol. Most often, your best bet is to skim through an entire alphabetical section looking for the symbol rather than figuring out and finding the correct subgroup.

Hydrographic offices often have national varia-

tions on the international theme, particularly so with older charts and those for which no new edition has been issued in recent years. In the United States, NOAA and NOS sometimes have different conventions than NIMA/NGA.

In our version of *INT-1*, we put the international symbol(s) on the left-hand side of the page (this is the most commonly used symbol), its label and explanation in the center, and any NOAA or NIMA/NGA national variations in columns on the right-hand side. Note that when the British Admiralty, the French, the Germans, and other national hydrographic offices have a symbol that differs from the international convention, one of the symbols on the right-hand side will likely closely replicate the variation.

All hydrographic offices supplement the international library of approved symbols with some of their own. In their national variation of *INT-1*, they are added to the end of the relevant alphabetical division and given a lower-case letter designator to distinguish them from the numbered international symbols. We included the U.S. supplementary symbols because many are similar to those of other countries.

A few other minor changes were made to the structure of *INT-1* to make it more user-friendly, re-

Schematic Layout

Schematic page layout for display of chart symbols.

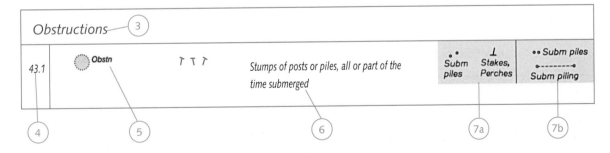

1 Alphabetic section
2 Section heading
3 Section subdivision
4 Column 1: symbol # in the IHO list
5 Column 2: international symbol
6 Column 3: description of symbol, term, or abbreviation
7a Column 4: representation used on charts produced by the National Ocean Service (NOS). In certain

instances, the representation is clarified by a label on the chart.

7b Column 5: representation used on charts produced by NIMA/NGA. In certain instances, the representation is clarified by a label on the chart.

Note: When the NOS and NIMA/NGA symbols are identical, columns 4 and 5 are combined to show only one set of symbols.

sulting in the typical page structure illustrated on page 89.

Generalizations Worth Knowing

Before getting into the details of *INT-1*, it is worth noting some recurring conventions and generalizations used by the hydrographic community that convey extremely useful information, but the significance of which is routinely missed by chart users.

First, a note on terminology. A common convention in charts is to distinguish labels typographically. *INT-1* has used the term "vertical" (or less frequently "upright") to refer to standard type (like this), which is sometimes also referred to as "regular" (in the word-processing world). This book uses the term "vertical." *INT-1* uses "sloping" to refer to italic type (*like this*); this book uses the term "italic." Charts also distinguish between "capital" letters (LIKE THIS—also called "upper case") and labels that have "initial capitals" only (Like This).

Positional Accuracy

- When something is precisely located, a small black dot is used to fix the location. It may be inside a circle or a triangle, or added to the base of a symbol, or incorporated in some other way into a symbol. IHO S-4 does not define the level of accuracy required for a precise location, but NOAA sets it at 3 meters (10 ft.).

- When something is approximately located, a small circle is used without a black dot. The circle may be incorporated into the base of a buoy symbol to indicate that the buoy has a turning circle ("watch" circle; note, however, that the circle on the chart is purely symbolic—it does not represent the turning circle itself). NOAA considers this symbol to mean that the position is accurate to within 30 meters (100 ft.).

- In cases where the margin of error may be higher (e.g., 100–300 ft. for NOAA), the letters "PA" (for Position Approximate) are added to the circle.

- If the position is even less certain but the existence of the feature itself is not in doubt, it is labeled "PD" (for Position Doubtful).

- If the existence of the feature itself is in doubt, it is labeled "ED" (for Existence Doubtful).

Capital and Lowercase Type

INT uses pictorial symbols for landmarks—"an object of enough interest or prominence in relation to its surroundings to make it outstanding or to make it useful in determining a location or a direction" (NOAA, *Nautical Chart Manual*). NOAA found U.S. chart users to be resistant to these pictorial symbols and so invariably adds labels. This has led to two somewhat different conventions when labeling landmarks.

- NOAA uses all capitals when the position is accurately known, and initial capitals followed by

Chesapeake Bay, Severn and Magothy Rivers — 12282 — 1:25,000

*Selected features: PA = **Position Approximate**. Vertical letters for **beacons** and topographic features (even if the label is over the water; e.g., St. Helena I), italic for hydrographic features (even if the label is placed on land; e.g., Old Place Cr). TR = **Tower** (it is in capitals, which means the position is accurate—which is confirmed by the dot inside the position circle—and/or it is conspicuous). **Vertical soundings**, because this is a NOAA imperial chart (ft.); if it were metric, the soundings would be italic. Labels on **depth contours** are italic to distinguish them from spot soundings, and also one font smaller and a lighter typeface. The blue denotes **shoal** water (on this chart, less than 10 ft.). ✺ = dangerous wreck (see chapter 7).*

lowercase letters when the position is approximate. However, all capitals may also be used for conspicuous features; they are routinely used for other information (e.g., bridge information, overhead power lines, and pipes).

- INT often does not use a label. When it does, if it uses all capitals, it indicates the landmark is conspicuous; initial capitals followed by lowercase letters indicates it is not as conspicuous. As with NOAA, all capitals may also be found on other information.

Vertical and Italic Type

- Topographic features—shoreside features and those firmly attached to the bottom and permanently above the high-water datum (e.g., lighthouses, fixed light structures, and beacons)—are labeled with vertical type.

- Hydrographic features—anything below the high-water datum (including features that dry out at low tide), names of water areas, underwater features, and all floating objects—are labeled with *italic* type.

Note: Imray, Laurie, Norie and Wilson, the well-known U.K. private chart-maker, uses vertical letters for both topographic and hydrographic features.

Vertical and Italic Numbers; Heights and Soundings

- In general, heights ashore are given in vertical numbers (consistent with the vertical type for topographic labels). However, to distinguish heights on contour lines (which do not represent specific measured points) from "spot" heights (which do represent specific measured points), the heights on contours are given at a marginally smaller font size than that used for spot heights (which is not always easy to detect). NOAA does not always adhere to this convention—see below.

- On rare occasions, the *approximate* height of something (usually trees) above the chart high-water datum is given (most likely used for wooded areas where the actual ground level is not visible). In this case, a straight line is drawn above the height, as in $\overline{123}$.

- If the same straight line in $\overline{123}$ is used on a

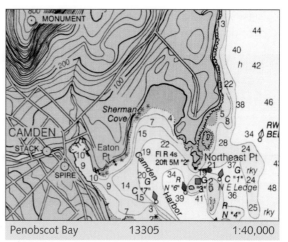

Penobscot Bay   13305   1:40,000

Selected features: Contour lines on land are every 20 feet, with every fifth one (100 ft. intervals) bolder. Contour labels are italic to differentiate them from soundings (vertical—this is a NOAA imperial chart, so the conventions are the opposite of INT conventions). MONUMENT, SPIRE, STACK are all accurately charted (positioning dot plus capital letters) and conspicuous (capital letters). Topographic labels are vertical, hydrographic italic. Beacon labels are vertical, buoys are italic.

sounding, generally in connection with a wreck or other obstruction, it indicates the safe clearance over the obstruction at the chart's low-water (sounding) datum.

- If a straight line is put above a sounding with a dot over the line, it indicates that no bottom was found at this depth, as in $\overset{\bullet}{\overline{136}}$—i.e., there is at least this much water.

- Small, subscript numbers are decimal fractions of a meter, as in 5_6, except on charts where soundings are given in fathoms and feet, in which case the subscript number is feet.

- In some areas, minimum depths are checked with a wire-drag apparatus. In this case, the minimum sounding found is given an inverted "hat" beneath it, as in $\underline{17}$.

- Occasionally the height of a feature is given above the seabed or above ground level, as opposed to its relationship to the low- or high-water datum. In this case, it is given a "hat," as in $\widehat{12}$.

- To comply with *INT-1*, soundings and drying heights (the height above the low-water datum of features covered at high tide) should be given in italic numbers (consistent with the italic type for hydrographic labels). However, to distinguish depths on depth contours (which do not represent specific measured depths) from soundings (which do represent specific measured depths), the contour depths are sometimes given in vertical numbers, and/or in a marginally smaller font size than that used for soundings (not always easy to detect). NOAA does not always adhere to this convention—see below.

Where it is deemed necessary to alert a navigator to the fact that a sounding may have come from a smaller-scale source (and therefore has an inherently higher potential for inaccuracy) or is unreliable in some other way (generally an older survey), the sounding may be shown in special type; IHO S-4 recommends vertical numbers formed from hairline lines (very fine lines, also not easy to detect).

NOAA does not fully adhere to these international conventions on heights and soundings. In particular, it uses italicized numbers—which are in compliance with *INT-1*—on its metric charts (depths in meters), but uses vertical numbers on its imperial charts (depths in fathoms and feet) to distinguish them from the metric charts. In both cases, the opposite type style is used to label contour lines (i.e., if the spot soundings are vertical, the contours are italicized and vice versa) and to warn of soundings that are unreliable. Given that most U.S. charts are still in imperial units, the conventions in effect are usually the opposite of the IHO conventions.*

For a rock that is covered when the water is at the level of the high-water datum but is uncovered when it is at the level of the low-water datum, a drying height may be given. This is

(Left) A beacon on the U.S. Intracoastal Waterway. Because it is fixed to the bottom, it is considered to be a topographic feature and will be labeled on the chart with vertical (upright, non-italic) type. (Right) All buoys are considered to be hydrographic features and as such are labeled on the chart with italic type.

---

* NOAA initiated a metrication program for its paper charts in 1972, but it soon stalled and is unlikely to be revived any time soon. In fact, those charts that were metricized have been converted back into imperial units. Vector-based electronic charts can be displayed either way.

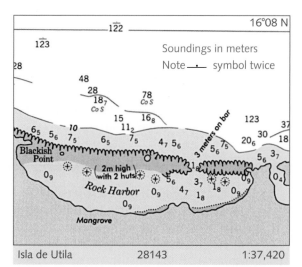

Isla de Utila   28143   1:37,420

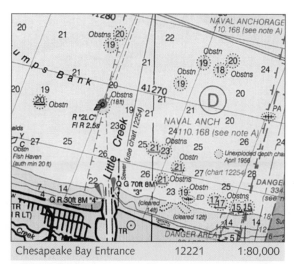

Chesapeake Bay Entrance   12221   1:80,000

Selected features: This is a metric chart. Soundings would normally be italic, but are upright to warn that they are from an old (in this case, 1835) survey. The small subscript numbers, as in 6_5, are decimal fractions of a meter. Depth contour labels are italic to differentiate from spot soundings, and also one font size smaller. Blue highlights shoal areas (in this case, less than 10 m). The deep-water soundings with the line and dot on top, as in $\overset{\cdot}{\underset{\cdot}{123}}$, indicate that no bottom was found at this depth. The label "(2m high with 2 huts)" has parentheses around it to indicate it is out of position (i.e., offset from its feature).

Selected features: Frequent use of the wire-drag symbol. Spot soundings vertical (NOAA imperial); depth contours (lower right corner) italic, with smaller and lighter font. Blue highlights shoal areas (in this case, less than 20 ft.). The dotted lines around various soundings and features warn of a potential danger. Various areas delineated in magenta (see chapter 7), with dashes, T-dashes, and continuous lines. A dangerous wreck almost on the beach whose existence is doubtful (ED). TR = tower, position accurate (position dot plus capitals and conspicuous).

its height above the low-water datum (i.e., the height to which it will be exposed when the water is at the level of the low-water datum). Drying heights are distinguished by underlining them, as in $\underline{9}$.

If depths (soundings) or heights are displaced from their actual position on the chart, they have parentheses around them, as in (30).

Dots and Dashes

In international symbology, dotted lines are used to indicate danger. They draw attention to a danger that would not stand out clearly enough if represented solely by its symbol (e.g., an isolated rock), or else they delimit an area containing numerous dangers, through which it is unsafe to navigate. In some cases, the danger area will be highlighted by coloring it blue (see the section on colors below). NOAA also uses dotted lines to delimit the chart low-water datum line (the seaward limit of the fore-shore—the area that dries out at low tide)

Not to be used for navigation

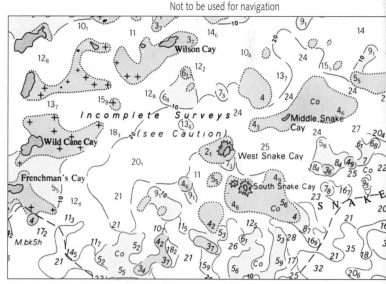

A mix of vertical and italic soundings on a British Admiralty (metric) chart of Belize. Selected features: Italic soundings are from more recent surveys, vertical from nineteenth-century surveys (INT conventions). Note the warning "Incomplete Surveys." The depth contour depths are given in vertical numbers (to differentiate them from italic spot soundings) and in a smaller font size.

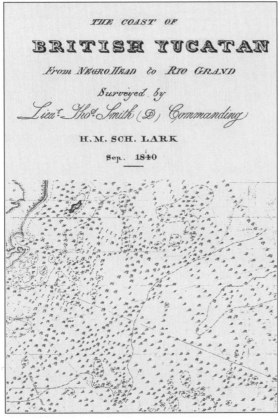

One of the source surveys for the nineteenth-century soundings on the Belize chart. This survey dates from 1840; the rest of them date from the 1830s!

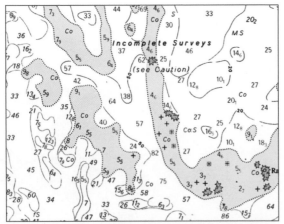

*More mixed older and newer soundings on the same Belize chart. **Selected features:** Mixed italic (newer and more reliable) and vertical (older and less reliable) soundings, with a warning of "Incomplete Surveys." **Depth contour depth** in smaller font, vertical numbers. Drying reef is given the **intertidal** color. Blue is used to highlight **shoal** areas (less than 10 meters). Dotted lines delineate **potential danger** areas. There are both "**rock awash**" and "**submerged rock**" symbols (these are coral heads)—see section K.*

whereas internationally the low-water datum line (also known as the *drying line*) will typically be shown by a standard depth contour, usually a continuous line.

- Dashed lines are used to delineate (1) maritime areas of one type or another (e.g., safety zones, fishing limits, the limits of surveyed areas, the sides of dredged channels); (2) tracks and the extension of leading lines beyond a navigable channel (the section of the leading line in the channel is a solid line); and (3) uncertainty in terms of shorelines, vegetative limits in marshes and mangrove swamps, and so forth (e.g., when used in connection with depth contour lines, the dashes indicate that the reliability of the contour is questionable).

- When defining areas, T-shaped dashes may be used, with the stem of the "T" pointing toward the inside of the area in question (generally, an area to be treated with caution or avoided).

Use of Color

The colors currently used on charts have been chosen in part because they are clearly visible under red nighttime lighting.

- Black is used for those features that need to be precisely located (e.g., shorelines, positions of objects, depth contours) and that constitute permanent physical obstructions (e.g., channel limits, dredged areas, spoil grounds, and works in progress that may impede safe navigation). This originated in the days of printing off plates because of the potential for registration errors between plates. By getting all the vital positioning information on one plate, together with the latitude and longitude grid, the consequences of such errors were minimized. Black is also used for some printed information (e.g., notes, titles) and for topographic features.

- Blue, in one or more tints, is used for shallow-water areas; how shallow is largely a function of chart scale. On large-scale charts, the definition is likely to be shallower than on small-scale charts. Blue is also used to highlight danger areas beyond the limit of coastal shoal water.

Somewhat counterintuitively, the deeper the shade of blue, the shallower the water, although both Stanfords Charts and Imray, Laurie, Norie

(continued page 97)

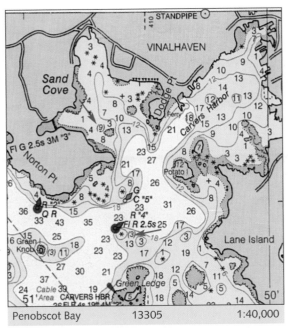

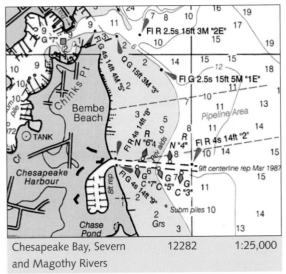

Penobscot Bay   13305   1:40,000

Chesapeake Bay, Severn   12282   1:25,000
and Magothy Rivers

*Selected features: Vertical **soundings** (NOAA imperial). There are errors on this chart, which are corrected in later editions (see below)—the chart compiler must have been having a bad day! The rock to the north of Green Ledge (just south of the buoy) is 3 feet above the LW datum. The "3" should be vertical and underlined. The **parentheses** are because its height is out of position (off to one side). Farther to the north (just above the center of the chart), we have an **out-of-position drying height** (9), indicated by the parentheses and underlined; this is the height above the low-water datum—it should be vertical and not italic. The STANDPIPE (northern edge) is accurately charted (position dot plus capitals, and conspicuous).*

*Selected features: The black dashed lines delineate the edge of the **dredged channel** (black is used for physical features, magenta for nonphysical information); the depth was last checked in 1987 (the date is a clue that this channel is not maintained at its charted depth). The dashed magenta lines indicate the limit of a **pipeline** area. The "**subm piles**" (submerged piles) are in italic typeface; if they stuck up above the high-water datum, the label would be in vertical type. The **buoys** and **beacons** can be differentiated by the type style: vertical for beacons (topographic features) and italic for buoys (hydrographic features).*

Corrected chart.

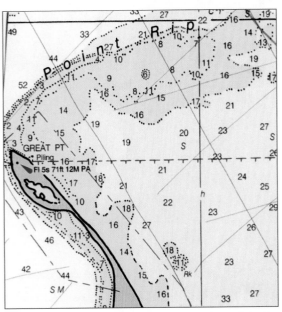

Magenta T-dashes to delineate an area; the base of the T points into the area in question.

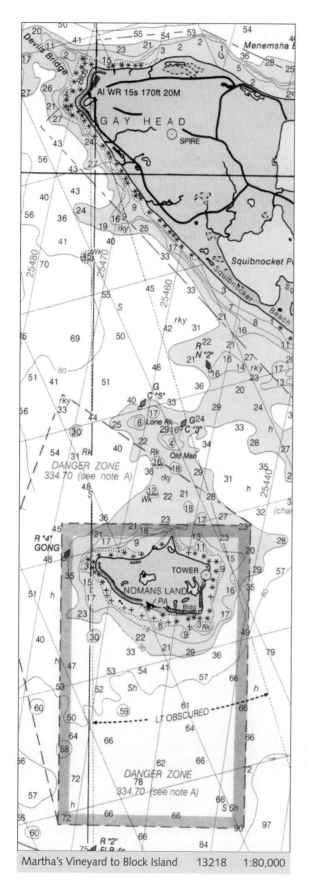

Martha's Vineyard to Block Island   13218   1:80,000

NOAA imperial chart (left) (vertical numbers are used for soundings, with italic in a smaller font size for depth contours). **Selected features:** *Two magenta danger areas around Nomans Land, with one highlighted with a magenta band, and with reference to a note. However, the note itself does not describe the danger zones and so is not much use to most users of this chart! Several* **wire-dragged depths** *between Nomans Island and Gay Head. The use of dotted* **danger lines** *around some of the shoal areas and the wreck south of Gay Head. Blue is used on some of the off-lying shoals and the* **wreck** *for emphasis. Both* **drying rock** *and* **submerged rock** *symbols.* **SPIRE** *and* **TOWER** *with position dot, and in capitals, indicating they are precisely located and conspicuous. The stranded* **wreck** *on the south side of Nomans Land is Position Approximate (PA).* **Hydrographic** *labels are italic;* **topographic** *vertical. Nomans Island obscures the light on Gay Head when approaching from the south.*

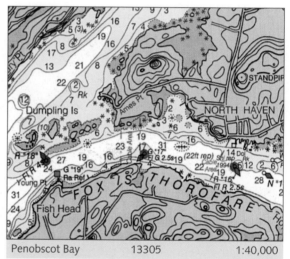

Penobscot Bay   13305   1:40,000

The chart above uses NOAA's color palette, which is a little different from that of the British Admiralty and some other hydrographic offices. **Selected features:** *Black for* **important physical features,** *soundings, heights, and other information. Buff for the* **land.** *Green for* **intertidal** *(with a different shade for green buoys). Blue for* **shallow water** *(two shades, although this is difficult to differentiate, with the deeper blue representing shallower water). White for* **deep water.** *Magenta for* **lit buoys,** *both red and green (the magenta circle; on INT charts it is a flare) and for red buoys (the red or green diamond is one of NOAA's supplementary national symbols, and is not an INT symbol), and also to define cautionary areas (the cable area). We have three different* **rock symbols:** *drying at low water; awash at low water; and permanently covered (see chapter 7).*

and Wilson reverse the water depth color conventions, using yellow (the color of sand) for intertidal areas, light blue for shoal water, and dark blue for deeper waters. Intuitively, this makes more sense than the IHO's scheme because it more nearly replicates real life.

Gold (or buff or gray) is used for land areas above the high-water datum (SPOR). It is overlain with a darker "screen" in built-up areas.

Green (which, in traditional offset lithographic printing, is generally achieved by overprinting the gold on the blue) is used for areas that cover and uncover; that is, the *intertidal zone* (foreshore)—the area between the high-water datum and the low-water (sounding) datum. A different shade of green is used for green buoys and beacons.

White, the background color of a paper chart, is used for deep water, dredged channels, and so forth in order to provide the greatest possible contrast under all lighting conditions, with dangers and other details shown in black. Because electronic charts are backlit when displayed on a screen, bright white areas can destroy night vision; therefore, the white areas on some charts can be turned black at night (this is an ECDIS requirement).

Magenta is used to do the following:

1. draw attention to features that have a significance extending beyond their immediate location

2. distinguish information superimposed on the physical features of the chart that does not imply any permanent physical obstruction (e.g., port authority limits and fisheries limits)

Features that warrant such treatment include the following:

1. lights and lighted buoys (red, green, white, and any other color; the color of the light is given in a label and is presumed to be white if not given): the light or buoy is generally given a magenta "flare" attached to the symbol, except that NOAA uses a magenta circle (disc) around a buoy's position circle to differentiate buoys (which move around) from beacons (which don't)

2. important caution and danger areas (e.g., safety zones, military firing ranges)

3. maritime boundaries (e.g., 3-mile limit)

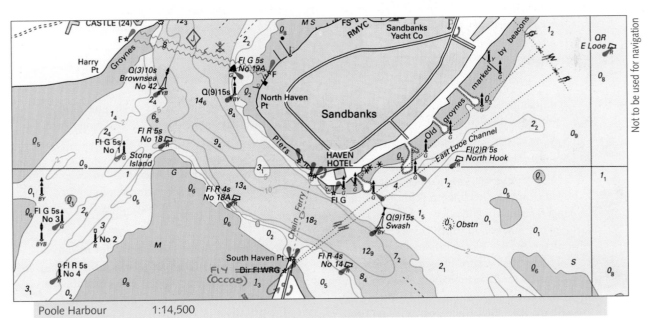

Poole Harbour   1:14,500

Privately produced chart (Stanfords Charts) with a color scheme different from that in INT-1. **Selected features:** *Yellow is used for* **intertidal** *(drying) areas, light blue for shoal water (less than 5 meters), and darker blue for deeper water. White is used for* **land**, *buff for* **built-up areas**. *Note the* **hand-corrected light** *in the lower center section of the chart —these charts are corrected up to date of sale (as opposed to NOAA charts, which are only corrected to the printing date). This area is in IALA* **Region A** *(see chapter 8) with the corresponding buoyage.*

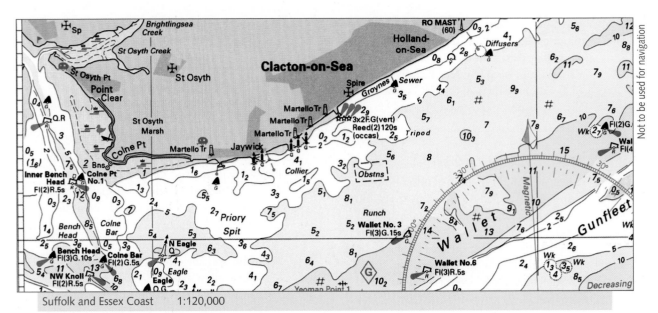

Suffolk and Essex Coast   1:120,000

*Another privately produced chart (Imray, Laurie, Norie and Wilson) with a different color scheme to the IHO. This chart is of my old stomping grounds! **Selected features:** Yellow is used for the **intertidal** zone, white for shallow water (to 5 meters), light blue from 5 to 10 meters, and darker blue above 10 meters. Land is green; **built-up** areas darker green. There is a **sunken wreck** in the lower center section of the chart (on the margin), a stranded wreck to the north of Colne Point, and numerous other wrecks with known least depths (see chapter 7), together with the "Foul Ground" symbol (#). We have a series of "**Martello Tr.**" (a defensive watchtower, many dating from the sixteenth century) with approximate position symbols (the small circle without a black dot in the base of the symbol). The "**RO MAST**" has an approximate position symbol (small circle in its base) but is conspicuous (capital letters). To seaward of this mast is a pipeline (the dashed line with dots on the end of the dashes) with "Diffusers" (see chapter 7). There is another pipeline to seaward of Jaywick. The dots indicate that the direction of flow is toward the dots; the black indicates the pipe carries nonvolatile liquids (this is probably a wastewater outfall). In the river estuary we have **marsh** and **wading bird** symbols (a nature preserve). This area is in IALA **Region A** (see chapter 8) with the corresponding buoyage.*

4. compass roses and lines of magnetic variation (*isogonic lines*)

5. miscellaneous information (e.g., ferry routes and recommended courses)

A wide magenta screened band may be added to any dashed line (to delineate various danger, restricted, and safety zones) to give it more prominence, in which case the band is added to the line on the inside of the zone. Note that black dashed lines are used for areas with potential navigational hazards (e.g., a dump site for spoil; dump sites for chemicals and explosives, however, are in magenta because they are always in deep water and therefore not a navigational hazard). Occasionally, other colors are used for special areas: for example, blue long-short dashed lines on NOAA charts for such things as national and state

parks, and wildlife parks; green long-short dashed lines represent an IMO-defined Particularly Sensitive Sea Area (PSSA), an area recognized as important for ecological, socioeconomic, or scientific reasons that "may be vulnerable to damage by international maritime activities" (NOAA, *Nautical Chart Manual*).

Notes are printed in the same color used to display the charted features to which they refer. On NOAA charts, Note A is reserved for a note listing publications with relevant navigation regulations. Other notes begin with a B, even if there is no A. Some other letters are reserved for specific notes. For example, Note S is reserved for information on dump sites, and Note Z is reserved for information on No-Discharge (of sewage) Zones (NDZ).

Notes are printed in the same color as the features to which they refer. Note A is reserved for information on navigation regulations. Notice the high-water datum: HEIGHTS—Heights in feet above Mean High Water. This is typically a small note at any point on the chart.

Place	Height referred to datum of soundings MLLW			
	Mean Higher High Water	Mean High Water	Mean Low Water	Extreme Low Water
	feet	feet	feet	feet
Tybee Light	7.4	7.0	0.2	-4.0
Savannah River Ent.	7.5	7.1	0.2	-4.5
Savannah	8.6	8.1	0.3	-4.5
Beach Hammock	7.5	7.1	0.2	-4.0

(288)

For Symbols and Abbreviations see Chart No. 1
COLREGS: International Regulations for Preventing Collisions at Sea, 1972 Demarcation lines are shown thus: — — — —

HEIGHTS
Heights in feet above Mean High Water.
AUTHORITIES
Hydrography and topography by the National Ocean Service, Charting and Geodetic Services with additional data from the Corps of Engineers and U.S. Coast Guard.

PLANE COORDINATE GRID
(based on NAD 1927)
Georgia State Grid, east zone, is indicated by dotted ticks at 16,000 foot intervals.

NOAA VHF-FM WEATHER BROADCASTS
The National Weather Service station listed below provides continuous marine weather broadcasts. The range of reception is variable, but for most stations is usually 20 to 40 miles from the antenna site.
Savannah, Ga.   KEC-85   162.40 MHz

NOTE A
Navigation regulations are published in Chapter 2, U.S. Coast Pilot 4. Additions or revisions to Chapter 2 are published in the Notices to Mariners. Information concerning the regulations may be obtained at the Office of the Commander, 7th Coast Guard District in Miami, Fla., or at the Office of the District Engineer, Corps of Engineers in Savannah, Ga. Refer to charted regulation section numbers.

Savannah River and Warsaw Sound   11512   1:40,000

It is worth noting that these colors derive from the days of printing from plates, when each new color required a new plate, which created considerable pressure to minimize the number of plates. In the future, plates will no longer be required: a nearly infinite number of colors can be used in the electronic world. A greater use of color on charts (both paper and electronic) can be expected, particularly more gradations of blue to give a better sense of changing depths. Finally, it should be noted that *many of the subtle details described above and in succeeding pages sometimes get lost when digitizing vector charts from paper and Mylars.* As noted in chapter 2, it takes educated and alert vectorizing personnel to detect and capture all the fine details created by a professional cartographer on a paper chart whereas many doing the vectorizing do not have cartographic training.

Now let's get into the details of *INT-1.*

General

THE FIRST MAJOR DIVISION in *INT-1* has the heading GENERAL. It covers most of the noncartographic details on a chart: the information that is printed in and under the title, around the margins, and in various notes scattered throughout the chart. This is the kind of information that can easily get lost on vectorized charts and can be hard to find on raster charts.

The "general" section is divided into two parts, A and B. A: Chart Number, Title, and Marginal Notes deals with most of this information; B: Positions, Distances, Directions, and Compass is more highly focused. Much of this information is routinely ignored by a typical mariner. Some of it is bureaucratic in nature and primarily of interest to hydrographic offices; however, there is also key information on horizontal and vertical datums, date of publication, source diagrams, units used for soundings, chart scale, and magnetic variation. *Mariners should automatically check these details before using a new chart and should look for this "meta" data before using an electronic chart.*

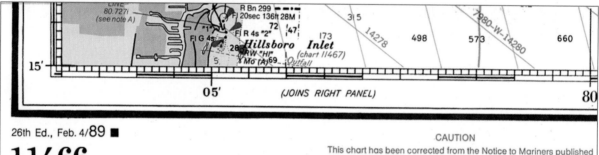

Publication note, giving the date of this edition and the latest date to which it has been corrected. U.S. charts are corrected to the date of printing. British Admiralty and other charts are then hand-corrected to the date of sale. Also present are the chart number (11466), a note to say it is Loran-C overprinted, and a reminder to check Notices to Mariners for changes subsequent to the date of the last corrections. Note that funding for Loran-C in the United States was cancelled in 2010; in European waters, Loran-C is being replaced by eLoran.

A *Chart Number, Title, and Marginal Notes*

Chart Corrections

As noted in chapter 4, hydrographic offices are constantly updating their databases and every time a chart is reprinted it is brought up to date. Some hydrographic offices (e.g., the British Admiralty, Canada, and Cuba) then require their chart agents to maintain databases of changes following the chart printing, and to bring paper charts fully up to date at the time of sale to the public. Other hydrographic offices (e.g., NOAA) require no further corrections beyond the date of printing. Once a chart is sold, it is the consumer's responsibility to find out when it was last corrected and to keep it updated via *Notices to Mariners* (see chapter 2).

In practice, few people outside of major shipping lines keep their charts updated (it can be quite a chore). We each have to make a judgment call about how much time and money to put into chart maintenance. Large-scale charts, especially those covering areas where there may have been changes with navigational significance (e.g., lots of new construction, a devastating hurricane), clearly require more attention than small-scale charts for offshore use. We need to be cognizant of the age of our charts and when they were last updated, factoring it into our navigational practices (e.g., don't rely on an old chart in poor visibility).

For those using electronic charts, it is important to note that the ability to correct them varies widely according to the method by which they were produced and by whom. In practice, many of the cheaper charts used in cockpit chart-plotters cannot be corrected; high-end charts issued by hydrographic offices may be easier to correct than paper charts (downloading corrections from the Internet). The ability to regularly update a chart is a requirement of ECDIS/RCDS, a consideration that is often overlooked when getting into electronic charting.

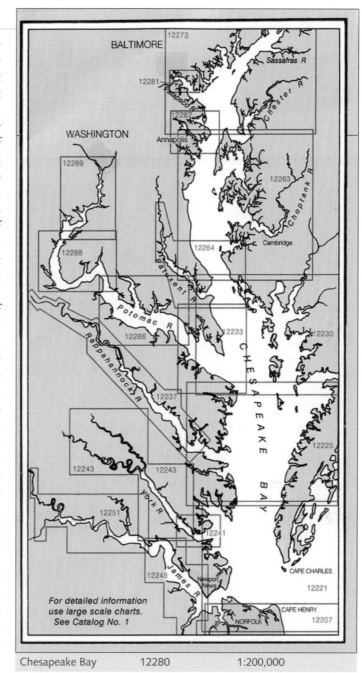

Chesapeake Bay 12280 1:200,000

Insert detailing larger-scale charts of the coverage area.

Schematic layout of a chart (reduced in size)

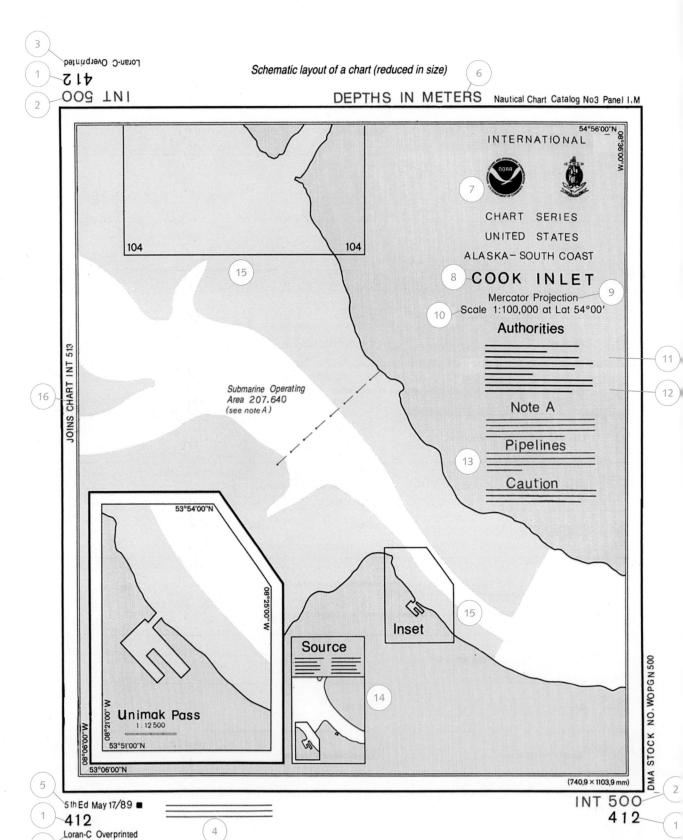

A Chart Number, Title, and Marginal Notes

①	Chart number in national series.
②	Chart number in international series (if any).
③	Identification of a latticed overprint, if any (Loran-C, Decca, or Omega; see chapter 8, section S).
④	Publication note (imprint): the date on which this chart was first published as a new chart (NC).
⑤	Edition note: the date of this edition of the chart (NE: new edition, sometimes also labeled LC for "large correction"). The dates of small corrections added to the chart may be listed separately from the edition information. To keep the chart current, it should be corrected with all relevant Notices to Mariners subsequent to the last date shown.
⑥	Units used for soundings: meters, feet, or fathoms and feet. The units are prominently displayed in the chart margin, as well as given in the notes under the title. Navigators using a mix of metric and imperial charts have to be especially diligent about checking the sounding units before using a chart.
⑦	The seal(s) of the issuing hydrographic office(s). If the chart was developed using data from another hydrographic office (the producer nation), the relevant seal is included alongside that of the publishing office (the printer nation). If it is an international chart, the IHO seal is included.
⑧	Chart title (the area it covers).
⑨	Chart projection (usually Mercator, transverse Mercator, or gnomonic).
⑩	Chart scale: the ratio of a given distance on the chart to the actual distance that it represents on the earth (see table, page 104). On a Mercator chart, on charts at a scale of 1:80,000 and smaller scales, the scale is only accurate at one specific latitude (see chapter 1), which is given in the title information. Measuring distances is discussed later in this chapter.
⑪	The horizontal datum (see chapter 1), which is WGS 84 (North American Datum 1983) on new charts, but often something different on older charts.
⑫	Units used for soundings, together with the low-water datum (see chapter 3). The high-water datum will be given in a note at any point on the chart.
⑬	Cautionary notes: these may appear at any point on the chart.
⑭	Source diagram, showing which parts of the chart have been compiled from which survey, and providing key data on the surveys (notably, the scale and date). More information follows.
⑮	Reference to a larger-scale (more detailed) chart of the outlined area (printed as an insert in this case, but usually consisting of a separate chart). Small-scale charts frequently have an insert that shows all the larger-scale charts covering the same area.
⑯	Reference to an adjoining chart at a scale similar to this chart.

Features highlighted on the schematic layout.

A *Chart Number, Title, and Marginal Notes*

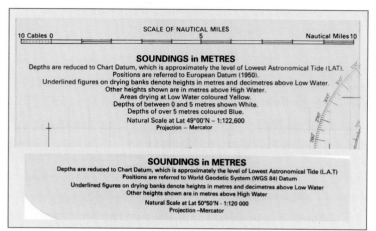

Part of the title block from two editions of the same chart (1995 and 2000). Note that in both cases the horizontal datum is given in the second line of the print. It has changed from ED (1950) to WGS 84, which, as we have seen, is a significant shift and vital to take into account if using a GPS for navigation. You have to read the small print on charts closely to pick up this kind of essential information.

Relationship between Chart Scale and the Distance on the Ground

Chart Scale	1 Inch in Nautical Miles	1 Nautical Mile in Inches	Chart Coverage Square NM[1]	Nautical Chart Type
5,000	0.069	14.58	6	Harbor
10,000	0.137	7.29	24	1:50,000 and
20,000	0.274	3.65	96	larger
30,000	0.411	2.43	217	
40,000	0.549	1.82	385	
50,000	0.686	1.46	601	
60,000	0.823	1.22	866	Coastal
70,000	0.960	1.04	1,179	1:50,000 to
80,000	1.097	0.91	1,540	1:150,000
90,000	1.234	0.81	1,949	
100,000	1.371	0.73	2,406	
150,000	2.057	0.49	5,413	
200,000	2.743	0.36	9,623	
300,000	4.114	0.24	21,651	General
400,000	5.486	0.18	38,491	1:150,000 to
500,000	6.857	0.15	60,142	1:600,000
600,000	8.229	0.12	86,605	
700,000	9.600	0.10	117,879	
800,000	10.972	0.09	153,964	Sailing
900,000	12.343	0.08	194,861	1:600,000 and
1,000,000	13.715	0.07	240,569	smaller
2,000,000	27.430	0.04	962,274	
3,500,000	48.002	0.02	2,946,965	International
10,000,000	137.149	0.01	24,056,854	

[1] *Assumes standard chart size of 750 mm x 1,100 mm*

A Chart Number, Title, and Marginal Notes

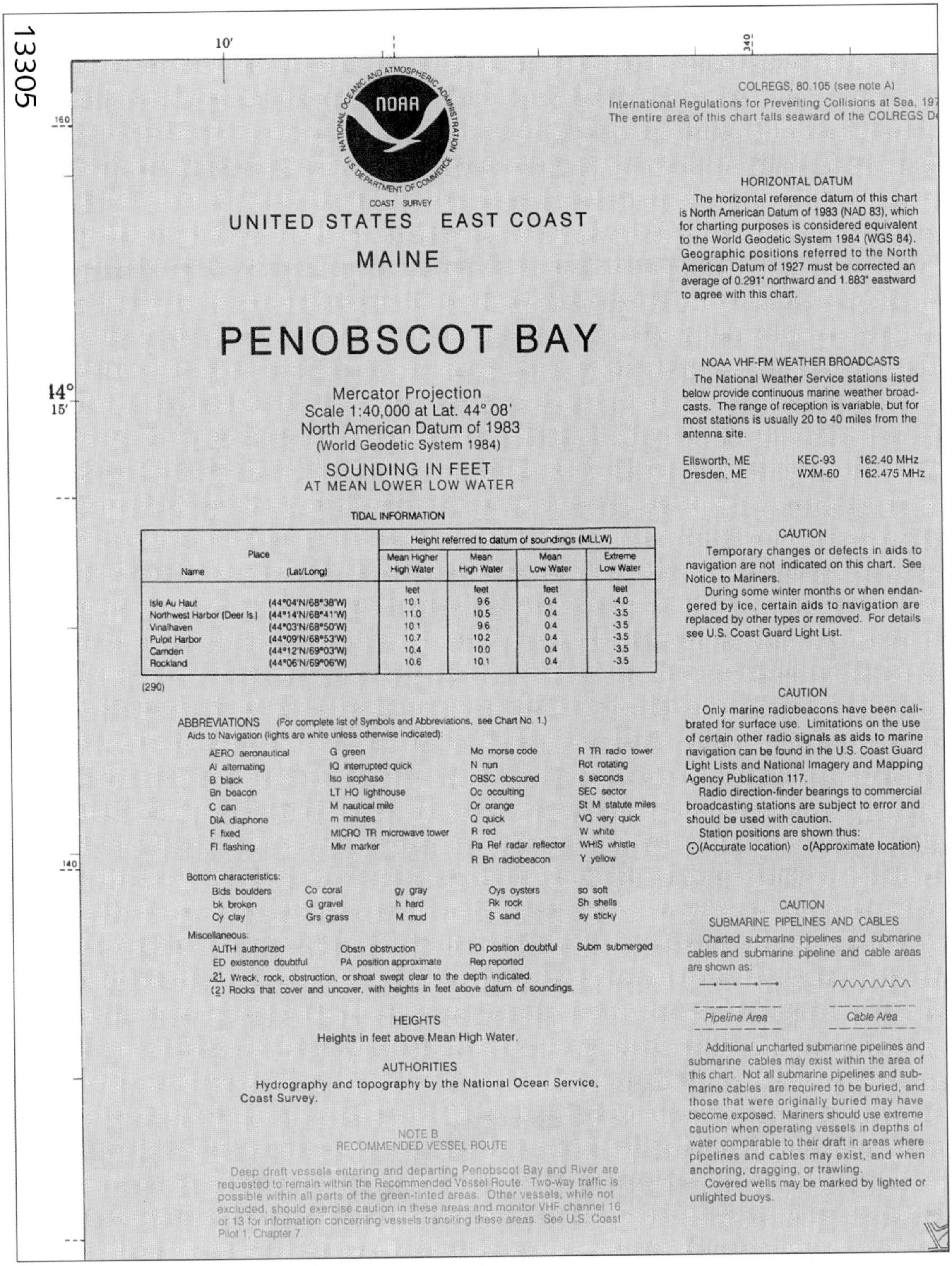

13305

COLREGS, 80.105 (see note A)
International Regulations for Preventing Collisions at Sea, 197
The entire area of this chart falls seaward of the COLREGS D

NOAA
NATIONAL OCEANIC AND ATMOSPHERIC ADMINISTRATION
U.S. DEPARTMENT OF COMMERCE
COAST SURVEY

UNITED STATES EAST COAST

MAINE

PENOBSCOT BAY

Mercator Projection
Scale 1:40,000 at Lat. 44° 08'
North American Datum of 1983
(World Geodetic System 1984)

SOUNDING IN FEET
AT MEAN LOWER LOW WATER

HORIZONTAL DATUM

The horizontal reference datum of this chart is North American Datum of 1983 (NAD 83), which for charting purposes is considered equivalent to the World Geodetic System 1984 (WGS 84). Geographic positions referred to the North American Datum of 1927 must be corrected an average of 0.291" northward and 1.883" eastward to agree with this chart.

NOAA VHF-FM WEATHER BROADCASTS

The National Weather Service stations listed below provide continuous marine weather broadcasts. The range of reception is variable, but for most stations is usually 20 to 40 miles from the antenna site.

Ellsworth, ME	KEC-93	162.40 MHz
Dresden, ME	WXM-60	162.475 MHz

TIDAL INFORMATION

Place		Height referred to datum of soundings (MLLW)			
Name	(Lat/Long)	Mean Higher High Water	Mean High Water	Mean Low Water	Extreme Low Water
		feet	feet	feet	feet
Isle Au Haut	(44°04'N/68°38'W)	10.1	9.6	0.4	-4.0
Northwest Harbor (Deer Is.)	(44°14'N/68°41'W)	11.0	10.5	0.4	-3.5
Vinalhaven	(44°03'N/68°50'W)	10.1	9.6	0.4	-3.5
Pulpit Harbor	(44°09'N/68°53'W)	10.7	10.2	0.4	-3.5
Camden	(44°12'N/69°03'W)	10.4	10.0	0.4	-3.5
Rockland	(44°06'N/69°06'W)	10.6	10.1	0.4	-3.5

(290)

CAUTION

Temporary changes or defects in aids to navigation are not indicated on this chart. See Notice to Mariners.

During some winter months or when endangered by ice, certain aids to navigation are replaced by other types or removed. For details see U.S. Coast Guard Light List.

CAUTION

Only marine radiobeacons have been calibrated for surface use. Limitations on the use of certain other radio signals as aids to marine navigation can be found in the U.S. Coast Guard Light Lists and National Imagery and Mapping Agency Publication 117.

Radio direction-finder bearings to commercial broadcasting stations are subject to error and should be used with caution.

Station positions are shown thus:
⊙(Accurate location) o(Approximate location)

ABBREVIATIONS (For complete list of Symbols and Abbreviations, see Chart No. 1.)

Aids to Navigation (lights are white unless otherwise indicated):

AERO aeronautical	G green	Mo morse code	R TR radio tower
Al alternating	IQ interrupted quick	N nun	Rot rotating
B black	Iso isophase	OBSC obscured	s seconds
Bn beacon	LT HO lighthouse	Oc occulting	SEC sector
C can	M nautical mile	Or orange	St M statute miles
DIA diaphone	m minutes	Q quick	VQ very quick
F fixed	MICRO TR microwave tower	R red	W white
Fl flashing	Mkr marker	Ra Ref radar reflector	WHIS whistle
		R Bn radiobeacon	Y yellow

Bottom characteristics:

Blds boulders	Co coral	gy gray	Oys oysters	so soft
bk broken	G gravel	h hard	Rk rock	Sh shells
Cy clay	Grs grass	M mud	S sand	sy sticky

Miscellaneous:

AUTH authorized	Obstn obstruction	PD position doubtful	Subm submerged
ED existence doubtful	PA position approximate	Rep reported	

21 Wreck, rock, obstruction, or shoal swept clear to the depth indicated.
(2) Rocks that cover and uncover, with heights in feet above datum of soundings.

CAUTION
SUBMARINE PIPELINES AND CABLES

Charted submarine pipelines and submarine cables and submarine pipeline and cable areas are shown as:

Pipeline Area   Cable Area

Additional uncharted submarine pipelines and submarine cables may exist within the area of this chart. Not all submarine pipelines and submarine cables are required to be buried, and those that were originally buried may have become exposed. Mariners should use extreme caution when operating vessels in depths of water comparable to their draft in areas where pipelines and cables may exist, and when anchoring, dragging, or trawling.

Covered wells may be marked by lighted or unlighted buoys.

HEIGHTS

Heights in feet above Mean High Water.

AUTHORITIES

Hydrography and topography by the National Ocean Service, Coast Survey.

NOTE B
RECOMMENDED VESSEL ROUTE

Deep draft vessels entering and departing Penobscot Bay and River are requested to remain within the Recommended Vessel Route. Two-way traffic is possible within all parts of the green-tinted areas. Other vessels, while not excluded, should exercise caution in these areas and monitor VHF channel 16 or 13 for information concerning vessels transiting these areas. See U.S. Coast Pilot 1, Chapter 7.

Here's the real thing (NOAA version): number, title, projection, datums (horizontal and sounding; high water near the bottom in a small note), scale, and miscellaneous tide and other information. All notes are in the same color as the features to which they refer. Much of this information is hard to find on electronic charts, and may not be available at all.

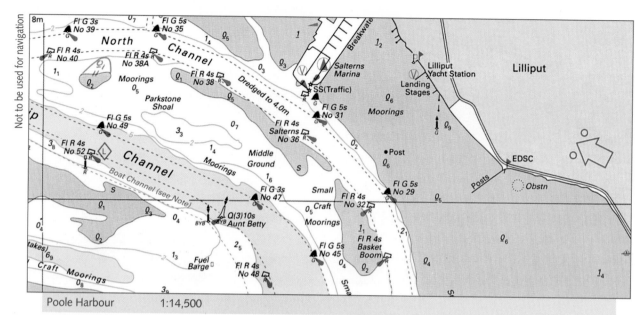

Poole Harbour   1:14,500

*Privately produced chart (Stanfords Charts) hand-corrected to the date of sale to the public. Note the hand correction in the northwest corner (the shoal has been extended, and a new drying height of 0.1 meter inserted). **Other selected features:** Color scheme with yellow for **drying**, light blue for **shoal** water, and darker blue for **deeper water**. IALA **Region A** buoyage. Note the **direction of buoyage** arrow on the right-hand side (see chapter 8).*

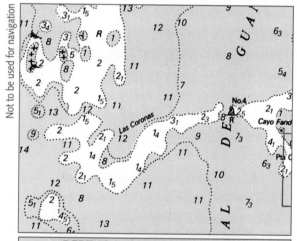

DEPTHS in FATHOMS and FEET
Heights in Feet above Mean High Water
Areas with depths of below 1 fathom coloured *Yellow*
Depths of between 1 and 5 fathoms shown *White*
Depths over 5 fathoms coloured *Blue*
Nat. Scale at Lat. 18° 10′ N − 1:116 700
Projection − Mercator

West Coast of Puerto Rico   1:116,700

Another privately produced chart (the popular Imray-Iolaire charts of the Caribbean) hand-corrected to the date of sale (the wreck in the northwest corner; we nearly piled up on this reef ourselves in 1986!). Note the non-INT colors (yellow is used for the intertidal zone, white for shoal water, and blue for deeper water). The depths on this chart are in fathoms and feet, not meters (a quirk of Don Street, who was the driving force behind this chart series) although the convention used is the same as meters on INT charts (italic soundings, with subscript numbers that look like decimal meters but are, in this case, feet). An end user who did not pay close attention to the general information on the chart could easily assume the depths are in meters.

A *Chart Number, Title, and Marginal Notes*

Producers and Printers

At one time, the major hydrographic offices maintained worldwide fleets of survey vessels and collected much of their own data. Today, they (including the British Admiralty, NOAA, and NGA) concentrate on their home waters and increasingly rely on other nations to supply the data for overseas editions of charts. As a general rule-of-thumb, charts published by the producer nation (the one originating hydrographic data) are likely to be more current and to contain more detail than those using the data secondhand (printer nations). Given a choice, it is generally best to obtain charts from the producer nation—unless, of course, the charts are in a foreign language. (I have some great Russian charts of Cuba in Cyrillic script!)

Measuring Distances

As mentioned in chapter 1, the scale on a Mercator chart is only accurate at one particular latitude—usually the midlatitude on the chart—although at scales larger than 1:80,000 the distortions toward the north and south margins are generally not great enough to be navigationally significant.

Measuring distance on paper charts is done with dividers. For short distances, the dividers are simply opened to span the distance and then taken to the scale bar (if present; on many charts it is not) or the latitude scales alongside the distance being measured

ЭЛЕМЕНТЫ ПРИЛИВА					
Пункт	Шир. N Долг. E	Высота над нулем глубин, м			
		ср сз ПВ	ср кв ПВ	ср кв МВ	ср сз МВ
Порт Рамсгит	51°20′ 1°25′	4,9	3,8	1,2	0,4
Порт Ричборо	51°18′ 1°21′	3,3	2,7	0,3	0,1

СВЕДЕНИЯ О ТЕЧЕНИЯХ			
Часы	A шир. 51°19,8′ долг. 1°27,7′		
	Направление	Скорость, уз	
		сз	кв
До полной воды в Дувре 6	203°	1,2	0,7
5	203°	1,3	0,7
4	210°	1,7	1,0
3	208°	1,9	1,1
2	215°	1,4	0,8
1	5°	0,6	0,4
Полная вода	21°	2,2	1,2
После полной воды в Дувре 1	30°	2,3	1,3
2	32°	1,9	1,1
3	43°	1,2	0,7
4	73°	0,4	0,2
5	195°	0,6	0,3
6	203°	1,1	0,6

Tidal information and a tidal stream table (see chapter 7) for the Ramsgate chart. Even this can be figured out without knowing the language!

(1 minute of latitude = 1 nautical mile [M or NM: just over 2,000 yd.]). Longer distances are measured by opening the dividers to a measured distance on the latitude scale (e.g., 5 minutes = 5 miles) and then "walking" them up the relevant course line, rotating the dividers around first one point and then the other, clocking the cumulative distance as each new move is made. Invariably, as the end of the line is neared, the final span will be less than that to which the dividers are set. The arms of the dividers are brought together to match the span, which is then transferred to the latitude scales to get an appropriate measurement. This is added to the running total to produce a final figure.

Source Diagrams

The purpose of a source diagram "is to guide navigators . . . on the degree of confidence they should have in the adequacy and accuracy of charted depths and positions" (IHO S-4). The more one goes sailing in areas that are unlikely to have been recently resurveyed, the more important the source diagram on a chart becomes—even in areas where up-to-date surveys might be expected (e.g., see the *QE2*'s encounter with an uncharted rock mentioned in chapter 3).

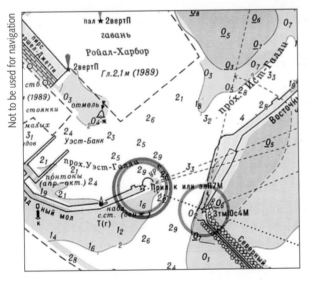

Not to be used for navigation

Details from an excellent Russian chart of Ramsgate, England. If you don't know Russian, it is a little difficult to read; nevertheless, it is surprising how much can be worked out because of the use of international symbology.

A *Chart Number, Title, and Marginal Notes*

Measuring distances with a pair of dividers.

1. *The dividers are opened to an appropriate distance (in this case, 10 minutes = 10 miles) on the adjacent latitude scale.*

2. *The dividers are . . .*

3. *"walked" along the course line . . .*

4. *tallying the distance.*

5. *The final length is less than 10 miles; the dividers are set to the distance and taken back to the latitude scale to see how much it is.*

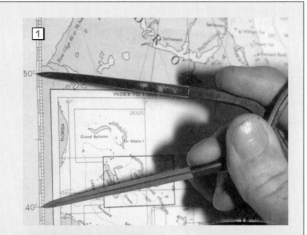

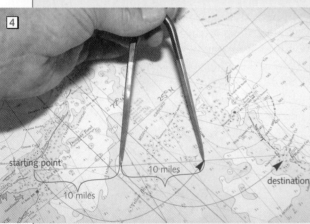

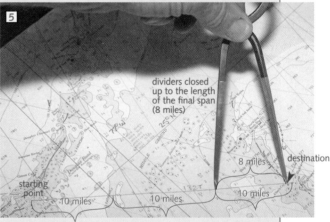

Measuring distances on a chart.

The three key pieces of information on a source diagram are the areas covered by the various surveys used to compile the chart, the date of the surveys, and the scale at which they were conducted. The area is more or less self-evident; it simply has to be visually correlated from the small source diagram with the chart as a whole.

The date of a survey "gives an indication of the adequacy of the equipment used, the maximum draught of vessel at that date (governing the thoroughness of examinations of dangers at particular depths), and the likelihood of later changes in depths" (IHO S-4). Note that lead-line surveys were the norm until the 1940s, after which single beam echo-sounding, later augmented with sidescan sonar, and finally multibeam echo-sounding became commonplace. As

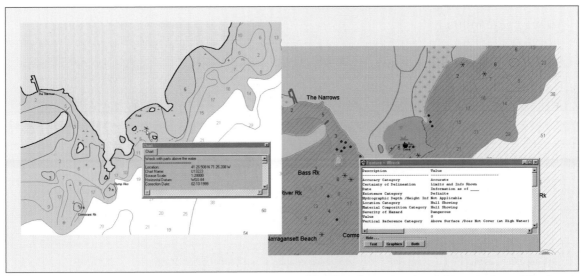

Metadata from vector-based electronic charts. The chart on the left is a moderately high-end chart from Transas; the chart on the right is from NIMA/NGA. Clicking on the wreck symbol produces the information shown.

noted in chapter 3, a lead line only samples the bottom over a small area, whereas more modern devices output a continuous scan; the newer devices have a wider scan width and, therefore, detect more bottom features and are less likely to miss isolated rocks, shoals, and other hazards.

The scale of a survey gives a sense of its thoroughness. If done at a small scale (e.g., 1:500,000), the bottom will have been sampled only at widely spaced intervals; if done at a very large scale (e.g., 1:5,000), almost all of the bottom features will have been detected. Details of the line spacing are sometimes given in a table (e.g., 200 m, meaning the survey vessel ran survey lines 200 m apart).

Occasionally (but not on current U.S. charts), a reliability diagram goes beyond the source diagram to provide quantifiable information on the reliability of the data used to compile the chart. More of this can be expected as we get into ECDIS/RCDS-compliant electronic charts based on new surveys and paper charts derived from them. The ultimate objective is attribute information "tagged" to every piece of data, giving its entire metadata (e.g., details of the survey from which it has been derived, together with a statement of its accuracy).

Annapolis Harbor	12283	1:10,000

A source diagram, giving the dates and bottom coverage of the surveys used to compile the chart. Anything before 1940 is likely to be a lead-line survey; hence, the partial bottom coverage. From 1940 to 1969 is probably echo-soundings, with more thorough but still not complete bottom coverage. Since 1990, we have sidescan sonar, with full bottom coverage.

SOURCE DIAGRAM

The outlined areas represent the limits of the most recent hydrographic survey information that has been evaluated for charting. Surveys have been banded in this diagram by date and type of survey. Channels maintained by the U.S. Army Corps of Engineers are periodically resurveyed and are not shown on this diagram. Refer to Chapter 1, United States Coast Pilot.

SOURCE			
A	1990–2001	NOS Surveys	full bottom coverage
B3	1940–1969	NOS Surveys	partial bottom coverage
B4	1900–1939	NOS Surveys	partial bottom coverage

B *Positions, Distances, Directions, and Compasses*

Geographical Positions			
1	Lat	Latitude	Lat
2	Long	Longitude	Long
3		International meridian (Greenwich)	
4	°	Degree(s)	°
5	′	Minute(s) of arc	′
6	″	Second(s) of arc	″
7	PA	Position approximate: the position has either not been accurately determined or does not remain fixed	PA
8	PD	Position doubtful: reported in various positions and not definitely determined in any way	PD
9	N	North, Northern	N
10	E	East, Eastern	E
11	S	South, Southern	S
12	W	West, Western	W
13	NE	Northeast	NE
14	SE	Southeast	SE
15	NW	Northwest	NW
16	SW	Southwest	SW

Control Points			
20	⚠	Triangulation point: a reference point for surveyors, accurately surveyed with respect to the horizontal datum of the chart	⚠
21	⊕	Observation spot: a reference point for astronomical observations	⊕ Obs Spot
22	⊙ ⊙	A fixed point whose position has been accurately determined and plotted	⊙

110

B Positions, Distances, Directions, and Compasses

23	大	Benchmark: a visible mark whose height is precisely known relative to a specific vertical datum	○ BM
24		Boundary mark	◆ Bdy Mon

Symbolized Positions (Examples)

30	:: # 18₃ Wk	Symbols in plan (viewed from above). The position of the feature is at the "center of gravity" of the symbol (in its center), unless the symbol includes a position identifier (e.g., a circle at the base of a chimney)	# 18₃ Wk (PA)
31		Symbols in profile (viewed from the side). There will either be a dot (indicating a precise location) or a small circle (indicating an approximate location, as here) incorporated into the base of the symbol to show the position of the feature	
32	⊙ Mast ⊙ MAST ★	Point symbols: the black dot indicates an accurate position	⊙
33	○ Mast PA	Approximate position: the absence of a black dot indicates an approximate position	○

Units

40	km	Kilometer(s)	km
41	m	Meter(s)	m
42	dm	Decimeter(s)	dm
43	cm	Centimeter(s)	cm
44	mm	Millimeter(s)	mm
45	M	Nautical mile(s) (1852 m) or sea mile(s)	M, Mi, NMi, NM
46		Cable (100 fathoms, 200 yds. or $1/10$ of 1 nautical mile—185.44 m or 608 ft.)	cbl
47	ft	Foot/feet	ft
48		Fathom(s) (1.83 m/6 ft.)	fm, fms

49	h	*Hour*	h, hr
50	m, min	*Minute(s) of time*	m, min
51	s, sec	*Second(s) of time*	s, sec
52	kn	*Knot(s)*	kn
53	t	*Ton(s) or Tonne(s) (metric ton equals 2,204.6 lb.)*	t
54	cd	*Candela (a measure of brightness of lights)*	cd

Magnetic Compass

The lines of longitude (meridians) on a Mercator chart are always aligned with true north. Magnetic north (shown by a compass) is rarely the same, and varies from place to place and in the same place over time. The degree to which magnetic north differs from true north at any particular place is its *variation*, expressed in degrees and minutes east or west of true north. The rate at which variation changes from year to year is expressed in minutes, either as east or west, or as increasing or decreasing (sometimes denoted as "incrg" or "decrg").

On relatively large-scale paper charts, one or more true compass roses are always shown (printed in magenta) aligned with the meridians, generally with a magnetic compass rose (aligned with magnetic north) on the inside (if shown, the magnetic rose is *always* on the inside). The magnetic rose *always* contains a printed statement of the magnetic variation (e.g., Variation 2°30' West), together with the date on which this is true (e.g., 2002). The rate of change in magnetic variation is printed next to this (e.g., 23' W). We get some variant of the following:

Variation 2°30' W (2002) (23' W), or, maybe 2°30' W (2002) (23' W)

When the rate of change has the same sign (east or west) as the magnetic variation, find the variation at the time of use of the chart by multiplying the number of years since the date on the chart by the rate of change, and add this to the variation. If the rate of change has the opposite sign as the magnetic variation, multiply the number of years since the date on the chart by the rate of change, and subtract it from the variation. Using the previous example, if the chart had been used in 2011, it would have been nine years since the variation date. With an annual rate of change of 23', this is 9 x 23 = 207'. There are 60 minutes in a degree; therefore, this is 3°37'. Because both the variation and the rate of change have the same sign (west), we add them together to find the variation in 2011:

$$2°30' \text{ W} + 3°37' = 5°67' = 6°07' \text{ W}$$

If the rate of change had been easterly, we would have subtracted this from the westerly variation, as follows:

$$2°30' \text{ W} - 3°37' = 1°07' \text{ E}$$

Note that the variation has now become easterly.

Most magnetic compasses fitted to boats don't actually line up with magnetic north. Onboard magnetic influences create a *deviation* from magnetic north, which varies from boat to boat according to the heading of the boat. Because deviation is peculiar to individual compasses and headings, it is *never* given on a chart, but must be considered by a navigator when determining compass courses. (I have seen a few English-language charts produced by non-English-speaking nations where the word *deviation* has been used in place of *variation*, but this is a translation error.)

If a chart issued by an official hydrographic office has a bearing, it is *always* in true degrees (reckoned clockwise from true north: 0° to 360°). Privately issued charts frequently have course lines and other information superimposed on an official government chart, in which case the bearings are likely to be in magnetic degrees. If this is the case, *on older charts the displayed bearings will not be correct because of the change in magnetic variation that will have occurred*

B Positions, Distances, Directions, and Compasses

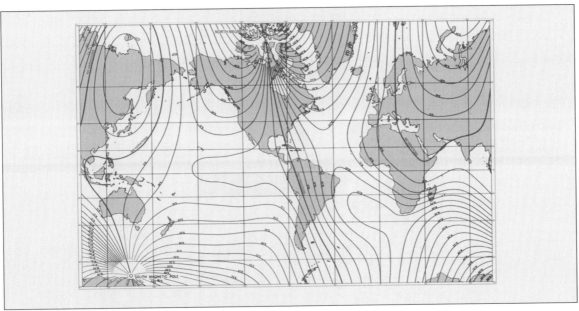

Worldwide lines of equal magnetic variation (isogonic lines).

since the chart was compiled. All such bearings need to be corrected before using them, especially in areas with a relatively high rate of annual change in variation. It is also important to distinguish superimposed bearings from those printed by the issuing hydrographic office (e.g., for sectored lights and leading lines), which will still be in true degrees (unless the private chart-maker changes them).

On smaller-scale charts, particularly those that have significant changes in magnetic variation over the area covered by the chart and on which the use of magnetic compass roses would consequently be confusing (e.g., a chart of Cuba, where the magnetic variation changes by 7 degrees from one end of the island to the other), compass roses may be omitted and replaced by *isogonic lines* (lines that connect all points that have the same magnetic variation: similar to magnetic contour lines).

Magnetic Compass			
60		Variation	var VAR
61		Magnetic	mag
62		Bearing	brg
63		True	T
64		Decreasing	
65		Increasing	
66		Annual change	
67		Deviation	dev
68.1	Magnetic Variation 4°31'W 1985 (8'E)	Note of magnetic variation, in position	

68.2	Magnetic Variation at 55°N 8°W 4°31'W 1985 (8'E)	*Note of magnetic variation, out of position*
70		*Compass rose, normal pattern (smaller patterns of compass rose may be used)*

International

Compass Roses, True and Magnetic.
4°30´W 1998 (9´E) on magnetic north arrow means
Magnetic Variation 4°30´W in 1998, annual change 9´E
(i.e., magnetic variation decreasing 9´ annually)

Magnetic Variation is expressed to the nearest 5´ and
relates to 1 January of the year stated. Annual change
E or W is given to the nearest minute.

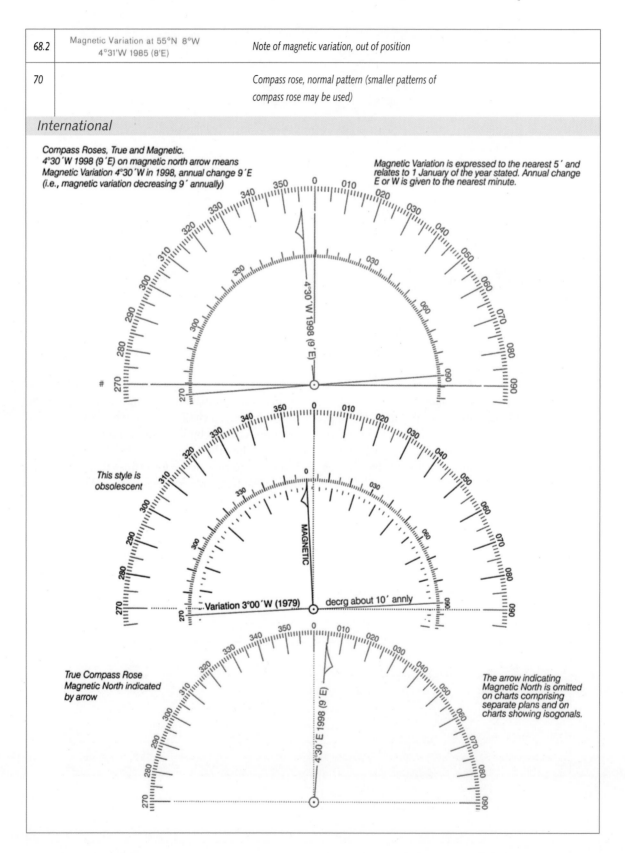

4°30´W 1998 (9´E)

This style is
obsolescent

MAGNETIC

Variation 3°00´W (1979)   decrg about 10´ annly

True Compass Rose
Magnetic North indicated
by arrow

4°30´E 1998 (9´E)

The arrow indicating
Magnetic North is omitted
on charts comprising
separate plans and on
charts showing isogonals.

B Positions, Distances, Directions, and Compasses

United States

Magnetic Variation (example): 4° 15′ W 1985 (8′ E) *on magnetic north arrow means Magnetic Variation 4° 15′ W* in 1985, annual change 8′ E *(i. e. magnetic variation decreasing 8′ annually).*

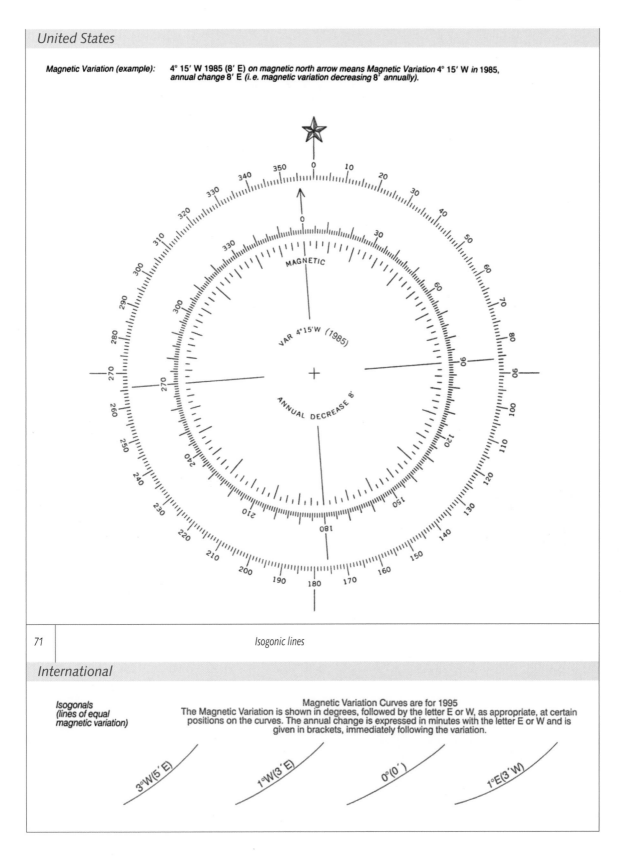

| 71 | Isogonic lines |

International

Isogonals
(lines of equal
magnetic variation)

Magnetic Variation Curves are for 1995
The Magnetic Variation is shown in degrees, followed by the letter E or W, as appropriate, at certain positions on the curves. The annual change is expressed in minutes with the letter E or W and is given in brackets, immediately following the variation.

3°W(5′E)   1°W(3′E)   0°(0′)   1°E(3′W)

B *Positions, Distances, Directions, and Compasses*

United States	

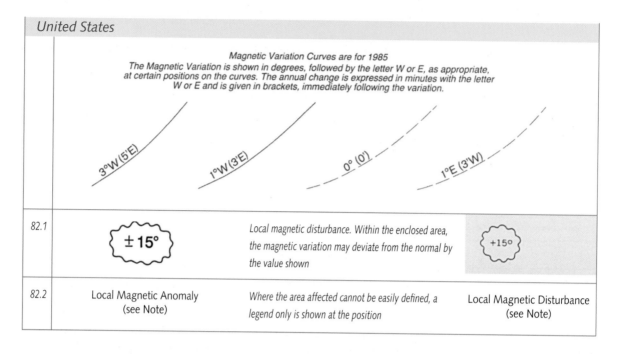

Magnetic Variation Curves are for 1985
The Magnetic Variation is shown in degrees, followed by the letter W or E, as appropriate,
at certain positions on the curves. The annual change is expressed in minutes with the letter
W or E and is given in brackets, immediately following the variation.

3°W (5'E)   1°W (3'E)   0° (0')   1°E (3'W)

82.1	± 15°	Local magnetic disturbance. Within the enclosed area, the magnetic variation may deviate from the normal by the value shown	+15°
82.2	Local Magnetic Anomaly (see Note)	Where the area affected cannot be easily defined, a legend only is shown at the position	Local Magnetic Disturbance (see Note)

Supplementary National Symbols		
a	Square meter	m²
b	Cubic meter	m³
c	Inch(es)	in, ins
d	Yard(s)	yd, yds
e	Statute mile	St M, St Mi
f	Microsecond	Msec, Ms
g	Hertz	Hz
h	Kilohertz	kHz
i	Megahertz	MHz
j	Cycles/second	cps, c/s
k	Kilocycle	kc
l	Megacycle	Mc
m	Ton (U.S. short ton equals 2,000 lb.). Note the use of a capital "T" (which is also used for "true north"; see B63) to distinguish this from a metric ton (a small "t"; see B53)	T
n	Degree(s)	deg

Topography

Natural Features, Cultural Features, Landmarks, Ports, and Topographic Terms

THIS CHAPTER discusses those sections of *INT-1* that come under the heading of "TOPOGRAPHY": generally speaking, shoreside features and man-made features both onshore and jutting out from the shoreline (e.g., breakwaters, piers, and all features associated with ports). Not included are any aids to navigation (e.g., lighthouses), whether or not they are on shore (these are discussed in chapter 8).

Because navigators see the coastline from a narrow perspective, their interest is in features that are conspicuous from seaward and in the immediate shoreline. IHO S-4 has this to say: "The navigator sees the coast in profile; the cartographer sees it in plan and must always be aware that the navigator's interest in land detail is at its greatest at the coastline and falls off rapidly inland." As a result, the shoreside features shown on charts are highly selective and incomplete. In general, the farther inland the chart goes, the fewer the details shown (mostly high ground and conspicuous buildings); however, airports are often shown—even though out of sight—because descending and ascending aircraft provide a good sense of the airport's direction.

The natural shoreline (also called the "coastline") is depicted with a relatively heavy black line. For charting purposes, it is the same as the line formed by the high-water datum, which is usually either MHWS (recommended by the IHO) or MHW (typically used by NOAA). In areas where there is no appreciable tide, it is likely to be MSL (see chapter 3 for more details on high-water datums). This high-water line is also sometimes known as the SPOR (shoreline plane of reference).

On NOAA charts a lighter line may be used where the actual shoreline is not clearly identifiable

(e.g., where marshes or mangrove swamps extend into the water, creating an "apparent" shoreline that may differ from the SPOR; see C9 following). In practice, the different line "weight" is often difficult to detect (it is likely to be 0.15 mm wide as opposed to 0.2 mm). This apparent shoreline should not be confused with an approximate or unsurveyed shoreline (shown with a dashed line; see C2): the former is known, the latter is not fully surveyed (NOAA may use a black dotted line in place of a dashed line if the unsurveyed area is considered to be a hazard to navigation).

If an island or a feature is too small to be shown

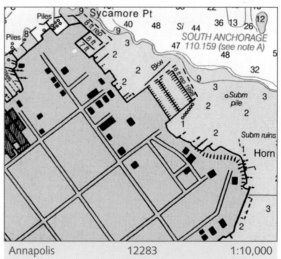

Even on large-scale charts (this one is 1:10,000), the charted shoreside detail decreases rapidly as you move inland. Note the steep coast symbol on the eastern shore. The "piles" labels (NW corner) use vertical letters (as opposed to italic on submerged piles) indicating that the piles stick out above the high-water datum.

C *Natural Features*

at its true scale, it is enlarged. The IHO rule-of-thumb is to make it large enough to not be confused with dots caused by pinhole imperfections in printing plates. This results in a minimum width the same as that of the line for the coastline (generally 0.2 mm, although NOAA's *Nautical Chart Manual* specifies the "minimum charting size for a bare rock [or inlet] is 0.65 mm by 0.5 mm").

The area between the high-water line and the chart's low-water line or datum (LAT in much of the world, but generally MLLW in the U.S., LLWLT in Canada, and MLWS in Germany; see chapter 3) is known as the *foreshore* or *intertidal* zone, and is given a distinctive color. Man-made features that rise above the SPOR are given a solid line and colored the same as the land; those in the intertidal zone that are below the SPOR are given a dashed line and colored the same as the intertidal zone or blue; and those that are always submerged are generally given a dotted outline (the dots warn of danger) and the shallow-water color (blue).

C *Natural Features*

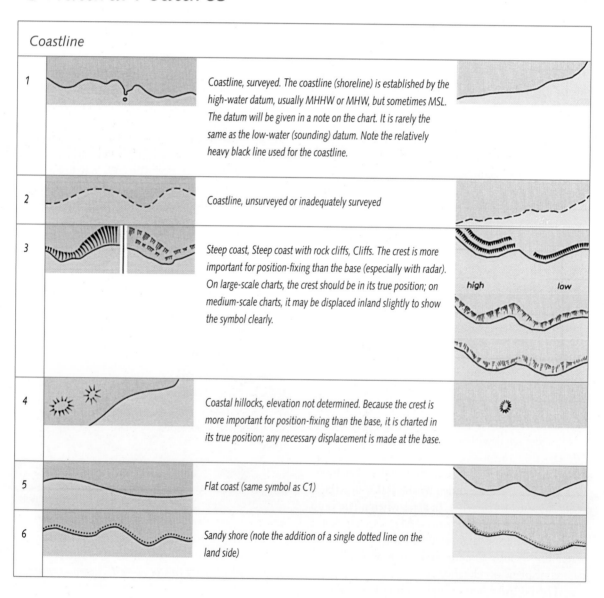

	Coastline	
1		Coastline, surveyed. The coastline (shoreline) is established by the high-water datum, usually MHHW or MHW, but sometimes MSL. The datum will be given in a note on the chart. It is rarely the same as the low-water (sounding) datum. Note the relatively heavy black line used for the coastline.
2		Coastline, unsurveyed or inadequately surveyed
3		Steep coast, Steep coast with rock cliffs, Cliffs. The crest is more important for position-fixing than the base (especially with radar). On large-scale charts, the crest should be in its true position; on medium-scale charts, it may be displaced inland slightly to show the symbol clearly.
4		Coastal hillocks, elevation not determined. Because the crest is more important for position-fixing than the base, it is charted in its true position; any necessary displacement is made at the base.
5		Flat coast (same symbol as C1)
6		Sandy shore (note the addition of a single dotted line on the land side)

C Natural Features

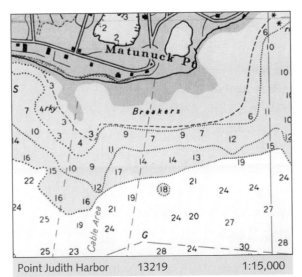

Point Judith Harbor   13219   1:15,000

*Above: The **dashed** line indicates inadequately surveyed (or constantly changing). **Right:** Note the cliff symbols at several points. Note also the **dam symbol*** just above the label: the direction of the "teeth" indicate the direction of flow.*

CARVERS HARBOR
AND APPROACHES
Scale 1:20,000

Penobscot Bay (Inset)   13305   1:40,000
(Inset 1:20,000)

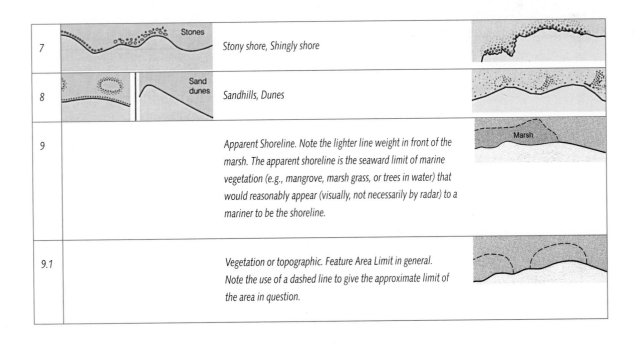

7		Stony shore, Shingly shore	
8		Sandhills, Dunes	
9		Apparent Shoreline. Note the lighter line weight in front of the marsh. The apparent shoreline is the seaward limit of marine vegetation (e.g., mangrove, marsh grass, or trees in water) that would reasonably appear (visually, not necessarily by radar) to a mariner to be the shoreline.	
9.1		Vegetation or topographic. Feature Area Limit in general. Note the use of a dashed line to give the approximate limit of the area in question.	

119

C Natural Features

Relief

The datum from which heights are measured is stated in a note on the chart. It is usually MHWS or MHW, but may be MSL (see C1). Note that when spot heights are given in vertical numbers, contour heights use italicized numbers, and vice versa, to distinguish precisely measured heights from cartographic generalizations.

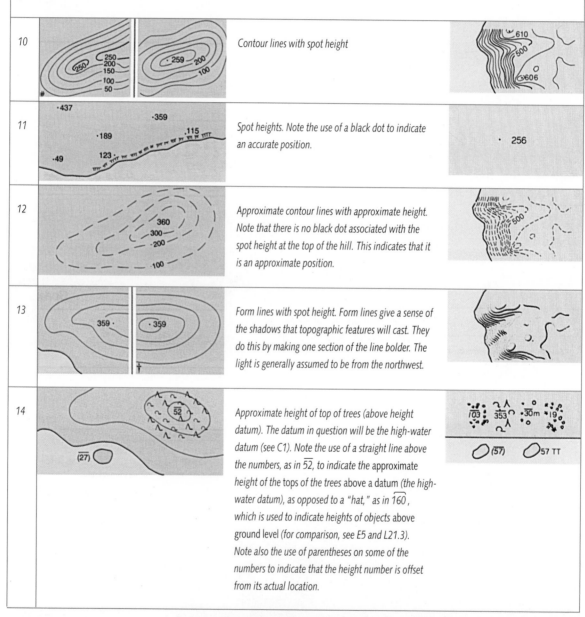

10		Contour lines with spot height	
11		Spot heights. Note the use of a black dot to indicate an accurate position.	
12		Approximate contour lines with approximate height. Note that there is no black dot associated with the spot height at the top of the hill. This indicates that it is an approximate position.	
13		Form lines with spot height. Form lines give a sense of the shadows that topographic features will cast. They do this by making one section of the line bolder. The light is generally assumed to be from the northwest.	
14		Approximate height of top of trees (above height datum). The datum in question will be the high-water datum (see C1). Note the use of a straight line above the numbers, as in $\overline{52}$, to indicate the approximate height of the tops of the trees above a datum (the high-water datum), as opposed to a "hat," as in $\overline{160}$, which is used to indicate heights of objects above ground level (for comparison, see E5 and L21.3). Note also the use of parentheses on some of the numbers to indicate that the height number is offset from its actual location.	

Soundings and heights in meters. Selected features: contour heights; deciduous and coniferous trees; marsh; boulders; cliffs; rocky foreshore.

Somerset and Devon BA 1160
1:20,000

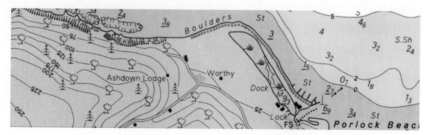

C Natural Features

Water Features, Lava

20		River, Stream	
21		Intermittent river (frequently dry)	
22		Rapids, Waterfalls	
23		Lakes	
24	Salt pans	Salt pans	
25		Glacier	
26		Lava flow	

Vegetation

30	Wooded	Wood, in general	Wooded
31		Prominent trees (in groups or isolated). Note the use of a small circle in the base of some of these symbols, which indicates the approximate position.	
31.1		Deciduous tree	
31.2		Evergreen (except conifer)	

121

C Natural Features

31.3	(symbols)	Conifer	(symbol)
31.4	(symbols)	Palm	(symbol)
31.5	(symbols)	Nipa palm	(symbols)
31.6	(symbols)	Casuarina	(symbols)
31.7	(symbols)	Filao	(symbol)
31.8	(symbols)	Eucalyptus	(symbol)

Where it is not possible to determine the high-water line with any certainty, it is shown as the outer limit of vegetation emerging at high water; that is, the apparent coastline (see C9).

32	(diagram)	Mangrove. The seaward limit is a fine dashed line; mangrove area should be covered by intertidal tint; if area is extensive, mangrove symbols may be spread across it.	(diagram: Mangrove (used in small areas))
33	(diagram)	Marsh, Swamp. If the seaward edge of a marsh is the only visible indication of a coastline, it is shown by a dashed line in addition to or in place of the high-water line.	(diagram: Marsh (used in small areas), Swamp)
34		Cypress	(diagram: Cypress)

	Supplementary National Symbols	
a	Chart sounding datum line (surveyed). The dotted line represents the low-water (sounding) datum (this is a NOAA convention; INT uses a solid line).	(diagram: Uncovers)
b	Approximate sounding datum line (inadequately surveyed). Note the absence of a dotted line to indicate that this is approximate.	(diagram)

C *Natural Features*

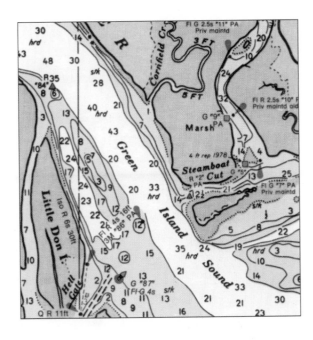

Savannah River and Warsaw Sound   11512   1:40,000

Selected features: The **marsh** *is identified with a label rather than a symbol. The use of a heavy black line in places to define the* **edge of the marsh**, *which is the visible high-water line (coastline) as far as a navigator is concerned. The use of a dotted line to define the* **low-water (LW) sounding datum** *(this is a NOAA convention; INT uses a continuous line). Vertical labels on all but one of the navaids indicates that they are* **beacons**; *note that most are "position approximate" (PA).*

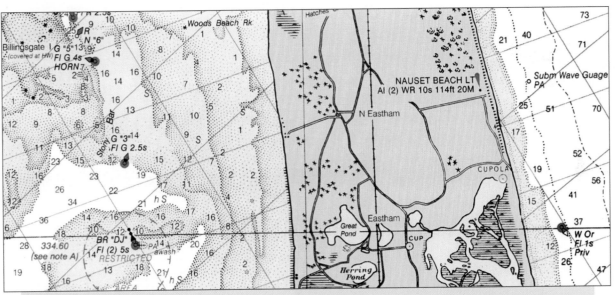

Cape Cod Bay   1:80,000

Cape Cod peninsula, Massachusetts. **Selected features:** *Deciduous woods with some conifers to the northeast.* **Coniferous woods** *to the west. Marsh in the south and northwest; the cross-hatching is not in INT-1 or Chart No. 1—it represents the chart compiler's license!* **Low cliffs** *in the northeast. Shading of the shoal water areas to indicate* **sandy or stony ridges.** *Restricted zone in southwest with T-dashes pointing into the zone, and an isolated danger buoy inside the zone (red and black with two spheres for a topmark—see chapter 8). This is situated on a dangerous wreck, position approximate (PA) that is noted as being "awash."* **Church CUPOLA** *on east coast, and another* **cupola** *("CUP") in the south center; both are accurately charted (the dot in the center of the circle) and conspicuous (capital letters), with the eastern one more conspicuous (larger font size and "cupola" spelled out in full). Nauset Beach Light is alternating white and red, with two flashes every 10 seconds, 114 feet high, range 20 miles.*

C *Natural Features*

c	Foreshore; Strand (in general). Stones; Shingle; Gravel; Mud; Sand	
d	Breakers along a shore	
e	Rubble	
f	Hachures. The light is generally assumed to be from the northwest.	
g	Shading	
h	Lagoon	
i	Deciduous woodland	
j	Coniferous woodland	
k	Tree plantation	
l	Cultivated fields	
m	Grass fields	
n	Paddy (rice) fields	
o	Bushes	

D *Cultural Features*

Settlements, Buildings

1		Urban area	
2		Settlement with scattered buildings. Usually, not all buildings are shown.	
3	o Name / ☐ Name / #	Settlement (on medium- and small-scale charts)	
4	✣ Name / Name ■ HOTEL	Village	Vil
5		Buildings in general	
6	Name Hotel	Important building in built-up area	
7	NAME	Street name, Road name — St Street / Ave Avenue / Blvd Boulevard	Church Street
8	Ru / # / 🏛 Ru	Ruins, Ruined landmark	Ruins / o Ru

Roads, Railways, Airfields

10		Motorway (Interstate)	
11		Road (hard surfaced)	
12		Track, Path (loose- or unsurfaced)	
13	# / #	Railway, with station	
14		Cutting. Note the shading is enclosed by a line, as opposed to outside the line, for an embankment; see D15.	
15		Embankment. Note the shading is outside the line, as opposed to enclosed by it, for a cutting; see D14.	

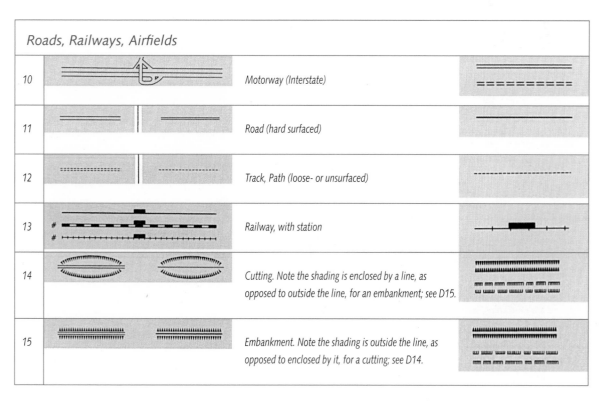

D Cultural Features

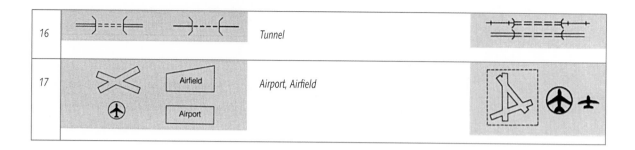

16		Tunnel	
17	Airfield / Airport	Airport, Airfield	

Other Cultural Features

All bridge clearances are given to the high-water datum, which is usually MHWS or MHW, but sometimes MSL (see chapter 3). The datum is stated in a note on the chart.

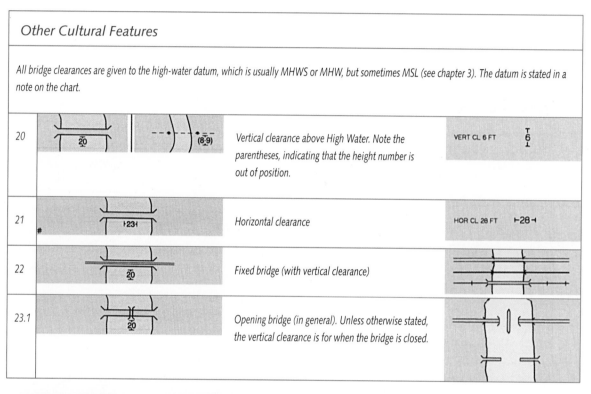

20	20 / (8·9)	Vertical clearance above High Water. Note the parentheses, indicating that the height number is out of position.	VERT CL 6 FT
21	⊢23⊣	Horizontal clearance	HOR CL 28 FT ⊢28⊣
22	20	Fixed bridge (with vertical clearance)	
23.1	20	Opening bridge (in general). Unless otherwise stated, the vertical clearance is for when the bridge is closed.	

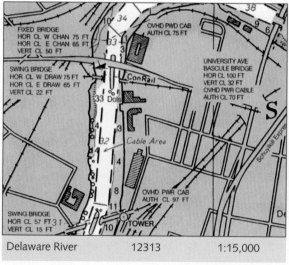

FIXED BRIDGE
HOR CL W CHAN 75 FT
HOR CL E CHAN 65 FT
VERT CL 50 FT

SWING BRIDGE
HOR CL W DRAW 75 FT
HOR CL E DRAW 65 FT
VERT CL 22 FT

ConRail

33 Dols

Cable Area

SWING BRIDGE
HOR CL 57 FT
VERT CL 15 FT

TOWER

UNIVERSITY AVE
BASCULE BRIDGE
HOR CL 100 FT
VERT CL 32 FT
OVHD PWR CABLE
AUTH CL 70 FT

OVHD PWD CAB
AUTH CL 75 FT

OVHD PWR CAB
AUTH CL 97 FT

Delaware River   12313   1:15,000

*Selected features: Figures are given for the **channel widths** at all the bridges (HOR CL) and the **vertical clearance** above the high-water datum when closed (VERT CL). When open, the limiting height at the southern bridge (swing bridge) is the overhead power cable (OVHD PWR CAB) with an authorized clearance of 97 feet above the high-water datum; at the central bridge (swing bridge and fixed bridge), it is the fixed bridge, with a vertical clearance of 50 feet (this is the limiting height in this stretch of the river); and at the northeastern bridge (bascule bridge) it is the overhead power cable with an authorized clearance of 70 feet. Note the **roads**, **railways**, and major **buildings** (drawn to scale). The dashed lines mark the sides of the **channels**. "Dols" = dolphins (see F20). The tower is accurately charted (position circle with position dot plus capitals), and conspicuous (capitals).*

D Cultural Features

23.2	Swing Bridge 7:8	Swing bridge. The bridge span swings horizontally—sideways—to open. (The vertical clearance is when closed.)	
23.3	Lifting Bridge (open 12) 4:2	Lifting bridge. The entire bridge span lifts vertically to open; the vertical clearance when closed, and the vertical clearance when open, is given.	
23.4	Bascule Bridge 12	Bascule bridge with vertical clearance when closed. The bridge has spans hinged at one end so that the spans pivot upward; note that if the spans do not go fully vertical, the vertical clearance at the sides of the channel will frequently still be restricted, whereas it is unlimited in the center.	
23.5	Pontoon Bridge	Pontoon bridge (supported by floating objects)	
23.6	Draw Bridge 5:5	Drawbridge, with vertical clearance when closed	
24	Transporter Bridge 20	Transporter bridge. A girder system suspended between two towers across which some kind of a carriage runs. The vertical clearance is to the lowest part of the structure.	
25	20	Overhead transporter, Telepheric with vertical clearance	
26	⊙ Pyl ⟨28⟩ ⊙ Pyl	Power transmission line with pylons. The minimum overhead clearance is given (in black). With very high voltages, a clearance of from 2 to 5 meters (6.6 to 16.5 ft.) may be needed between a vessel and the cable to avoid electrical discharge. If the overhead clearance is printed in magenta, this has been considered and is defined as the "safe overhead clearance" (on NOAA charts, the safe overhead clearance is defined as 3.5 m/11.55 ft.). NOAA also explicitly labels all power cables as "POWER," whereas INT does not.	OVERHEAD POWER CABLE AUTHORIZED CL 140 FT ⊙ TOWER ⊙ TOWER
27	20	Overhead cable, Telephone line, Telegraph line, with vertical clearance	Tel
28	Overhead pipe 20	Overhead pipe with vertical clearance	OVHD PIPE VERT CL 6 FT
29		Pipeline on land. The flow is toward the dots.	

D *Cultural Features*

	Supplementary National Symbols	
a	Highway markers	
b	Railway (Ry) (single or double track) Railroad (RR)	CONRAIL Same grade Ry above Ry below
c	Abandoned railroad	
d	Bridge under construction	
e	Footbridge	
f	Viaduct	Viaduct
g	Fence	
h	Power transmission line	

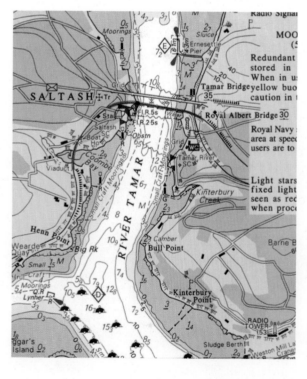

Note the vertical bridge clearances (35 and 30), the railway (which is a solid black line—INT convention), embankments, and numerous other features associated with built-up areas, including power or telephone cables crossing the river (magenta), a water pipeline (black, but labeled in magenta), individual buildings, a church tower, a water tower, and a radio tower (conspicuous). Immediately to the west of the "WC" label is a gridiron ("grid").

Rivers Tamar, Lynher, and Tavy   BA 5602.9
1:25,000

E *Landmarks*

A landmark is defined as any object (natural or artificial) on land that is prominent from seaward and can be used in determining a direction or position, but not including "objects expressly erected for navigational purposes" (e.g., lighthouses, discussed in section P). Prominence is the first requisite for a landmark, but ease of positive identification is almost as important. In general, features that are not particularly conspicuous from seaward are portrayed with just a symbol, whereas those that are conspicuous have a label added.

General

1	✦ Factory ⊚ Hotel ⊓	Examples of landmarks. Note the small positioning circle, which indicates that the feature is not particularly conspicuous, as opposed to the larger circle in E2, which indicates that the feature is conspicuous. Lowercase letters also indicate it is not so conspicuous (INT) and/or its position is approximate (NOAA); capital letters indicate it is conspicuous (INT) and/or accurately positioned (NOAA). A dot within the circle indicates an accurate position.	⊙TANK o Tk ⊕ ⊘
2	✦ FACTORY ⊙ HOTEL ⊓ WATER TOWER	Examples of conspicuous landmarks. Note the larger positioning circle than in E1, indicating a conspicuous feature, and the capital letters. Once again, the dot indicates an accurate position.	⊙ CAPITOL DOME
3.1	 🏠 🏢	Pictorial symbols (in true position). Note the use of black as opposed to magenta in E3.2. This tells us the symbol is in position. The position of the landmark is indicated by the small circle in its base. NOAA does not use these pictorial representations.	
3.2	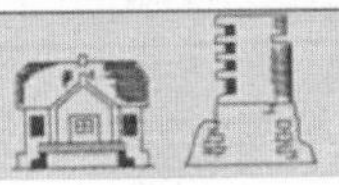 🏠 🏛	Sketches, Views (out of position). The magenta is the clue that this is out of position; there is also no positioning circle.	
4	⊓ (30)	Height of top of a structure above plane of reference for heights. The heights are above the high-water datum (given in a note somewhere on the chart). The parentheses indicate that the height number is out of position (the actual position is given by the small positioning circle at the base of the symbol).	(30)
5	⊓ (30̅)	Height of structure above ground level. The "hat" over the height, as in 30̅, indicates that it is above ground level (this is the actual height of the feature itself), as opposed to above the high-water datum (see also C14 and L21.3).	(30̅)

E Landmarks

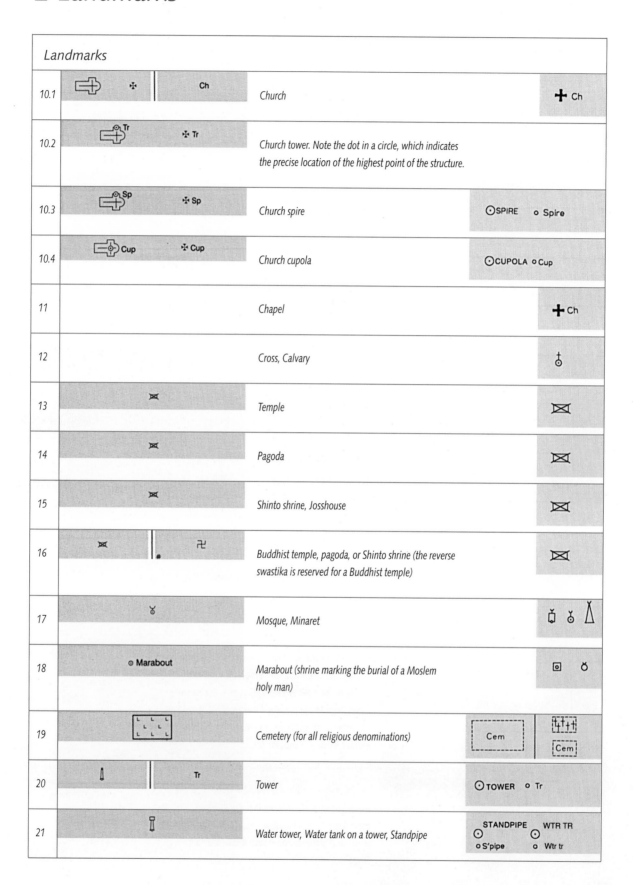

Landmarks

10.1	Church	✚ Ch
10.2	Church tower. Note the dot in a circle, which indicates the precise location of the highest point of the structure.	
10.3	Church spire	⊙SPIRE o Spire
10.4	Church cupola	⊙CUPOLA oCup
11	Chapel	✚ Ch
12	Cross, Calvary	
13	Temple	
14	Pagoda	
15	Shinto shrine, Josshouse	
16	Buddhist temple, pagoda, or Shinto shrine (the reverse swastika is reserved for a Buddhist temple)	
17	Mosque, Minaret	
18	Marabout (shrine marking the burial of a Moslem holy man)	
19	Cemetery (for all religious denominations)	Cem / Cem
20	Tower	⊙TOWER o Tr
21	Water tower, Water tank on a tower, Standpipe	STANDPIPE WTR TR o S'pipe o Wtr tr

No.	Symbol 1	Symbol 2	Description	Variant A	Variant B
22		Chy	Chimney	⊙ CHIMNEY o Chy	
23			Flare stack (on land)	⊙ FLARE o Flare	
24		Mon	Monument	MONUMENT ⊙ o Mon	
25.1	×		Windmill	⊙ WINDMILL o Windmill	⊙ WINDMILL
25.2	× Ru		Windmill (wingless)		
26			Windmotor (wind generator)	⊙ WINDMOTOR o Windmotor	
26.2			Windfarms		
27	P	FS	Flagstaff, Flagpole	⊙ F S o F S	⊙ F P o F P
28			Radio mast, Television mast (a mast is supported by guy wires)	⊙ R MAST o R Mast	⊙ MAST o TV Mast
29			Radio tower, Television tower (a tower is self-supporting)	⊙ R TR o R Tr	⊙ TV TR o TV Tr
30.1	⊙ Radar Mast		Radar mast	⊙ RADAR MAST o Radar Mast	
30.2	⊙ Radar Tr		Radar tower	⊙ RADAR TR o Radar Tr	
30.3	⊙ Radar Sc		Radar scanner		
30.4	⊙ Radome		Radar dome	⊙ DOME (RADAR) o Dome (Radar)	⊙ RADOME o Radome
31			Dish aerial (ANT = antenna/aerial)	⊙ ANT (RADAR) o Ant (Radar)	
32		Tanks	Tanks	⊙ TANK ⊘ o Tk ⊕	⊙ TANK o Tk
33	⊙ Silo	⊙ Silo	Silo, Elevator	⊙ SILO o Silo	

E *Landmarks*

34.1	Fort (disused)	Fortified structure (on large-scale charts)	
34.2		Castle, Fort, Blockhouse (on smaller-scale charts)	Cas
34.3		Battery, small fort, or "pillbox" (on smaller-scale charts)	
35.1		Quarry (on large-scale charts)	
35.2		Quarry (on smaller-scale charts)	
36		Mine	

Supplementary National Symbols				
a	Moslem shrine		l	Magazine	Magz
b	Tomb		m	Government house	Govt. Ho
c	Watermill		n	Institute	Inst
d	Factory	Facty	o	Courthouse	Ct Ho
e	Well	○ Well	p	Pavilion	Pav
f	School	■ Sch	q	Telephone	T
g	Hospital	■ Hosp	r	Limited	Ltd
h	University	■ Univ	s	Apartment	Apt
i	Gable	⊙ GAB ○ Gab	t	Capitol	Cap
j	Camping site		u	Company	Co
k	Telegraph, Telegraph office	Tel Tel Off	v	Corporation	Corp

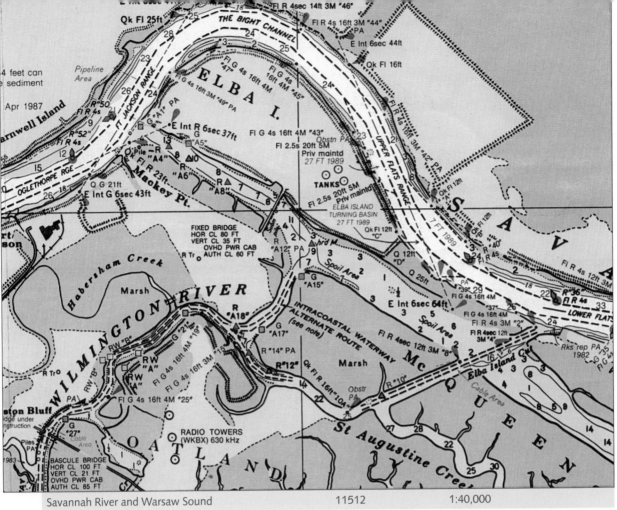

Savannah River and Warsaw Sound   11512   1:40,000

*Look for the following features, moving clockwise from the western edge of the chart: A **railway line** with a building alongside it drawn to scale. Levees throughout the chart area. The **OGLETHORPE RGE** (Range), with a continuous line within the navigable area, and a dashed line where the range line continues outside the navigable area; the range lights are Q Fl R 23ft (Quick Flash Red, 23 feet high) and E Int R 6 Sec 37ft (Equal Interval Red, with a 6-second cycle, 37 feet high). The back light is higher than the front light (this is always the case). For more on lights, see chapter 8. The **FT (Fort) JACKSON RANGE**, with lights at both ends (Quick Flash and Equal Interval, red at one end, green at the other). The pipeline crossing area (magenta dashed lines). The **UPPER FLATS RANGE**, with range lights at both ends that have a similar flash pattern, and which are white (no color is given). ELBA ISLAND TURNING BASIN 27 FT 1989: the date indicates it is not necessarily maintained at this depth. **Buoys** and **beacons** differentiated by the type style on their labels: buoys are italic (hydrographic features), while beacons are vertical (topographic features). **Green buoys** and **beacons** with odd numbers (1, 3, 5, etc.) and red even (2, 4, 6, etc.). This area is in IALA Region B; if it was in Region A, the colors and numbers would be reversed (on the other side of the river to where they are now, see chapter 8). The buoy and beacon numbers increase from the SE to the NW, so the seaward end of the channel is to the SE (lower numbers). All **lit structures** (buoys, beacons, etc.) are given a magenta flare or circle, irrespective of the light color. If no light color is given, it is white. Otherwise, it is given in a label (R or G), and/or via a red or green diamond emanating from the positioning circle (this is a NOAA, not an INT, convention). **Unlit beacons** are identified by the shape of the symbol: a green square for a green beacon; a red triangle for a red beacon (this is a NOAA, not an INT, convention). In this case, the position of the beacon is presumed to be at the center of the symbol. The **high-water line** (SPOR) is not accurately charted in a number of places (dashed lines); where shown, the low-water (sounding) datum is shown with a dotted line. Dashed lines are also used to show the limits of the **navigable channels**. There are a number of conspicuous (capital letters) **tanks** and **radio towers**, accurately positioned (a positioning dot inside a circle). At the mouth of the Elba Island Cut in the SE, **rocks** reported, position approximate, 1982 (Rks rep PA 1982). At the other end of the cut, an **obstruction**, position approximate (the dotted circle, Obstr PA). A **stranded wreck** (see chapter 7) in the Wilmington River. A **bascule bridge**, with a channel width of 100 feet (HOR CL 100 FT) and a closed vertical clearance from the high water datum of 21 feet (VERT CL 21 FT), with the open height limited by an overhead power cable with an authorized vertical clearance of 85 feet (OVHD PWR CAB AUTH CL 85 FT).*

F *Ports*

If piers, docks, and so forth fall below a certain length when plotted at chart scale, they are not charted (for NOAA, if they are less than 0.8 mm long at chart scale, they are not charted). Similarly, if below a certain width (0.3 mm at chart scale), the actual width is not shown—the feature is represented by a single black line.

Hydraulic Structures in General

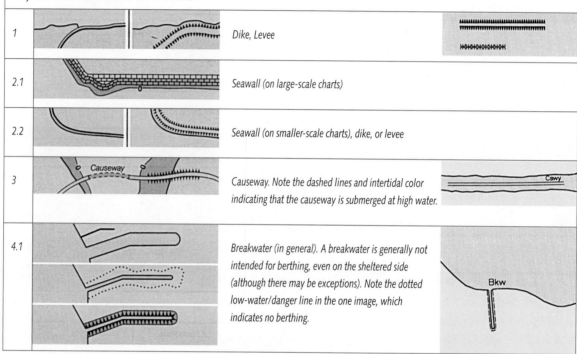

1		Dike, Levee
2.1		Seawall (on large-scale charts)
2.2		Seawall (on smaller-scale charts), dike, or levee
3		Causeway. Note the dashed lines and intertidal color indicating that the causeway is submerged at high water.
4.1		Breakwater (in general). A breakwater is generally not intended for berthing, even on the sheltered side (although there may be exceptions). Note the dotted low-water/danger line in the one image, which indicates no berthing.

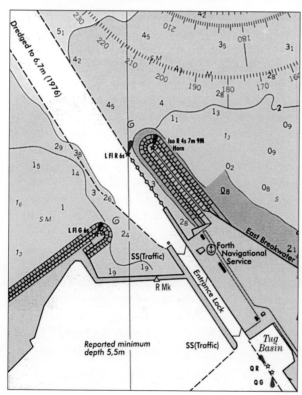

Firth of Forth	NIMA 35082	1:25,052

Selected features: Note the graphic depiction of the **seawall** *on this large-scale chart (1:25,052). On the end of the seawall, we have an isophase* **red light flashing** *every 4 seconds, 7 meters high, with a range of 9 miles (Iso R 4s 7m 9M: see chapter 8 for lights). This area is in IALA Region A (see chapter 8), so the red lights are to port when entering harbor. Either side of the channel, we have a* **long flash light** *(L Fl). In the shoal water to the west of the harbor, we have* **two soundings** *in a smaller font, and italicized (this is hard to decipher), whereas the rest are vertical: this is to warn that these soundings have been taken from an older or less reliable survey. There is another of these soundings to the east (1.3 m). The fact that there is a* **date** *on the dredged channel indicates that it is not necessarily maintained and may not be the same today. SS = signal station.* ⊞ *= harbormaster's office (port captain).* ⓖ *= eddies: off the ends of the seawalls.*

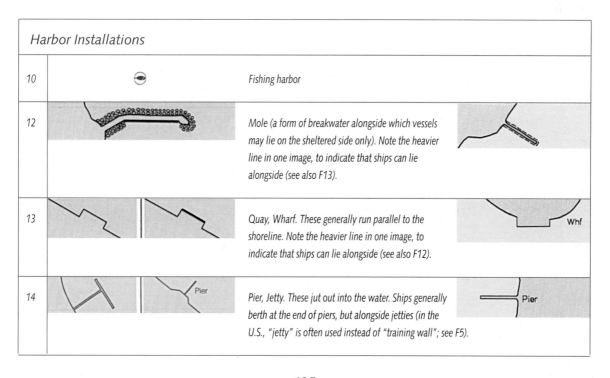

4.2		Breakwater (loose boulders, tetrapods, etc.)	
4.3		Breakwater (slope of concrete or masonry)	
5		Training wall (partly submerged at high water). A training wall (often called a "jetty" in the U.S.; see F14) is a structure built alongside a channel to direct the tidal stream or current through the channel to promote a scouring action (see also F14). The solid portion is permanently above the high-water datum. The dashed section is covered at times.	
6.1		Groin (always dry). A groin (or groyne) is a low, wall-like structure built to prevent coast erosion. The section drawn with a solid line is permanently above the high-water datum; that with a dashed line is covered at times (intertidal); the dotted extension is a danger signal to alert navigators to the fact that this portion is permanently submerged (below the chart sounding datum).	
6.2		Groin (intertidal)	
6.3		Groin (always under water)	

Harbor Installations

10		Fishing harbor	
12		Mole (a form of breakwater alongside which vessels may lie on the sheltered side only). Note the heavier line in one image, to indicate that ships can lie alongside (see also F13).	
13		Quay, Wharf. These generally run parallel to the shoreline. Note the heavier line in one image, to indicate that ships can lie alongside (see also F12).	
14		Pier, Jetty. These jut out into the water. Ships generally berth at the end of piers, but alongside jetties (in the U.S., "jetty" is often used instead of "training wall"; see F5).	

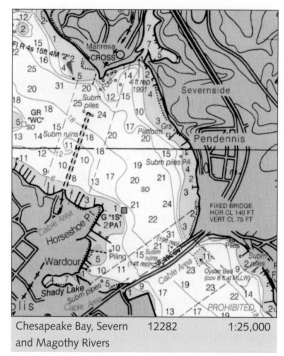

Chesapeake Bay, Severn
and Magothy Rivers | 12282 | 1:25,000

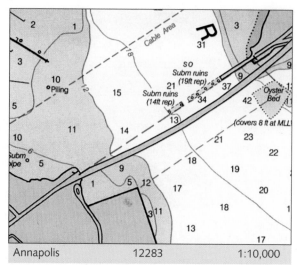

Annapolis | 12283 | 1:10,000

Selected features: *A* **discontinued railway line** *(dashed) with the ruins of a causeway in the northern half of this chart, and a similar road feature just above the road in the southern half. The blue color on the causeways'* **ruins** *indicates that they are below the low-water datum. All* **docks** *are too small to show at chart scale, so a single black line is used. In the southeast corner, we have* **"Subm piles"** *in italic typeface, and* **"Piles"** *in vertical, indicating the former is below the high-water datum, and the latter above it. In the northwest corner, we have* **"Dol"** *= dolphin (vertical type; therefore, above the high-water datum).*

Detail shot (1:10,000) of the previous chart (1:25,000). There is not a single additional sounding, so in one sense no more information, but it is much easier to read. Note also the submerged ruins in the center, which are in the center of the ruined causeway of a bridge, whereas in the previous chart, they are offset just to the south (perhaps due to a registration error). The larger scale chart is always more accurate.

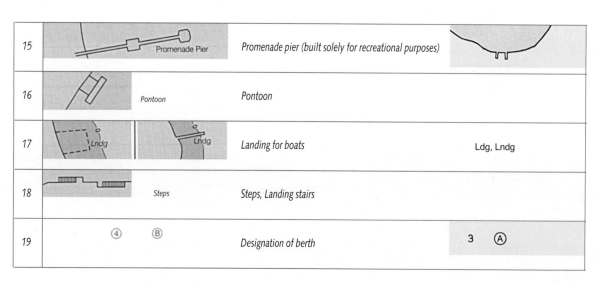

15		Promenade pier (built solely for recreational purposes)	
16	Pontoon	Pontoon	
17	Lndg	Landing for boats	Ldg, Lndg
18	Steps	Steps, Landing stairs	
19	④ Ⓑ	Designation of berth	3 Ⓐ

F Ports

20	◯　　▫　　▫ Dn　　▯ Dns	Dolphin (a very substantial post, group of posts, or structure used for mooring or hauling off vessels, or for the protection of other ships)	◦ Dol • Dol
21	⚓	Deviation dolphin (a dolphin around which a vessel may swing for compass adjustment)	
22	·　　•	Minor post or pile	◦ Pile　　• Pile

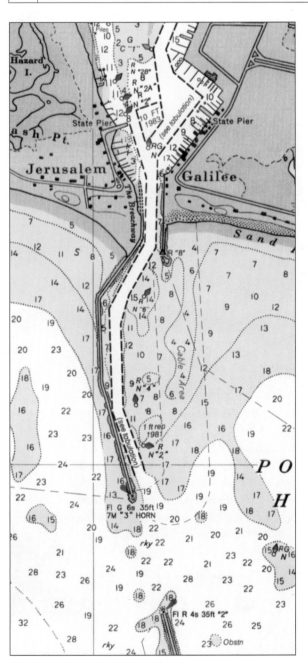

Point Judith Harbor　　　13219　　　1:15,000

Selected features: Breakwaters (jetties). Sand dune symbol ▨▨▨ *on the beach south of Galilee. Some individual **houses** are shown to scale (this is a large-scale chart: 1:15,000). A mix of **symbolic piers** (single black line) and piers drawn to chart scale (e.g., the two "State Piers").*

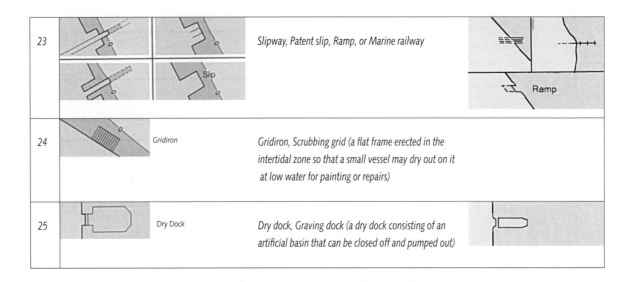

23		Slipway, Patent slip, Ramp, or Marine railway	
24	Gridiron	Gridiron, Scrubbing grid (a flat frame erected in the intertidal zone so that a small vessel may dry out on it at low water for painting or repairs)	
25	Dry Dock	Dry dock, Graving dock (a dry dock consisting of an artificial basin that can be closed off and pumped out)	

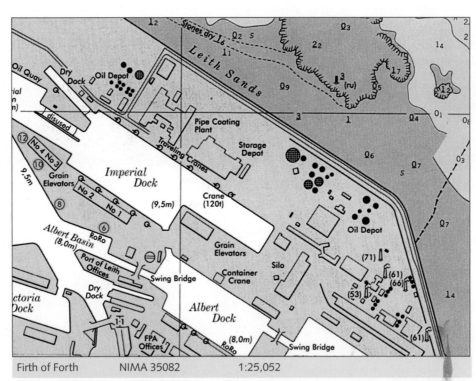

Firth of Forth   NIMA 35082   1:25,052

*Selected features: **Vertical clearance** of 1.1 (⊞) meters in the southwest corner. Roll-On, Roll-Off (RoRo) ferry terminal. **Lock gates** in the NW quadrant (disused). **Crane** symbols, as in ⊙ , on the docks. **Drying height**s (e.g., 3) along the shoreline. An old **stone causeway** in the north. A **ruin** ("ru") on the rocks, with a drying height (3). Various **chimneys**, with their heights above the high-water datum, in the southeast corner. Because the heights are out of position (not exactly over the location for the chimneys), they are in parentheses.*

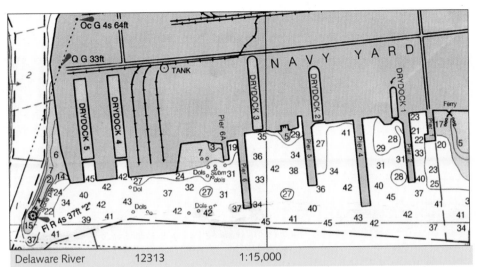

Delaware River   12313   1:15,000

*The Philadelphia U.S. Navy base, drawn to a large scale (1:15,000). **Selected features:** The individual **piers** and **drydocks** are at chart scale. **Roads** and **railways**. **Range lights** (the solid line in the channel with the dashed line going to the two lights in line; see chapter 8). "**Dols**" = dolphins above the high-water datum (vertical letters); "**Subm dols**" = dolphins below the level of the high-water datum (italic). The **tank** is accurately located and conspicuous (positioning dot plus capitals).*

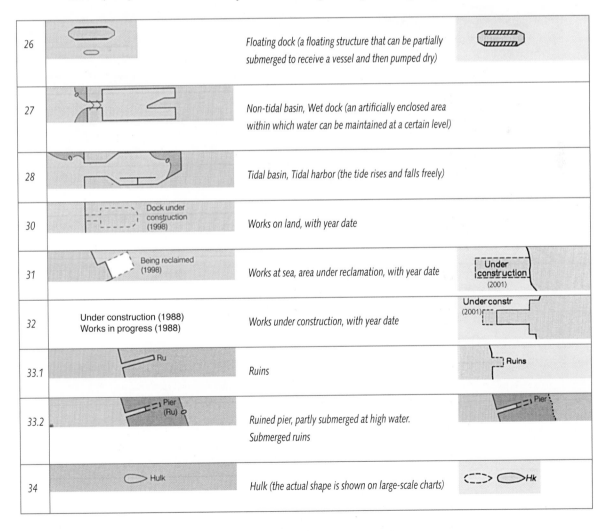

26		Floating dock (a floating structure that can be partially submerged to receive a vessel and then pumped dry)
27		Non-tidal basin, Wet dock (an artificially enclosed area within which water can be maintained at a certain level)
28		Tidal basin, Tidal harbor (the tide rises and falls freely)
30	Dock under construction (1998)	Works on land, with year date
31	Being reclaimed (1998)	Works at sea, area under reclamation, with year date
32	Under construction (1988) Works in progress (1988)	Works under construction, with year date
33.1	Ru	Ruins
33.2	Pier (Ru)	Ruined pier, partly submerged at high water. Submerged ruins
34	Hulk	Hulk (the actual shape is shown on large-scale charts)

F *Ports*

Canals, Barrages

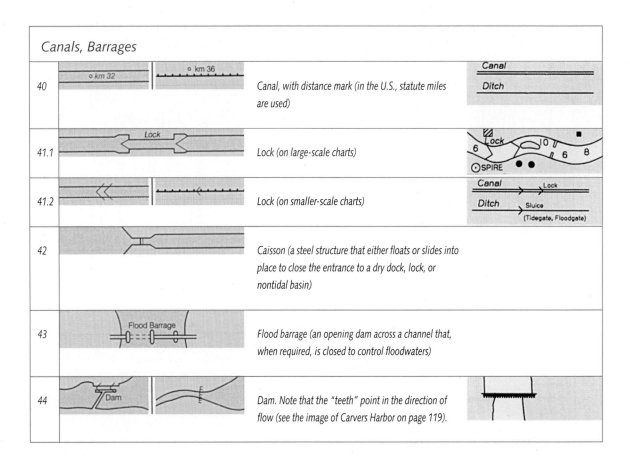

40		Canal, with distance mark (in the U.S., statute miles are used)	
41.1		Lock (on large-scale charts)	
41.2		Lock (on smaller-scale charts)	
42		Caisson (a steel structure that either floats or slides into place to close the entrance to a dry dock, lock, or nontidal basin)	
43		Flood barrage (an opening dam across a channel that, when required, is closed to control floodwaters)	
44		Dam. Note that the "teeth" point in the direction of flow (see the image of Carvers Harbor on page 119).	

Transhipment Facilities

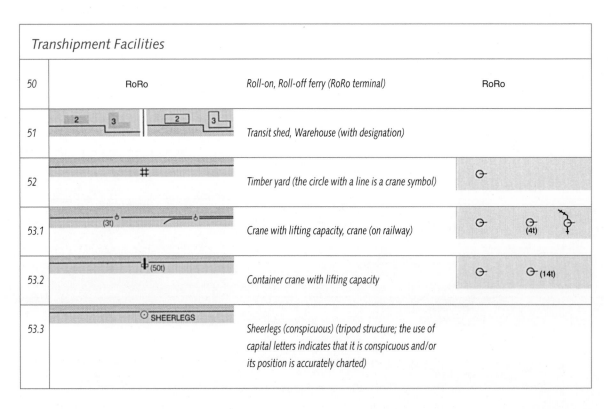

50	RoRo	Roll-on, Roll-off ferry (RoRo terminal)	RoRo
51		Transit shed, Warehouse (with designation)	
52		Timber yard (the circle with a line is a crane symbol)	
53.1		Crane with lifting capacity, crane (on railway)	
53.2		Container crane with lifting capacity	
53.3		Sheerlegs (conspicuous) (tripod structure; the use of capital letters indicates that it is conspicuous and/or its position is accurately charted)	

F *Ports*

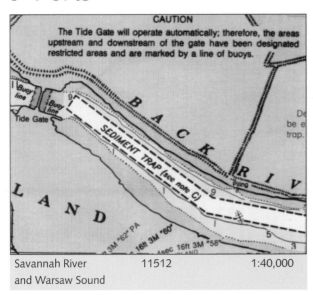

Savannah River
and Warsaw Sound   11512   1:40,000

*Selected features: A **tide gate**, with a note explaining its operation. The **embankment** symbol. A lighter line weight for the **coastline** in the mid- to western section of the southern coastline (this is hard to detect), indicating less certainty as to the high-water line (this may be a drafting anomaly).*

Public Buildings			
60	⊕	Harbormaster's office	Hbr Mr
61	⊖	Customhouse	▪ Cus Ho
62.1	⊕	Health officer's office	⊕ Health Office
62.2	⊕ Hospital	Hospital	▪ Hosp
63	✉	Post office	▪ PO

Supplementary National Symbols		
a	Jetty (partly below MHW)	
b	Submerged jetty	
c	Jetty (small-scale)	
d	Pump-out facilities	℗
e	Quarantine	⊕ Quar

G Topographic Terms

TOPOGRAPHY: G *Topographic Terms*

Coast

1	Island	6	Atoll	11	Rock
2	Islet	7	Cape	12	Salt marsh, Saltings
3	Cay	8	Head, Headland	13	Lagoon
4	Peninsula	9	Point		
5	Archipelago	10	Spit		

Natural Inland Features

20	Promontory	27	Hill	34	Vegetation
21	Range	28	Boulder	35	Grassland
22	Ridge	29	Tableland	36	Paddy field
23	Mountain, Mount	30	Plateau	37	Bushes
24	Summit	31	Valley	38	Deciduous woodland
25	Peak	32	Ravine, Cut	39	Coniferous woodland
26	Volcano	33	Gorge		

Settlements

50	City, Town	52	Fishing village	54	Saint
51	Village	53	Farm		

Buildings

60	Structure	74	Institute	87	Refinery
61	House	75	Cathedral	88	Power station
62	Hut	76	Monastery, Convent	89	Electric works
63	Multistory building	77	Lookout station, Watchtower	90	Gas works
64	Castle	78	Navigation school	91	Water works
65	Pyramid	79	Naval college	92	Sewage works
66	Column	80	Factory	93	Machine house, Pump house
67	Mast	81	Brick kiln, Brick works	94	Well
68	Lattice tower	82	Cement works	95	Telegraph office
69	Mooring mast	83	Water mill	96	Hotel
70	Floodlight	84	Greenhouse	97	Sailors' home
71	Town hall	85	Warehouse, Storehouse	98	Spa hotel
72	Office	86	Cold store, Refrigerating storage house		
73	Observatory				

G Topographic Terms

Road, Rail, and Air Traffic

110	Street, Road	113	Viaduct	116	Runway
111	Avenue	114	Suspension bridge	117	Landing lights
112	Tramway	115	Footbridge	118	Helicopter landing site

Ports, Harbors

130	Tidal barrier	139	Haven	148	Building harbor
131	Boat lift, Ship lift, Hoist	140	Inner harbor	149	Oil harbor
132	Loading canal	141	Outer harbor	150	Ore harbor
133	Sluice	142	Deep-water harbor	151	Grain harbor
134	Basin	143	Free port	152	Container harbor
135	Reservoir	144	Customs harbor	153	Timber harbor
136	Reclamation area	145	Naval port	154	Coal harbor
137	Port	146	Industrial harbor	155	Ferry harbor
138	Harbor	147	Commercial port, Trade port	156	Police

Harbor Installations

170	Terminal	176	Tanker cleaning facilities	182	Conveyor
171	Building slip	177	Cooling water intake/outfall	183	Storage tanker
172	Building yard	178	Floating barrier, Boom	184	Lighter Aboard Ship—LASH
173	Buoy yard, Buoy dump	179	Piling	185	Liquefied Natural Gas—LNG
174	Bunker station	180	Row of piles	186	Liquefied Petroleum Gas—LPG
175	Reception facilities for oily wastes	181	Bollard	187	Very Large Crude Carrier—VLCC

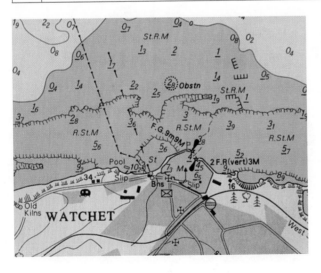

Selected features: post office (✉), customs house (⊜), caravan park (🚐), churches (✠), old kilns precisely located (the black dot in the circle) but not particularly conspicuous (initial capitals in the label but otherwise lowercase letters).

Somerset and Devon   BA 1160   1:20,00

Hydrography

Tides, Currents, Depths, Nature of the Seabed, Rocks, Wrecks, Obstructions, Offshore Installations, Tracks, Routes, Areas, Limits, and Hydrographic Terms

THE SECTIONS ON HYDROGRAPHY in *INT-1* discuss the shape of the bottom, depths, obstructions, tides and currents, traffic-separation schemes (TSSs), and other regulated areas: all core information for navigators. *Familiarity with these sections is essential.* More than any other sections, they warrant independent study with a chart in hand, in the quiet of your home rather than under the stress of a voyage. In particular, *sections I (Depths) and K (Rocks, Wrecks, Obstructions) should be committed to memory.*

Section H: Tides and Currents

Section H begins with "Terms Relating to Tidal Levels" (H1–17); it continues with "Tidal Levels and Charted Data" (H20), illustrating various vertical datums. *It is important to understand these datums, particularly their implications in use on any specific chart for the actual water depth—especially at low tide—and the real-life clearance under bridges and overhead cables—especially at high tide.* Refer to chapter 3 for a full explanation of these terms and issues, as well as the following paragraph.

Charts generally do not carry substantial tidal information—it is relegated to separate tide tables published by hydrographic offices. However, there is frequently a table that references the state of different tides to the low-water (sounding) datum in use on a chart (H30). This particularly useful table is underutilized by many mariners. It gives the height of the tide above the sounding datum for such conditions as MHWS and MHHW; more importantly, it provides the anticipated variance from charted soundings at various low-water conditions. If the sounding datum is the LAT, these variances are rarely negative; however, if it is another datum, such as MLLW (used by NOAA), at certain times the low-water level may be *well below* the sounding datum. *The depths will be below charted depths by the amount of the variance* (e.g., 5.0 ft. in the case of Chesapeake Bay; the "Extreme Low Water" shown in the table is the lowest tide recorded and can be more or less equated with LAT). In areas with a substantial tidal range, it is not unusual for these variances to be as great as 2 meters

TIDAL INFORMATION				
Place	Height referred to datum of soundings (MLLW)			
Name (LAT/LONG)	Mean Higher High Water	Mean High Water	Mean Low Water	Extreme Low Water
	feet	feet	feet	feet
Betterton, Sassafras River entr. (39°22'N/76°04'W)	2.4	2.0	0.4	-5.0
Baltimore, Ft. McHenry (39°16'N/76°35'W)	1.7	1.4	0.2	-4.9
Annapolis, U.S. Naval Academy (38°59'N/76°29'W)	1.4	1.2	0.2	-4.0
Drum Point, Patuxent River (38°19'N/76°25'W)	1.8	1.5	0.3	-3.5
Point No Point (38°08'N/76°18'W)	2.0	1.6	0.3	--
Smith Point Light (37°53'N/76°11'W)	1.4	1.3	0.1	--
Wolf Trap Light (37°23'N/76°11'W)	1.8	1.7	0.1	-3.0
Hampton Roads, Sewells Point (36°57'N/76°20'W)	2.8	2.6	0.1	-3.5
(396)				

Chesapeake Bay	12280	1:200,000

The low-water (sounding) datum on this chart is Mean Lower Low Water (MLLW). Note that this is very close to Mean Low Water (the differences are a fraction of a foot), which is the average of all low tides. This suggests that somewhere on the order of one of every two low tides will be lower than this. As can be seen from the Extreme Low Water column, some of these will be several feet lower (up to 5.0 ft.).

144

(6 ft. or more). *This is critical information for navigators*, especially during spring tides (of course, you also have to know the state of the moon). It is information that may not show up on vector charts, and for which you will have to hunt around on raster charts.

Given the typical situation of diurnal tides (two tides a day) with no unusual characteristics, the rule of twelfths can be used to approximate the changes in water depth during a tidal cycle. The depth is considered to change by one twelfth of the tidal range in each of the first and sixth hours of the ebb and flood, two twelfths in each of the second and fifth hours, and three twelfths in each of the third and fourth hours (see the diagram).

Tidal-stream (current) tables (H31), which are placed on some charts (NOAA does not), are another piece of invaluable information in areas subject to strong tidal streams. For a given location, the table provides the direction of the flow (in true degrees) and its speed (in knots) on an hour-by-hour basis. At the top of the table is a reference letter inside a diamond (or circle, on some private charts), printed in magenta (which indicates that this is data superimposed on the physical features of the chart; see chapter 5). This letter is then printed on the chart at the location to which the table applies. Where strong tidal streams occur in narrow channels, there often may be a significant time delay between the times of slack water (high and low) in the channel and the times of high and low tide in other parts of the area. To use the tidal-stream table effectively, you need to know the times of slack water in the channel, not somewhere else.

TIDAL INFORMATION

Place	Height above datum of soundings			
	Mean High Water		Mean Low Water	
	Springs	Neaps	Springs	Neaps
	meters	meters	meters	meters
Leith..............	.... 5.6	.... 4.5	.... 0.8	.... 2.1 ....
Granton..........	.... 5.6	.... 4.5	.... 0.8	.... 2.1 ....
Burntisland......	.... 5.6	.... 4.5	.... 0.8	.... 2.1 ....

Tidal Streams referred to HW at LEITH

Hours		Geographical Position		A 56°01'.9N 3°16'.4W		B 56°02'.4N 3°10'.1W		C 56°00'.6N 3°07'.2W		D 56°04'.5N 3°02'.3W	
Before High Water	6	Directions of streams (degrees)	-6	060	0.2 0.1	135	0.3 0.2	290	0.1 0.0	156	0.1 0.1
	5		-5	234	0.4 0.2	209	0.3 0.1	272	0.4 0.2	209	0.4 0.2
	4		-4	241	1.5 0.8	255	1.0 0.5	260	1.0 0.5	237	0.8 0.4
	3		-3	246	1.5 0.8	258	1.1 0.6	264	0.7 0.3	239	0.7 0.3
	2	Rates at spring tides (knots)	-2	247	0.9 0.5	264	0.8 0.4	263	0.4 0.2	255	0.5 0.3
	1		-1	246	0.6 0.3	263	0.7 0.3	250	0.2 0.1	267	0.4 0.2
High Water	0	Rates at neap tides (knots)	0	243	0.4 0.2	268	0.4 0.2	225	0.1 0.0	297	0.2 0.1
After High Water	1		+1	124	0.1 0.1	039	0.2 0.1	077	0.6 0.3	046	0.4 0.2
	2		+2	070	1.0 0.5	055	0.8 0.4	080	0.8 0.4	051	0.7 0.4
	3		+3	059	1.6 0.8	066	1.2 0.6	085	0.8 0.4	054	0.9 0.4
	4		+4	052	1.3 0.7	078	1.1 0.5	092	0.5 0.2	073	0.7 0.3
	5		+5	052	0.7 0.3	092	0.7 0.4	095	0.2 0.1	098	0.3 0.2
	6		+6	056	0.3 0.2	126	0.4 0.2		0.0 0.0	122	0.1 0.1

Firth of Forth   NIMA 35082   1:25,052

The low-water (sounding) datum on this chart is Lowest Astronomical Tide (LAT). Note that even the Mean Low Water Spring Tides (MLWS) are above this (top table), which suggests that, in practice, the water will almost never go much below chart datum. The tidal-stream table gives the tidal stream for four different locations (A, B, C, and D), for both spring tides and neap tides.

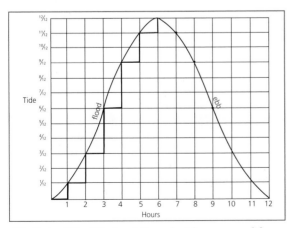

The Rule of Twelfths (semidiurnal with no unusual features).

Approx Direction and Rate of Tidal Streams
Based upon HW at St Helier

Not to be used for navigation

Position 49°05'.8N 2°09'.9W	(A)	Hours before H.W.						Hours after H.W					
		6	5	4	3	2	1	HW	1	2	3	4	5	6
Direction °		270	099	106	107	104	094	054	309	289	282	280	277	273
Rate in Knots — Springs		0.8	0.7	2.5	3.5	3.1	1.9	0.6	1.0	2.1	2.9	2.8	2.1	1.2
Rate in Knots — Neaps		0.4	0.3	1.1	1.5	1.3	0.8	0.3	0.4	0.9	1.2	1.2	0.9	0.5

Position 49°02'.0N 2°34'.2W	(B)	Hours before H.W.						Hours after H.W					
		6	5	4	3	2	1	HW	1	2	3	4	5	6
Direction °		293	161	145	140	131	112	064	002	330	312	300	297	293
Rate in Knots — Springs		0.9	0.1	1.9	2.9	2.1	1.2	0.7	0.8	1.3	1.8	2.1	1.9	1.1
Rate in Knots — Neaps		0.4	0.1	0.8	1.3	0.9	0.6	0.3	0.3	0.6	0.8	0.9	0.8	0.6

Position 49°00'.0N 1°51'.0W	(C)	Hours before H.W.						Hours after H.W					
		6	5	4	3	2	1	HW	1	2	3	4	5	6
Direction °		216	179	144	123	107	056	358	344	335	318	292	251	227
Rate in Knots — Springs		1.0	1.1	1.8	2.0	1.5	0.7	1.2	1.5	1.6	1.4	1.1	1.1	1.0
Rate in Knots — Neaps		0.4	0.5	0.7	0.8	0.6	0.3	0.5	0.6	0.7	0.6	0.5	0.4	0.4

Position 48°51'.5N 2°38'.0W	(D)	Hours before H.W.						Hours after H.W					
		6	5	4	3	2	1	HW	1	2	3	4	5	6
Direction °		350	101	127	129	130	133	124	310	306	310	310	309	308
Rate in Knots — Springs		0.8	0.3	1.9	2.8	2.5	1.5	0.4	0.6	1.7	2.1	2.1	1.8	1.2
Rate in Knots — Neaps		0.4	0.1	0.9	1.2	1.1	0.6	0.2	0.3	0.8	1.0	0.9	0.8	0.5

Position 48°48'.5N 2°08'.0W	(E)	Hours before H.W.						Hours after H.W					
		6	5	4	3	2	1	HW	1	2	3	4	5	6
Direction °		263	218	108	102	097	094	083	320	292	283	276	273	267
Rate in Knots — Springs		1.1	0.3	1.5	2.3	2.3	1.5	0.6	0.4	1.1	1.9	1.6	1.5	1.2
Rate in Knots — Neaps		0.5	0.2	0.6	1.0	1.0	0.7	0.3	0.2	0.5	0.8	0.7	0.7	0.5

A tidal-stream table for the Channel Islands (off the north coast of France). The same kind of information as in the table above, but in a somewhat different format.

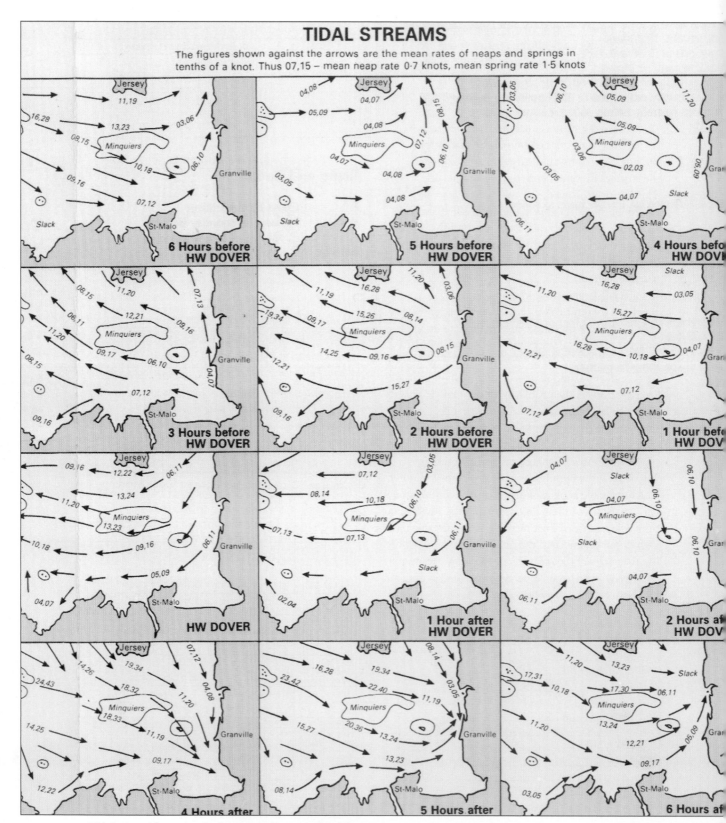

Tidal-stream data may also be presented in a graphical format.

H *Tides, Currents*

Terms Relating to Tidal Levels

#			
1	CD	*Chart Datum, Datum for sounding reduction*	
2	LAT	*Lowest Astronomical Tide*	
3	HAT	*Highest Astronomical Tide*	
4	MLW	*Mean Low Water*	MLW
5	MHW	*Mean High Water*	MHW
6	MSL	*Mean Sea Level*	MSL
7		*Land survey datum*	
8	MLWS	*Mean Low Water Springs*	MLWS
9	MHWS	*Mean High Water Springs*	MHWS
10	MLWN	*Mean Low Water Neaps*	MLWN
11	MHWN	*Mean High Water Neaps*	MHWN
12	MLLW	*Mean Lower Low Water*	MLLW
13	MHHW	*Mean Higher High Water*	MHHW
14	MHLW	*Mean Higher Low Water*	
15	MLHW	*Mean Lower High Water*	
16	Sp	*Spring tide*	Sp
17	Np	*Neap tide*	Np

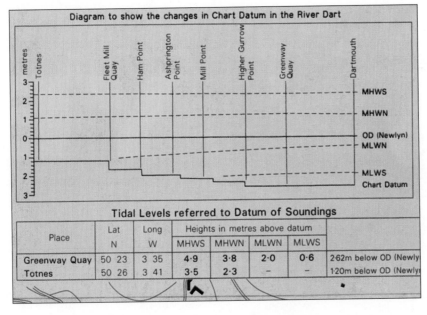

A somewhat unusual tide diagram showing how the tide varies as you head up the River Dart in southern England. The chart sounding datum is LAT.

Diagram to show the changes in Chart Datum in the River Dart

Totnes — Fleet Mill Quay — Ham Point — Ashprington Point — Mill Point — Higher Gurrow Point — Greenway Quay — Dartmouth

MHWS
MHWN
OD (Newlyn)
MLWN
MLWS
Chart Datum

Tidal Levels referred to Datum of Soundings

Place	Lat N	Long W	Heights in metres above datum				
			MHWS	MHWN	MLWN	MLWS	
Greenway Quay	50 23	3 35	4·9	3·8	2·0	0·6	2·62m below OD (Newly
Totnes	50 26	3 41	3·5	2·3	–	–	1·20m below OD (Newly

BA 5602.12

147

H *Tides, Currents*

Tidal Levels and Charted Data—International

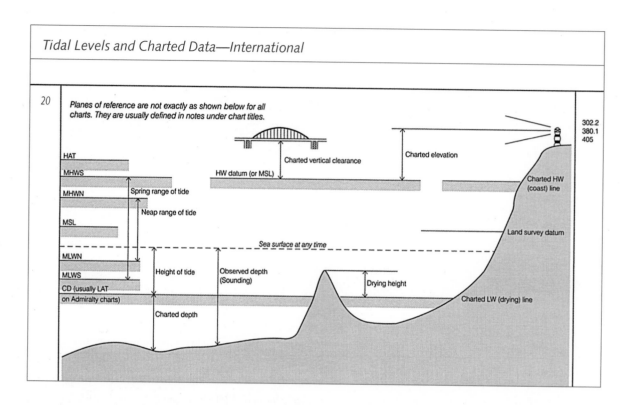

20

Planes of reference are not exactly as shown below for all charts. They are usually defined in notes under chart titles.

302.2
380.1
405

Charted vertical clearance

Charted elevation

HW datum (or MSL)

Charted HW (coast) line

HAT
MHWS
MHWN — Spring range of tide
Neap range of tide
MSL

Land survey datum

Sea surface at any time

MLWN
MLWS
CD (usually LAT on Admiralty charts)

Height of tide

Observed depth (Sounding)

Drying height

Charted LW (drying) line

Charted depth

Tidal Levels and Charted Data—United States

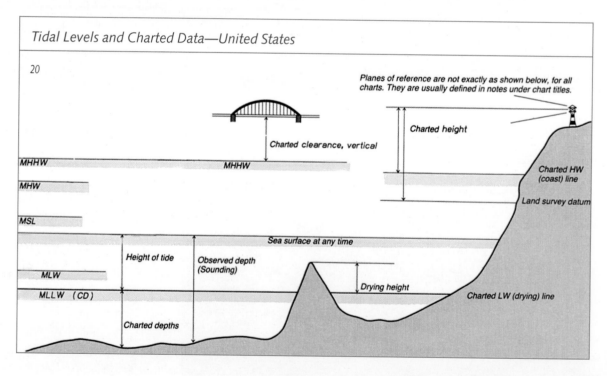

20

Planes of reference are not exactly as shown below, for all charts. They are usually defined in notes under chart titles.

Charted height

Charted clearance, vertical

MHHW   MHHW

Charted HW (coast) line

MHW

Land survey datum

MSL

Sea surface at any time

Height of tide

Observed depth (Sounding)

MLW

Drying height

MLLW (CD)

Charted LW (drying) line

Charted depths

Tide Tables

30 Tabular statement of semi-diurnal or diurnal tides

Tidal Levels referred to Datum of Soundings

Place	Lat. N/S	Long. E/W	Heights in metres/feet above datum				Datum and Remarks
			MHWS	MHWN	MLWN	MLWS	
			MHHW	MLHW	MHLW	MLLW	

Offshore position for which tidal levels are tabulated

a

31 Tidal stream table

Tidal streams referred to....

Hours	◇	Geographical Position			ⒶA	ⒷB	ⒸC	ⒹD	ⒺE
Before High Water: 6 5 4 3 2 1 / High Water / After High Water: 1 2 3 4 5 6	Directions of streams (degrees)	Rates at spring tides (knots)	Rates at neap tides (knots)	-6 -5 -4 -3 -2 -1 0 +1 +2 +3 +4 +5 +6					No / Maximum Rates / For predictions, use Admiralty Tide Tables

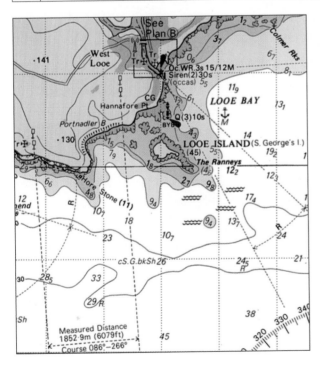

Selected features: overfalls (〰), measured distance, shoal patch offshore highlighted in blue (9₄), sectored lighthouse at West Looe, spot heights ashore, coast guard station (CG), cliffs, and churches. Note the cardinal beacon (chapter 8) to the south of the lighthouse. This is IALA Region A (chapter 8), so the buoy and beacon conventions will be a little unfamiliar to U.S. navigators.

Fowey to Plymouth	BA 5602.3	1:75,000

Tidal Streams and Currents

Tidal streams are defined in IHO S-4 as "periodic and astronomical in origin" (i.e., related to tides, and generally reversing in direction with the tide), whereas currents are not considered to be dependent on astronomical conditions but rather are created by river flows and the wind (e.g., the equatorial current generated by the trade winds); as such, they are generally consistent in direction. This distinction between streams and currents is often not adhered to (particularly in the U.S., where it is common to refer to tidal currents).

40		Flood stream (current) with rate. Note the tail feathers on just one side of the arrow, to denote a flood stream. On some charts, there are black dots on the arrow. When present, they denote the number of hours after low water that the stream is running.	
41		Ebb stream (current) with rate. Note the lack of tail feathers on the arrow to denote an ebb stream. On some charts, black dots are on the arrow. When present, they denote the number of hours after high water that the stream is running.	
42		Current in restricted waters. Note the tail feathers on both sides of the arrow to denote a current that is relatively constant in direction.	
43		Ocean current with rates and seasons. The squiggly arrow indicates that the current is variable or the information is uncertain.	
44		Overfalls, tide rips, races	
45		Eddies	
46		Position of tabulated tidal data with designation. See previous text for further information on tidal-stream (current) tables.	

H *Tides, Currents*

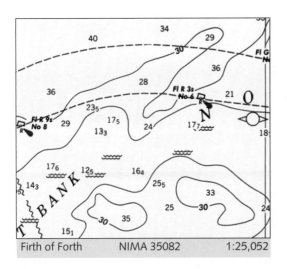

Firth of Forth   NIMA 35082   1:25,052

Overfalls (tide rips). Note the "reporting in" symbol ( ) on the east side of the chart. The double arrowhead indicates that both inbound and outbound shipping must report in. Note also that the can buoys flash red—this is IALA Region A (see chapter 8, section Q).

Supplementary National Symbols

a	HW	High Water		l	Str	Stream
b	HHW	Higher High Water		m	2kn	Current, general, with rate. Note the feathers on both sides of the arrow (as in H42) to denote a current that is relatively consistent in direction, as opposed to a tidal stream.
c	LW	Low Water				
d	LWD	Low-water datum		n	vel	Velocity; Rate
e	LLW	Lower Low Water		o	kn	Knots
f	MTL	Mean Tide Level		p	ht	Height
g	ISLW	Indian spring low water		q	fl	Flood
h	HWF&C	High-water full and change (vulgar establishment of the port)		r	●	New moon
i	LWF&C	Low-water full and change		s	☺	Full moon
j	CRD	Columbia River Datum		t		Current diagram
k	GCLWD	Gulf Coast Low Water Datum				

151

I Depths

Section I: Depths

The key point to remember in connection with depths is that they are all relative to a particular low-water (sounding) datum (also known as the *Chart Datum* [CD] or *Chart Sounding Datum*). *One of the first things a navigator should do when looking at a new chart is establish this sounding datum*, and determine from it whether the actual water depth is ever likely to be less than that shown and, if so, when. (If the sounding datum is MLLW, as it is on NOAA's charts, the water level at low tide will *frequently* be less than the charted depth, sometimes by a considerable amount.)

Shoal water is colored blue. What is considered shoal varies with the scale of the chart (on a large-scale chart, the shoal water line may be drawn at 2 m/6 ft.; on a small-scale chart, it may be at 20 m/60 ft.). In the future, we can expect to see more charts with gradations of blue—the darker the blue, the shallower the water (with the exception of certain private chartmakers, such as Stanfords Charts and Imray, Laurie, Norie and Wilson, in the U.K., which reverse this convention: darker blue represents deeper water).

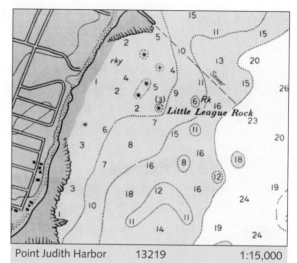

| Point Judith Harbor | 13219 | 1:15,000 |

Selected features: Soundings, with upright numbers (NOAA imperial units). The use of a dotted line, rather than a solid line, for contours is unusual. Normally, dotted lines are used to highlight dangers (shoals, wrecks, etc.). Little League Rock has a **drying height** *(height above the low-water datum) of 3 feet (note the line under it, which is difficult to see). Because it is out of position (alongside its rock), it is in parentheses. Between the 20- and 30-foot contour lines, there are* **shoal** *patches below 20 feet. These are highlighted by coloring them blue.*

I Depths

General			
1	ED	Existence doubtful. Existence doubtful means just that—the feature itself is in question.	ED
2	SD	Sounding doubtful. The feature itself is not in question, but its charted depth is and, in fact, is strongly suspected to be less than is shown.	SD
3.1	Rep	Reported, but not surveyed. The "reported" label is added if a feature is considered dangerous to navigation, but its existence is not officially confirmed.	Rep
3.2	⋮3⋮ Rep (1983)	Reported with year of report, but not surveyed	Rep (1983)

Depths

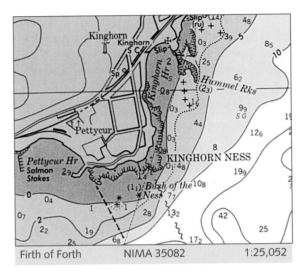

Firth of Forth　　　NIMA 35082　　　1:25,052

Selected features: *Drying heights are underlined; out-of-position heights have parentheses. The "Bush of the Ness" has a* **drying rock** *symbol but its height (1.1 m) is not underlined, so must be a height above the high-water datum (or else the chart compiler has made a mistake). Because it is out of position, it is in parentheses. Note three symbols for* rocks: ✛ = *submerged rock (below the low-water datum);* ✳ = *a rock awash at the level of the low-water datum;* ✻ = *a rock above the level of the low-water datum, but below that of the high-water datum. The* **salmon stakes** *are labeled with italic typeface and, therefore, are below the level of the high-water datum (covered at high tide). On shore we have a* **cemetery**, *a* **church** *with a spire ("sp"), a church with a tower* ✠, *and a chimney* ▯.

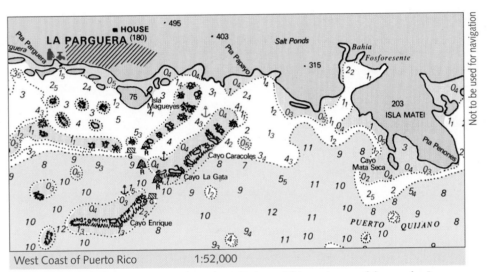

West Coast of Puerto Rico　　　1:52,000

Private chart with a different color scheme to INT charts. This one is part of the popular Imray Iolaire charts of the Caribbean. The intertidal zone is yellow (sand color), shoal water white, and deeper water blue. **Other features include:** *Off-lying shoal areas are highlighted with white (the opposite of the INT convention). Considerable* **reef** *areas.* **Soundings** *in fathoms and feet (not common these days).*

4	(184)	(212)	Reported but not confirmed sounding or danger	(3) Rep

As noted in chapter 5, features may also be tagged with the label PA for "Position Approximate," which means the feature is known to exist but its position has not been accurately determined; or PD for "Position Doubtful," which also means the feature is known to exist but has been reported in various positions, with no one position confirmed.

Depths

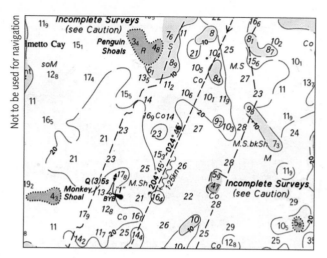

Not to be used for navigation

INT-1 *chart, in meters and decimal meters, with a combination of italicized soundings and vertical soundings (the latter are from older, less reliable, surveys).* **Other features include:** *Contour lines with* **depth labels** *in vertical type and a smaller font size. The use of a dotted line and blue color to highlight* **shoal** *areas. Dashed lines to delineate the* **approximate boundary** *of more recent surveys, with a dashed recommended track down the center together with its bearing (204–024 degrees). A* **cardinal style buoy** *(see chapter 8) with a diamond topmark. Ocean current symbol* 〰 *with a rate of 1.25 knots.*

Soundings

On INT charts, spot soundings are in italicized numbers (I10), with vertical numbers (and "hairline numbers"; not shown) denoting soundings that are older or less reliable (I14). On NOAA's charts, italicized numbers are used for meters, and vertical numbers for imperial units (feet and fathoms). Whatever the convention, depth labels on contour lines use the opposite (i.e., if spot soundings are italic, contour depths are vertical, and vice versa; this distinguishes the precise spot soundings from the generalized contour lines). The position of a sounding is assumed to be at the "center of gravity" of the number. Out-of-position soundings are indicated by parentheses, with or without a dot or other marker for the sounding location, or else with a line from the sounding to its marked location (I11). All text (both INT and NOAA) is italicized to identify hydrographic features (in contrast to the vertical text used for shoreside features; see chapter 5).

10	*12* *9₂* # *9,7*	Sounding in true position—the soundings are italic (NOAA/NOS uses vertical soundings on imperial unit charts and italic soundings on metric charts).	19 8₂ 6¾ 8₂ 19	19 8₂ 6¾
11	+(12) ⊙ 3349	Sounding out of position (in parentheses)	(23) .—1036
12	(14,7)	Least depth in narrow channel. Note that because the sounding is out of position (not in the channel), it is in parentheses.	(5)
13	330̇	No bottom found at depth shown	65̇
14	*12* *9₁*	Soundings that are unreliable or taken from a smaller-scale source (NOAA/NOS uses italic soundings on English unit charts and vertical soundings on metric charts).	8₂ 19 8₂ 19	8₂ 19
15	4₉ 4 0₉ 3₄ 2 0	Drying heights above chart datum (they are underlined)	6

Depths

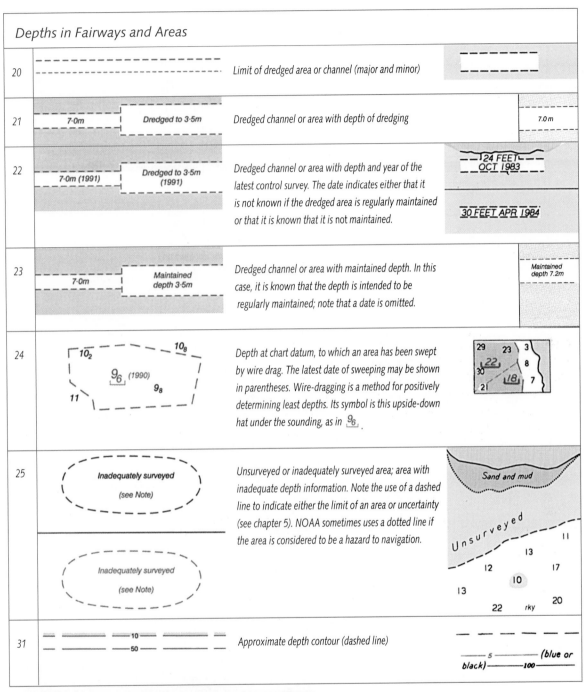

Depths in Fairways and Areas

20	‑ ‑ ‑ ‑ ‑ ‑ ‑ ‑ ‑ ‑ ‑ ‑ ‑ ‑ ‑ ‑ ‑ ‑	Limit of dredged area or channel (major and minor)	‑ ‑ ‑ ‑ ‑ ‑ ‑ ‑
21	7·0m Dredged to 3·5m	Dredged channel or area with depth of dredging	7.0 m
22	7·0m (1991) Dredged to 3·5m (1991)	Dredged channel or area with depth and year of the latest control survey. The date indicates either that it is not known if the dredged area is regularly maintained or that it is known that it is not maintained.	24 FEET OCT 1983 30 FEET APR 1984
23	7·0m Maintained depth 3·5m	Dredged channel or area with maintained depth. In this case, it is known that the depth is intended to be regularly maintained; note that a date is omitted.	Maintained depth 7.2m
24	10₂ 10₈ 9₆ (1990) 9₈ 11	Depth at chart datum, to which an area has been swept by wire drag. The latest date of sweeping may be shown in parentheses. Wire-dragging is a method for positively determining least depths. Its symbol is this upside-down hat under the sounding, as in $\underline{9}_6$.	29 23 3 / 22 / 8 / 30 18 7 / 21
25	Inadequately surveyed (see Note) Inadequately surveyed (see Note)	Unsurveyed or inadequately surveyed area; area with inadequate depth information. Note the use of a dashed line to indicate either the limit of an area or uncertainty (see chapter 5). NOAA sometimes uses a dotted line if the area is considered to be a hazard to navigation.	Sand and mud Unsurveyed 11 13 12 17 13 10 13 20 22 rky
31	‑‑‑ 10 ‑‑‑ ‑‑‑ 50 ‑‑‑	Approximate depth contour (dashed line)	‑‑ 5 ‑‑ (blue or black) ‑‑ 100 ‑‑

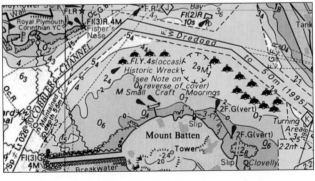

A very busy chart! **Selected features:** dredged channel with date (which means the depth may now be different), numerous ship moorings, a magenta T-dashed area boundary, lights in line symbol (✳), a vertically disposed light ("vert").

Cattewater	BA 5602.8
1:12,500	

Depth Contours

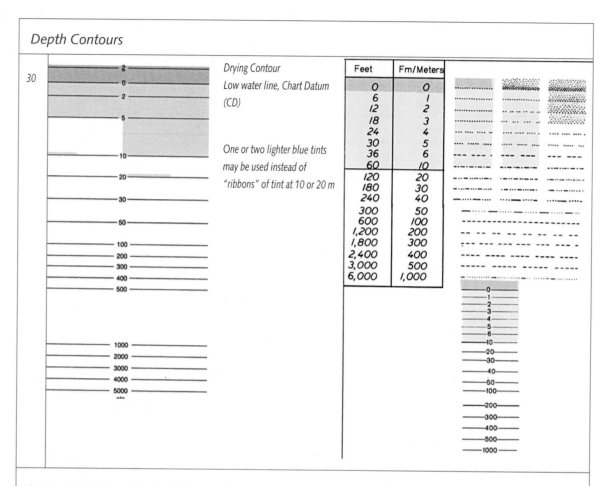

Drying Contour

Low water line, Chart Datum (CD)

One or two lighter blue tints may be used instead of "ribbons" of tint at 10 or 20 m

Feet	Fm/Meters
0	0
6	1
12	2
18	3
24	4
30	5
36	6
60	10
120	20
180	30
240	40
300	50
600	100
1,200	200
1,800	300
2,400	400
3,000	500
6,000	1,000

Note: The extent of the blue tint varies with the scale and purpose of the chart, or its sources. On some charts, contours and figures are printed in blue.

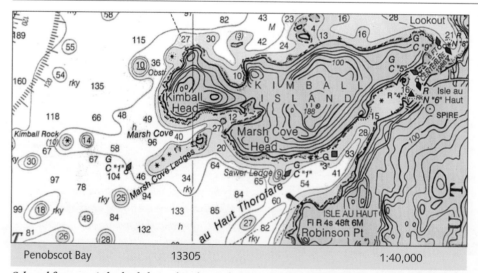

Penobscot Bay   13305   1:40,000

Selected features: *A **dredged channel** in the northeast corner, delineated with black (physical feature) dashed lines with the least depth at the time of dredging (6 ft 1986). "**Kimball Rock**" to the west has a drying height of 10 feet (underlined; the parentheses indicate the sounding is out of position; it should not be italicized—this is a mistake). The 10-foot spot to the northeast of Kimball Rock has been swept by a wire drag to establish a minimum depth. Kimball Island has a spot height (note the black dot) of 188 feet above the high-water datum.*

J Nature of the Seabed

Section J: Nature of the Seabed

Most of the time, mariners are not especially concerned with the nature of the seabed, except when there are minimal underkeel clearances (it is good to know there is mud and not rock just below the boat) and when anchoring. Numerous abbreviations are used to describe the bottom and there is no way to remember all of them; if it becomes important, you'll just have to look them up.

J Nature of the Seabed

Types of Seabed			
1	S	Sand	S
2	M	Mud	M
3	Cy	Clay	Cy; Cl
4	Si	Silt	Si
5	St	Stones	St
6	G	Gravel	G
7	P	Pebbles	P
8	Cb	Cobbles	Cb
9	R	Rock; Rocky	Rk; rky
10	Co	Coral and Coralline algae	Co
11	Sh	Shells	Sh
12	S/M	Two layers; e.g., sand over mud	S/M
13.1	Wd	Weed (including Kelp)	Wd

J *Nature of the Seabed*

13.2	ﻌﺡ	Kelp, Seaweed	᚛᚛᚛ Kelp
14	∿	Mobile bottom (sand waves)	∿ Sandwaves
15	⊤	Freshwater springs in seabed	⊤ Spring

Types of Seabed, Intertidal Areas

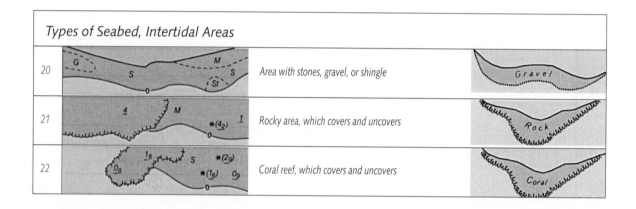

20		Area with stones, gravel, or shingle	Gravel
21		Rocky area, which covers and uncovers	Rock
22		Coral reef, which covers and uncovers	Coral

Qualifying Terms

30	f	fine—only used in relation to sand (i.e. fS = fine sand)	f; fne
31	m	medium—only used in relation to sand (i.e. = mS)	m
32	c	coarse—only used in relation to sand (i.e. = cS)	c; crs
33	bk	broken	bk; brk
34	sy	sticky	sy; stk
35	so	soft	so; sft
36	sf	stiff	stf
37	v	volcanic	Vol
38	ca	calcareous	Ca
39	h	hard	h; hrd

J Nature of the Seabed

Supplementary National Abbreviations

a	Grd	Ground	ad	Po	Polyzoa
b	Oz	Ooze	ae	Cir	Cirripedia
c	Ml	Marl	af	Fu	Fucus
d	Sn	Shingle	ag	Ma	Mattes
e	Blds	Boulders	ah	sml	Small
f	Ck	Chalk	ai	lrg	Large
g	Qz	Quartz	aj	rt	Rotten
h	Sch	Schist	ak	str	Streaky
i	Co Hd	Coral head	al	spk	Speckled
j	Mds	Madrepores	am	gty	Gritty
k	Vol Ash	Volcanic ash	an	dec	Decayed
l	La	Lava	ao	fly	Flinty
m	Pm	Pumice	ap	glac	Glacial
n	T	Tufa	aq	ten	Tenacious
o	Sc	Scoriae	ar	wh	White
p	Cn	Cinders	as	bl; bk	Black
q	Mn	Manganese	at	vi	Violet
r	Oys	Oysters	au	bu	Blue
s	Ms	Mussels	av	gn	Green
t	Spg	Sponge	aw	yl	Yellow
u	K	Kelp	ax	or	Orange
v	Grs	Grass	ay	rd	Red
w	Stg	Sea-tangle	az	br	Brown
x	Spi	Spicules	ba	ch	Chocolate
y	Fr	Foraminifera	bb	gy	Gray
z	Gl	Globigerina	bc	lt	Light
aa	Di	Diatoms	bd	dk	Dark
ab	Rd	Radiolaria	be	vard	Varied
ac	Pt	Pteropods	bf	unev	Uneven

K Rocks, Wrecks, Obstructions

Section K: Rocks, Wrecks, Obstructions

An entire set of conventions already referred to comes into play in this important section, notably those concerning soundings (vertical and italic numbers, parentheses for out-of-position soundings, and the wireline symbol); the use of blue to highlight shoal water; the use of a dotted line to highlight the limits of shoal areas and isolated dangers; and the use of italic type for labels on hydrographic features.

Rocks

Several important new symbols must be learned that distinguish one rock from another in terms of their relationship to the high- and low-water (sounding) datums used on the chart. Following are the four categories of rocks:

1. **BARE ROCKS.** Those that are permanently above the high-water datum (generally MHWS, MHW, or MSL; see chapter 3). In areas with a significant tidal range, *they may be submerged at high tide during abnormally high tides*. If a height is given, it is *the height above the high-water datum* (not the sounding datum). It will use the same typeface convention as for spot heights on shore (vertical numbers with INT; italic with NOAA imperial).

2. **ROCKS THAT COVER AND UNCOVER.** These are rocks that are between the high- and low-water datums (i.e., covered at high tide and uncovered at low tide). If a height is given, it is *the height above the low-water (sounding) datum*. To indicate that it is a drying height, it is underlined, as in <u>6</u>. It uses the same typeface convention as for soundings (italic numbers on INT charts and NOAA metric, vertical on NOAA imperial).

3. **ROCKS AWASH AT THE LEVEL OF THE CHART'S LOW-WATER (SOUNDING) DATUM.** These rocks are only visible, if at all, at low water. If the low-water (sounding) datum is a conservative one (e.g., LAT), the rocks are rarely visible; if it is less conservative (e.g., MLLW), they are visible at most low tides, and at some lows will be partially uncovered (e.g., spring tides). Typeface conventions are the same as for rocks that cover and uncover.

4. **SUNKEN ROCKS.** These rocks are always covered at the level of the chart's low-water (sounding) datum. However, if they are only a little beneath the surface and the sounding datum is not that conservative, they may be partially uncovered on abnormally low tides. Typeface conventions are the same as for rocks that cover and uncover.

Each rock category has its own symbol or symbols; it is advisable to memorize them (K10, 11, 12, and 13). *Note that as a result of poor vectorizing practices, many vector-based electronic charts fail to differentiate rocks awash at low tide from sunken rocks, and may also fail to differentiate rocks that cover and uncover from sunken rocks.*

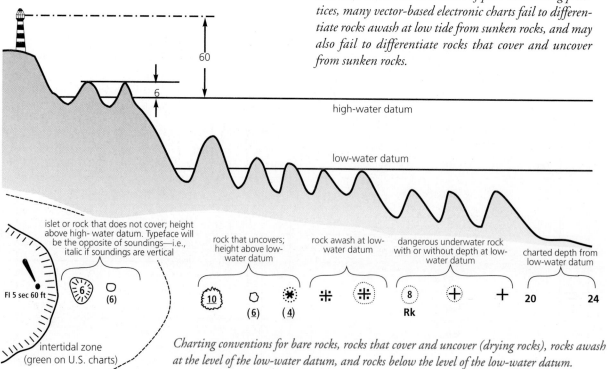

islet or rock that does not cover; height above high- water datum. Typeface will be the opposite of soundings—i.e., italic if soundings are vertical

Fl 5 sec 60 ft

rock that uncovers; height above low-water datum

rock awash at low-water datum

dangerous underwater rock with or without depth at low-water datum

charted depth from low-water datum

high-water datum

low-water datum

intertidal zone (green on U.S. charts)

Charting conventions for bare rocks, rocks that cover and uncover (drying rocks), rocks awash at the level of the low-water datum, and rocks below the level of the low-water datum.

K *Rocks, Wrecks, Obstructions*

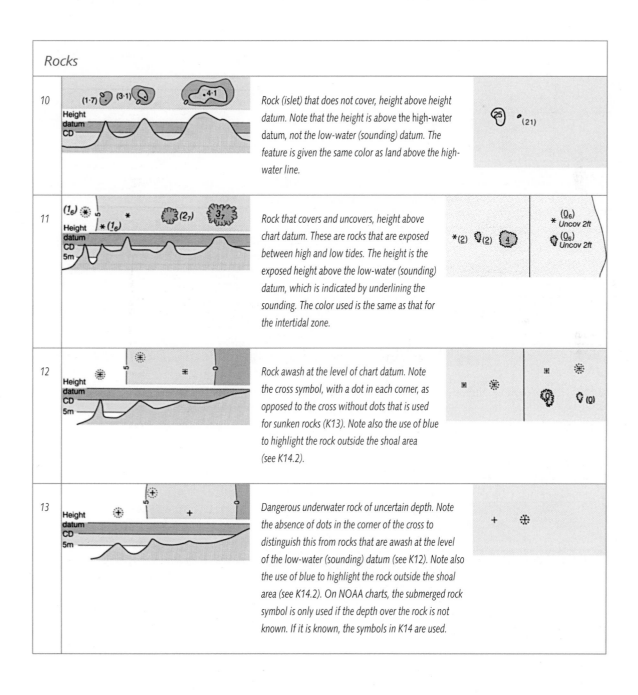

	General	
1		Danger line, in general. (It is the dotted line that warns of danger, with added emphasis provided by the blue.)
2		Swept by wire drag or diver

	Rocks	
10		Rock (islet) that does not cover, height above height datum. Note that the height is above the high-water datum, not the low-water (sounding) datum. The feature is given the same color as land above the high-water line.
11		Rock that covers and uncovers, height above chart datum. These are rocks that are exposed between high and low tides. The height is the exposed height above the low-water (sounding) datum, which is indicated by underlining the sounding. The color used is the same as that for the intertidal zone.
12		Rock awash at the level of chart datum. Note the cross symbol, with a dot in each corner, as opposed to the cross without dots that is used for sunken rocks (K13). Note also the use of blue to highlight the rock outside the shoal area (see K14.2).
13		Dangerous underwater rock of uncertain depth. Note the absence of dots in the corner of the cross to distinguish this from rocks that are awash at the level of the low-water (sounding) datum (see K12). Note also the use of blue to highlight the rock outside the shoal area (see K14.2). On NOAA charts, the submerged rock symbol is only used if the depth over the rock is not known. If it is known, the symbols in K14 are used.

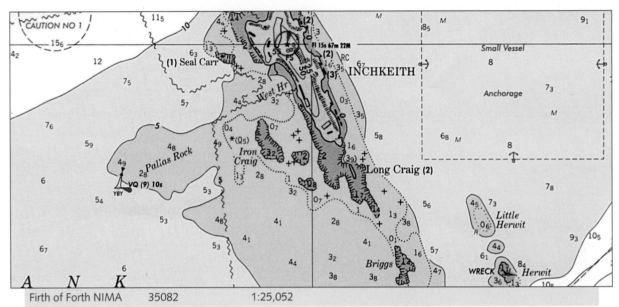

Firth of Forth NIMA   35082   1:25,052

Selected features: ⬩ = *stranded wreck* (at least partially above the level of the low-water datum). ✳ = *drying rock* (above the level of the low-water datum, often with the height above the datum, underlined). ✢ = *underwater rock* (below the level of the low-water datum). (2) = *out-of-position height* above the high-water datum. VQ = *Very Quick* (in this case, a group of nine very quick flashes every 10 seconds; see chapter 8). ∿ ∿ = *disused* (the line is periodically broken) *underwater cable.*

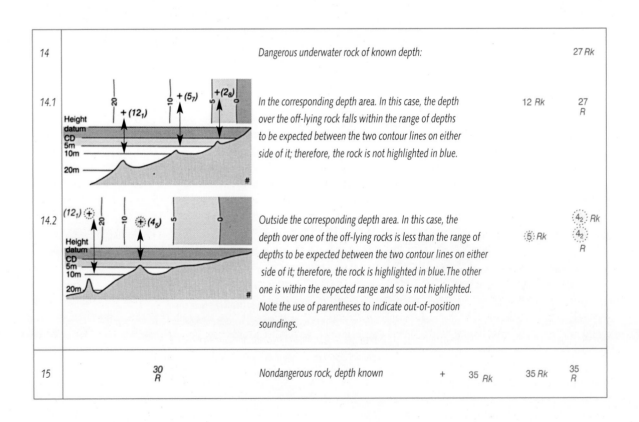

14	Dangerous underwater rock of known depth:	27 *Rk*
14.1	In the corresponding depth area. In this case, the depth over the off-lying rock falls within the range of depths to be expected between the two contour lines on either side of it; therefore, the rock is not highlighted in blue.	12 *Rk* 27 R
14.2	Outside the corresponding depth area. In this case, the depth over one of the off-lying rocks is less than the range of depths to be expected between the two contour lines on either side of it; therefore, the rock is highlighted in blue. The other one is within the expected range and so is not highlighted. Note the use of parentheses to indicate out-of-position soundings.	5 *Rk* 4₂ *Rk* / 4₂ R
15	Nondangerous rock, depth known	30 R + 35 *Rk* 35 *Rk* 35 R

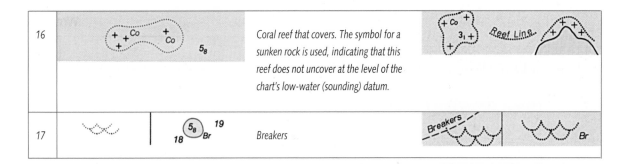

| 16 | | Coral reef that covers. The symbol for a sunken rock is used, indicating that this reef does not uncover at the level of the chart's low-water (sounding) datum. | |
| 17 | | Breakers | |

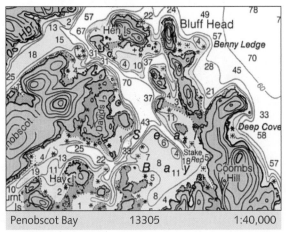

| Penobscot Bay | 13305 | 1:40,000 |

Selected features: ✳ = *drying rocks (above the level of the low-water datum).* ✳ = **rock awash** *at the level of the low-water datum.* + = **submerged rock** *(below the level of the low-water datum).*

| Jupiter Inlet to Fowey Rocks | 11466 | 1:80,000 |

Note the use of blue to highlight the **fish havens** *despite the fact that their minimum authorized depths exceed the depth contour below which blue is used (30 ft.). Note also the* **territorial sea** *boundary that marks the 12-mile limit.*

Wrecks and Obstructions

Wrecks are classified as stranded or sunken. A stranded wreck is one that has any portion of the hull or superstructure above the level of the low-water (sounding) datum. A sunken wreck is entirely below the level of the low-water (sounding) datum, with the possible exception of its masts. Wrecks are normally labeled in italic type to indicate a hydrographic feature. However, if a significant portion of a wreck is above the level of the high-water datum, it may be considered a topographic feature, in which case it will be labeled with vertical (shoreside) type (refer to chapter 5 for more on type conventions).

On large-scale charts, the physical outline of a wreck may be charted, in which case it will be given an appropriate color (land color if above the high-water datum, intertidal color if stranded, and blue if sunken). On smaller-scale charts, there is either a line with three crossed lines—with or without a dotted

oval (the position of the wreck is at the point where the center cross line crosses the long line)—or the notation "Wk" placed alongside a dotted circle. The inclusion of the dotted oval or circle indicates that it is considered a "dangerous" wreck. If the least depth over the wreck is less than what is expected in the surrounding depth area (see K14.2), the area inside the dotted circle is colored blue; otherwise, it may be white (not always; it depends on how much attention the chart compiler wants to draw to the wreck).

Different hydrographic offices use different depth criteria to define dangerous wrecks, and within individual hydrographic offices the definition has changed over time. For example, prior to 1960, the British Admiralty depth criterion was 8 fathoms; from 1960 to 1963, it was 10 fathoms; from 1963 to 1968, 11 fathoms; and, since 1968, 28 meters (15 fathoms). This change reflects the increasing draft of ships. Other hydrographic offices currently use from 18 to 30 meters

K *Rocks, Wrecks, Obstructions*

(60–100 ft.). NOAA uses 11 fathoms (20 m/66 ft.) In all cases, on a modern chart, the dangerous-wreck symbol is used for many wrecks that pose no hazard to recreational boats; however, if there is no associa-ted sounding, the boater should avoid the wreck.

Similar conventions regarding italic or vertical type, dotted (danger) lines, and the use of the color blue apply to obstructions and other hazards.

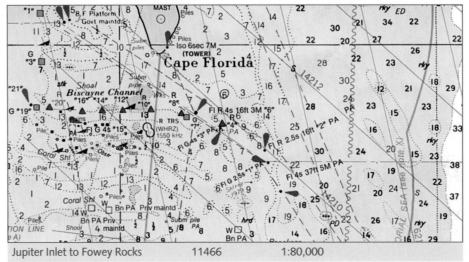

Jupiter Inlet to Fowey Rocks   11466   1:80,000

*Selected features: Numerous **stranded wrecks** (in the Biscayne Channel) and a couple of danger-ous **sunken wrecks** ▦. Some **soundings** and one **sunken wreck** symbol are bold, while others are not. This is a convention I have not seen explained anywhere! The limit of the territorial sea is to the east (12-mile limit) with a disused cable to the west of this (broken magenta "squiggly" line). There is an **out-of-position** shoal reported, 1979 ("shl rep 1979" with an arrow to its loca-tion) just south of the entrance to the channel. There are all kinds of **obstructions**, piles, and dry-ing shoals: I would not want to navigate this channel without a larger scale chart (this one is 1:80,000)!*

	Wrecks		
20	Mast (1·2) Wk	*Wreck, hull always dry, on large-scale charts. Note the use of land color.*	Hk
21	Mast (1₂) Wk	*Wreck, covers and uncovers, on large-scale charts. Note the use of intertidal color.*	Hk
22	Wk	*Submerged wreck, depth known, on large-scale charts. Note the use of shoal-water color to indicate that the wreck is below the level of the low-water (sounding) datum.*	
23	Wk	*Submerged wreck, depth unknown, on large-scale charts*	Hk

24		Wreck showing any portion of hull or superstructure at level of chart datum. This is the symbol for a stranded wreck most commonly found on charts. The small circle on the baseline indicates the position of the wreck.	
25	Masts	Wreck showing mast or masts above chart datum only. This is a sunken wreck, in the sense that the entire hull and superstructure are below the level of the low-water (sounding) datum; hence, the blue.	Masts Mast (10 ft) Funnel
26	4 Wk 25 Wk	Wreck, least depth known by sounding only	5₄ Wk
27	4 Wk 25 Wk	Wreck, least depth known, swept by wire drag or diver	2₁ Wk 5₃ Wk 2₁ Wk 5₄ Wk 5 Wk
28		Dangerous wreck, depth unknown. The position of the wreck is where the center cross line crosses the long line. The dotted line indicates danger.	
29		Sunken wreck; not dangerous to surface navigation. There is no dotted line or blue.	
30	20 Wk	Wreck, least depth unknown, but considered to have a safe clearance to the depth shown. The line above the sounding indicates that the depth is at least as great as is shown (compare this to C14).	8 Wk
31	# Foul	Remains of a wreck or other foul area, non-dangerous to navigation, should be avoided by vessels anchoring, trawling etc. The absence of blue indicates that this is not dangerous to navigation.	Foul # Foul
32		Foul area. Foul with rocks or wreckage, dangerous to navigation. The addition of blue indicates that this is dangerous to navigation.	Foul Wks Wreckage

Obstructions

40	Obstn Obstn	Obstruction, depth unknown	Obstn Obstn
41	4 Obstn 16₈ Obstn	Obstruction, least depth known	5₁ Obstn 5₁ Obstn
42	4 Obstn 16₈ Obstn	Obstruction, least depth known, swept by wire drag or diver	21 Obstn 21 Obstn 5 Obstn 5 Obstn
43.1	Obstn T T T	Stumps of posts or piles, all or part of the time submerged	Subm piles Stakes, Perches
43.2	T	Submerged pile, stake, snag, well, or stump (with exact position). The small circle indicates the position. The italic letters in the labels indicate that these are hydrographic features (below the level of the high-water datum).	Snags Stumps
44.1		Fishing stakes. The use of vertical letters indicates that the fish stakes are permanently above the level of the high-water datum (topographic features).	Fsh stks
44.2		Fish trap, fish weirs, tunny nets	
45	Fish traps Tunny nets	Fish trap area, tunny nets area	Fish traps Tunny nets
46.1		Fish haven (artificial fishing reef, often formed by dumping stones, concrete, scrap vehicles, and similar material on the seabed)	Obstruction (fish haven) Obstn (fish haven) (actual shape)
46.2	(2₄) 2₄	Fish haven with minimum depth	Obstn Fish haven (Auth min 42ft)
47	Shellfish Beds	Shellfish cultivation (stakes visible)	Oys
48.1		Marine farm (on large-scale charts)	
48.2		Marine farm (on small-scale charts)	

K Rocks, Wrecks, Obstructions

	Supplementary National Symbols	
a	Rock awash (height unknown). This symbol is used extensively on NOAA's charts.	∗ ⁂
b	Shoal sounding on isolated rock or rocks	5̲ Rk 5̲ Rks
c	Sunken wreck covered 20 to 30 meters (i.e., not considered hazardous to navigation, and therefore not given a dotted oval)	+⊦+
d	Submarine volcano	◯ Sub vol
e	Discolored water	◯ Discol water
f	Sunken danger with depth cleared (swept) by wire drag (note the dotted danger line)	2̲₁ Rk 3̲₂ 3̲₂
g	Reef of unknown extent	Reef
h	Coral reef, detached (uncovers at sounding datum; therefore, given the intertidal color)	◯ ⁂ Co Coral Co Co ⁂ Co
i	Submerged crib	⊡ Subm Crib ⊡ Crib
j	Crib, Duck blind (above water)	▢ Crib ▪ Duck Blind
k	Submerged duck blind	⊡ Duck Blind
l	Submerged platform	⊡ Platform

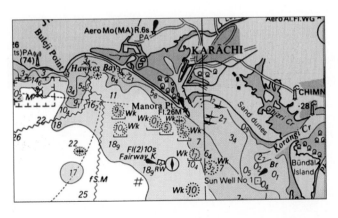

Karachi, Pakistan. **Selected features:** *numerous wire-dragged depths, some highlighted in blue, foul ground symbol (#), dangerous sunken wreck (⊛), stranded wrecks (⊥), no anchoring area (⨯) delineated by magenta T-dashes, dangerous submerged rocks (⊛), offshore oil platform (⌂), pilot boarding area (①).*

Karachi (Pakistan)	BA 39
1:500,000	

L *Offshore Installations*

Section L: Offshore Installations

This section discusses a mixed bag of potential hazards—oilfield platforms and wells, offshore mooring buoys, and submarine pipelines and cables. In any area that has such activities, the mariner needs to be especially careful because there is often new construction underway or old, abandoned facilities on which the navigational aids are not being properly maintained. (I speak from experience: I was once an oilfield mechanic responsible for the navigation lights on approximately thirty platforms and wellheads in the Gulf of Mexico. Despite my best efforts, at any given time, up to a third of the lights were out of commission for one reason or another.) If at all possible, passage through oilfields should be made only in daylight, and with due recognition that many oilfield workboats pay scant attention to the rules of the road. Be aware that some nations place a 500-meter safety zone, into which entry is prohibited by general shipping and boating, around oil and gas platforms (e.g., in the North Sea).

In areas with numerous platforms, a "selection of platforms shall be charted to avoid covering the area with overlapping symbols. The selection shall include the outermost platforms and a selection of the inner platforms where necessary" (NOAA, *Nautical Chart Manual*). In other words, some may not be charted. This is particularly important to recognize when zooming in with electronic charts (see chapter 2). You may well appear to have clear water in areas that are full of obstructions!

L *Offshore Installations*

	General		
1	**EKOFISK** **OILFIELD**	Name of oilfield or gas field	DURRAH OILFIELD
2	⊡ Z-44	Platform with designation/name. A label is not required for all structures; only those that are isolated, or selected outer structures in a group.	▣ ■ "Hazel" ⊡ "Hazel"
3	⊡	Limit of safety zone around offshore installation. Note that the stems of the T-shaped dashes forming the boundary to the safety zone point in toward the safety zone. The use of magenta indicates that this is information superimposed on the chart rather than a permanent physical feature (see chapter 5).	⊡
4		Limit of development area	
5.2	⌖	Windfarms	
6.1	⌖	Wave energy	

L Offshore Installations

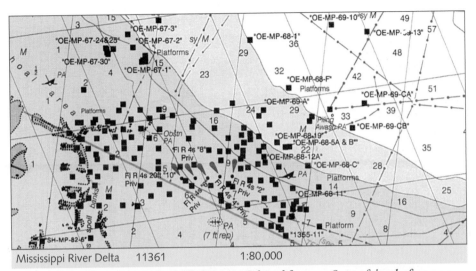

Mississippi River Delta   11361   1:80,000

*A crowded offshore oilfield in the Gulf of Mexico. **Selected features:** Some of the **platforms** are named, others are not. There are **stranded wreck** symbols (among the platforms and in the northwest quadrant) and a dangerous **sunken wreck** symbol (center south), all PA (position approximate). Just outside of the blue **shoal** water zone, in the white area, midway up the chart, is a "piling awash PA"—potentially a particularly dangerous feature. This is a NOAA imperial chart (soundings in feet), so the soundings use vertical numbers. Various **pipelines** are shown in magenta (volatile liquids) with the direction of flow indicated by the dots on the ends of the dashes (toward the dots). This chart is overprinted with a **Loran-C lattice**.*

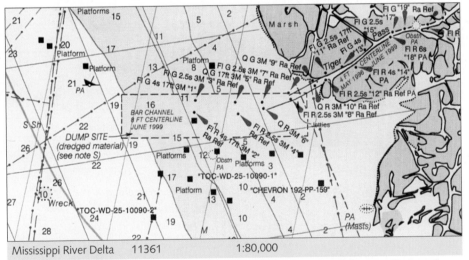

Mississippi River Delta   11361   1:80,000

*Gulf of Mexico oilfield near the mouth of the Mississippi River. **Selected features:** Various **platforms** with a marked channel up the middle into Tiger Pass. The **channel markers** are beacons not buoys (the labels use vertical letters, not italic letters, indicating that these are topographic rather than hydrographic features). The channel had 8 feet on the centerline in June 1999, Tiger Pass 4 feet. The **dates** indicate that these depths are not necessarily maintained. There is a **stranded wreck** just to seaward of the 20-foot line, and a dangerous sunken wreck in the SW quadrant (highlighted with a dotted line and dark blue). Various **pipelines** are shown in magenta (volatile liquids) with the direction of flow indicated by the dots on the ends of the dashes (toward the dots).*

L *Offshore Installations*

Platforms and Moorings

10	Production platform, Platform, Oil derrick (see also L2).	■ "Exxon MP–236"	⊡	⊡
11	⊡ Fla	Flare stack (at sea)		⸙
12	⊡ SPM	Mooring tower, Articulated Loading Platform (ALP), Single Anchor Leg Mooring (SALM), Single Point Mooring (SPM).		⊡ SPM
13		Observation/research platform (with name)	■ "Hazel"	⊡ "Tuna"
14		Disused platform		
15		Artificial island	⬭ Artificial Island (Mukluk)	
16	⌖	Oil or Gas installation buoy, Catenary Anchor Leg Mooring (CALM), Single Buoy Mooring (SBM). These are all large tanker mooring buoys.	⌖	
17		Moored storage tanker, used for storing crude oil prior to shipping out.	⌖	⌖ tanker

Underwater Installations

20	15 Prod Well Prod Well	Submerged production well. In the absence of a depth sounding, the blue inside a dotted circle indicates that the feature is covered at all times, but calls attention to it as potentially hazardous.	Well (cov 21ft) Well (cov 83ft) ✦ ✦	⬭ Well
21.1	⬭ Well	Suspended (i.e., not in production) well, depth over wellhead unknown. A wellhead is a submarine structure projecting above the seabed and capping a temporarily abandoned or suspended oil or gas well.	⬭ Pipe	⬭ Well
21.2	15 Well	Suspended well, with depth over wellhead	Pipe (cov 24ft) Pipe (cov 92ft)	15 Well

170

L *Offshore Installations*

21.3	○ Well (5.7)	Wellhead with height above the bottom. Note the use of the "hat" over the sounding to indicate the height above the seabed, as opposed to the depth of water over the feature (see also E5). The absence of blue inside the dotted circle indicates that this feature is not hazardous to navigation.
22	⧉	Site of cleared platform. Note that this is the same symbol as for a small area of foul ground (K31).
23	● Pipe	Above water wellheads ● **Pipe**
24	Turbine	Underwater turbines

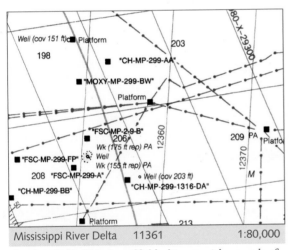

Mississippi River Delta   11361   1:80,000

Another Gulf of Mexico oilfield, this one with a couple of capped oil wells. These have been capped near the seabed, and each has the depth over it given—for example, Well (cov 151 ft).

Firth of Forth   NIMA 35082   1:25,052

*Selected features: The **pipelines** are black, indicating non-volatile liquids. The flow is seaward (these are probably wastewater outfalls). The **submarine cable** (magenta) is discontinued (broken). We have **out-of-position drying heights** (underlined and in parentheses), and an out-of-position chimney height (above the high-water datum).*

Submarine Cables and Pipelines

Similar symbols are used for submarine cables and pipelines, and there are certain common conventions. Magenta, the color used for designating danger and restricted areas (see section N) is used for cables and for pipelines carrying volatile materials. Black is used for pipelines carrying nonvolatile materials (e.g., water, nonvolatile waste). Where an area is enclosed, T-shaped dashes are used in the relevant color, with the stems pointing in toward the cable or pipeline area.

If the pipeline symbol includes a dot, the direction of flow within the pipeline is presumed to be toward the dot (I don't know why a mariner would need to know this). Potable-water intakes (rare in saltwater but sometimes found in lakes, especially the Great Lakes in the U.S.) may be offset from the bottom (to avoid sucking in sediment), in which case there may be a note stating how far off the bottom. The pipeline may also include some kind of a screen (a "crib") at its intake end.

L Offshore Installations

Submarine Cables

30.1	~~~~~~~~~~~~~	Submarine cable. (Generic symbol for both power and communications)	~~~~~~
30.2	T T T T ~~~~~ T T T T / ⊥ ⊥ ⊥ ⊥ ~~~~~ ⊥ ⊥ ⊥ ⊥	Submarine cable area. Note that the stems of the T's point in toward the cable area.	Cable Area / T T TMMM T T T / ⊥ ⊥ MMM ⊥ ⊥ ⊥
31.1	~~~~~ ∫ ~~~~~	Submarine power cable. Note the lightning-flash power symbol; when present, it indicates high voltage.	~~∫~~∫~~∫~~
31.2	T T T T ~~~∫~~~ T T T T / ⊥ ⊥ ⊥ ⊥ ~~~∫~~~ ⊥ ⊥ ⊥ ⊥	Submarine power cable area	~~T T ~~∫~~T / ~~⊥ ⊥ ⊥~~∫~~⊥
32	∿ ∿ ∿ ∿ ∿ ∿ ∿	Disused submarine cable	∿ ∿ ∿ ∿ ∿

Submarine Pipelines

40.1	Oil — — — Gas / Chem — — — Water	Oil, Gas and other pipelines. The use of magenta indicates volatile liquids. The dots give the direction of flow (toward the dots).	•—•—•—•
40.2	T T T T T T T T / ⊥ ⊥ ⊥ ⊥ ⊥ ⊥ ⊥ / Oil T T T / Gas ⊥ ⊥ ⊥ / Chem / Water	Oil, Gas and other pipeline areas. Note that the stems of the T's point in toward the pipeline area.	Pipeline Area / T T T T / ⊥ ⊥ ⊥ ⊥
41.1	Water / Sewer / Outfall / Intake	Waterpipe, sewer, outfall pipe, intake pipe. Note the use of black for nonvolatile liquids. The dots give the direction of flow (toward the dots).	Water / Sewer / Outfall / Intake
41.2	T T T T T T T T T / ⊥ ⊥ ⊥ ⊥ ⊥ ⊥ ⊥ ⊥ / Water / Sewer / Outfall / Intake	Discharge pipeline areas	Pipeline Area / ⊥—⊥ T T / —⊥ ⊥ ⊥ / T T—•—T T

42	············ Buried 1·6m ············	Buried pipeline/pipe (with nominal depth to which buried)
43	·····················⦿ 3₂ *Obstn*	Potable Water intake, diffuser, or crib. These are usually elevated above the bottom.
44		Disused pipeline/pipe

	Supplementary National Symbol
a	Submerged well (buoyed)

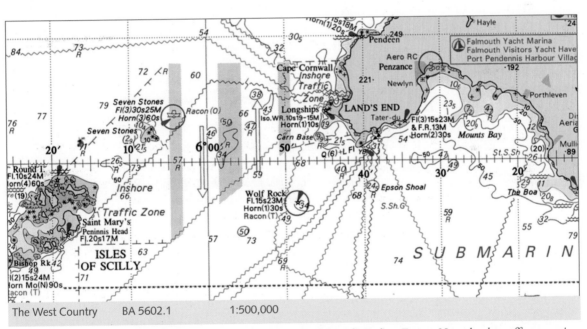

No shortage of cables here running from the western tip of England (Land's End) to France. Note also the traffic separation zone (see section M), which is mandatory (arrows have solid, not dashed, lines), with inshore traffic zones on either side delineated by magenta T-dashes, the lightship, and several powerful lighthouses (see chapter 8).

M *Tracks, Routes*

Recommended tracks are long-established features of charts. They are not generally subject to regulation, whereas routes are generally regulated. Tracks are mostly established for hydrographic reasons—to lead safely between shoals—whereas routes are established for nonhydrographic reasons, such as the prevention of collisions or avoidance of pollution risks. Routes are usually mandated by national or international agencies (e.g., the IMO, an agency of the United Nations) and not by hydrographic offices (routes are discussed in more detail later in this chapter).

M *Tracks, Routes*

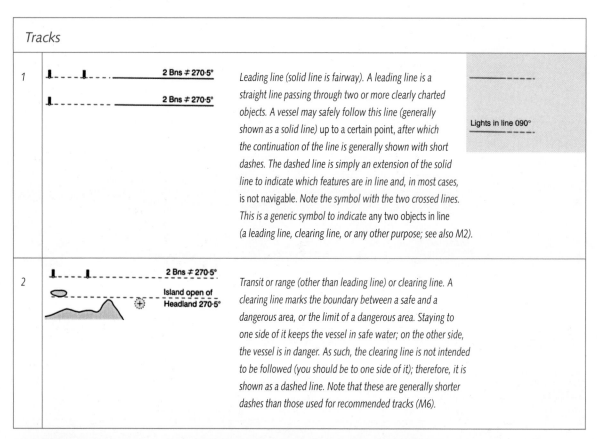

Tracks		
1	2 Bns ≠ 270·5° 2 Bns ≠ 270·5°	Leading line (solid line is fairway). A leading line is a straight line passing through two or more clearly charted objects. A vessel may safely follow this line (generally shown as a solid line) up to a certain point, after which the continuation of the line is generally shown with short dashes. The dashed line is simply an extension of the solid line to indicate which features are in line and, in most cases, is not navigable. Note the symbol with the two crossed lines. This is a generic symbol to indicate any two objects in line (a leading line, clearing line, or any other purpose; see also M2).
		Lights in line 090°
2	2 Bns ≠ 270·5° Island open of Headland 270·5°	Transit or range (other than leading line) or clearing line. A clearing line marks the boundary between a safe and a dangerous area, or the limit of a dangerous area. Staying to one side of it keeps the vessel in safe water; on the other side, the vessel is in danger. As such, the clearing line is not intended to be followed (you should be to one side of it); therefore, it is shown as a dashed line. Note that these are generally shorter dashes than those used for recommended tracks (M6).

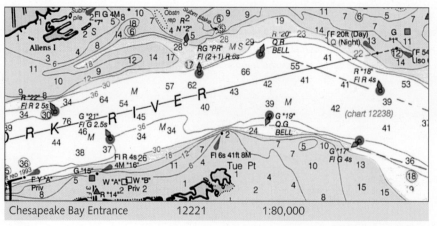

Chesapeake Bay Entrance   12221   1:80,000

A leading line (the solid portion) with a dashed extension where it runs out of the channel to the two lights. Note the use of different light patterns for day and night (not common).

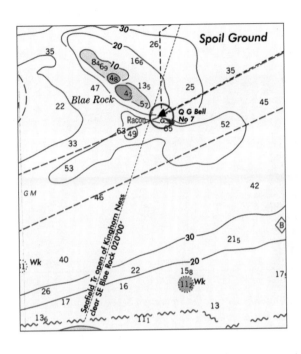

Firth of Forth NIMA　　35082　　　　　1:25,052

A transit (range) consisting of two distant objects (Seafield Tower and Kingdom Ness; Ness is a Scottish word for cape), which are to be kept "open" (i.e., with a small space visible between the two) to clear the Blae Rock. The bearing is 020° True.

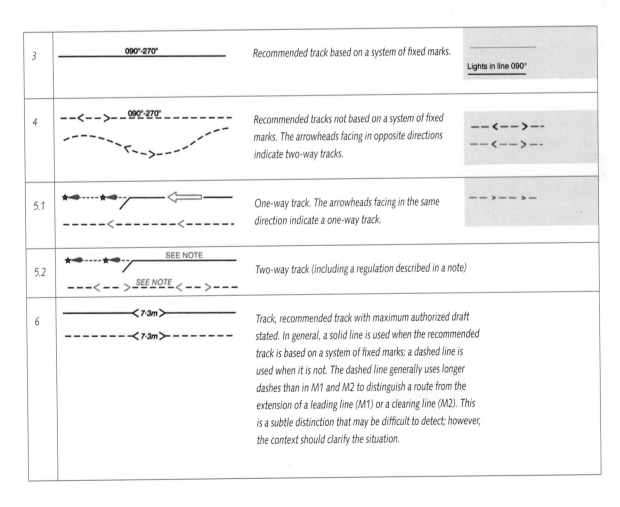

3	090°-270°	Recommended track based on a system of fixed marks.	Lights in line 090°
4	090°-270°	Recommended tracks not based on a system of fixed marks. The arrowheads facing in opposite directions indicate two-way tracks.	
5.1		One-way track. The arrowheads facing in the same direction indicate a one-way track.	
5.2	SEE NOTE	Two-way track (including a regulation described in a note)	
6	7·3m	Track, recommended track with maximum authorized draft stated. In general, a solid line is used when the recommended track is based on a system of fixed marks; a dashed line is used when it is not. The dashed line generally uses longer dashes than in M1 and M2 to distinguish a route from the extension of a leading line (M1) or a clearing line (M2). This is a subtle distinction that may be difficult to detect; however, the context should clarify the situation.	

M *Tracks, Routes*

Routing Measures

IHO S-4 notes that routing measures, as designated by the IMO, consist of the following:

- traffic separation schemes (TSSs), with any associated inshore traffic zones
- precautionary areas
- deep-water routes
- recommended routes
- recommended directions of traffic flow
- two-way routes
- areas to be avoided by certain classes of ships (routing in a negative sense)

These measures are all represented by magenta symbols. There may also be nationally adopted types of routing, such as safety fairways (used extensively in the U.S.) and controlled-access channels to certain ports.

The outer limits of traffic lanes are indicated by dashed lines (the symbol for maritime limits in general). Other areas to be avoided or treated with caution are also shown with dashed lines or T-shaped dashes, with the stems of the T's pointing in toward the relevant area. Separation zones, which boats should stay out of, are shown with a magenta band, as are roundabouts (traffic circles) and similar areas. There may be separation zones between both traffic lanes and the outside of the lanes and surrounding waters (which separate traffic using the scheme from that outside it).

An inshore traffic zone may be identified between the inner boundary of a TSS and the coastline. The inshore zone is not normally to be used by through traffic, although boats less than 20 meters in length and sailboats are exempt.

At roundabouts, the direction of traffic flow is generally counterclockwise. At crossings (junctions),

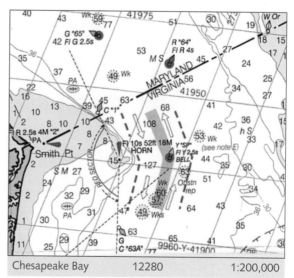

*Chesapeake Bay Traffic Separation Scheme (TSS). The outer limits of the area covered by the scheme are shown by dashed magenta lines, the separation zone by a magenta band. The fact that the arrows are solid (not dashed) indicates that the directions are mandatory. Note also various dangerous **wreck** symbols and some **wire-drag soundings**.*

arrows are omitted so as not to imply any right-of-way of one traffic lane over another.

Mandatory direction arrows are drawn with solid lines, recommended arrows with dashed lines. Where directions are not mandatory, the general rule is "keep to starboard." Deep-water routes for deep-draft vessels may be labeled DW and given a minimum depth. The limits of a deep-water channel are shown with a dashed line. Some TSSs have associated shoreside radar surveillance and control stations, which are indicated on charts.

Boats are not obliged to use a TSS. However, if not using it, it must be avoided "by as wide a margin as is practicable" (rule 10 of the International Navigation Rules). When joining or leaving a traffic lane, it should be done at as shallow an angle as possible. Once in it, boats must comply with the general direction of traffic flow and other requirements. Note that "a vessel of less than 20 meters in length or a sailing vessel shall not impede the safe passage of a power-driven vessel following a traffic lane."

If it is necessary to cross a TSS, it should be crossed "on a heading as nearly as practicable at right angles to the general direction of traffic flow." In recent years, several recreational boat owners in Europe have been arrested and prosecuted for not complying with this regulation.

NOTE F
TRAFFIC SEPARATION SCHEME

The traffic separation scheme is designed to aid in the prevention of collisions at the approaches to Chesapeake Bay and does not supersede or alter the applicable Rules of the Road.

The RECOMMENDED routes for entering and departing from Chesapeake Bay are overprinted on this chart. The Northeast Approach is marked by a tinted magenta line centered on a line of fairway buoys which separates the courses of inbound and outbound vessels. Vessels should leave all buoys on their port hand.

It is RECOMMENDED that the following ships use the Southern Approach deep-water route when bound for Chesapeake Bay from sea or to sea from Chesapeake Bay: Deep-draft ships, drafts defined as greater than 13.5 meters/45 feet in fresh water, and naval aircraft carriers.

Chesapeake Bay	12280	1:200,000

Chart notes describing the Chesapeake Bay TSS. Note the use of magenta, the same color used to depict the TSS on the chart.

It is RECOMMENDED that a ship using the deep-water route:

Announce its intention on VHF-FM channel 16 as it approaches Chesapeake Bay Southern Approach Lighted Whistle Buoy "CB" on the south end, or Chesapeake Bay Junction Lighted Buoy "CBJ", on the north end of the route;

Avoid, as far as practicable, overtaking other ships operating in the deep-water route;

Keep as near to the outer limit of the route which lies on the starboard side as is safe and practicable.

All other ships approaching the Chesapeake Bay traffic separation scheme should use the appropriate inbound or outbound traffic lane of the traffic separation scheme.

Traffic within the precautionary area may consist of vessels operating between Thimble Shoal and Chesapeake Channels and one of the established traffic lanes. Mariners are advised to exercise extreme care in navigating within this area. The pilotage area is marked by a tinted magenta band.

Routing Measures

10	⇒	Established (mandatory) direction of traffic flow	⇒
11	⊏===⇒	Recommended direction of traffic flow	⇒
12	▬▬▬	Separation line	⇐ ⇒
13	▬▬▬	Separation zone	⇐ ⇒
14	⌐ᴛᴛᴛᴛᴛᴛᴛᴛᴛ	Limit of restricted area	RESTRICTED AREA
15	⌐− − − − − −	Maritime limit in general	− − − − −
16	⚠ Precautionary Area	Precautionary area	PRECAUTIONARY AREA ⚠
18	⌐‐‐‐‐‐‐‐‐¬ *FAIRWAY 7,3m (see Note)* ⌐‐‐‐‐‐‐‐‐¬	A Fairway is delimited by bold magenta dashed lines; a minimum depth may also be indicated	
24	Precautionary Area	An area with within defined limits (often in TSSs), where ships must navigate with particular caution and within which the direction of traffic flow may be recommended	

M *Tracks, Routes*

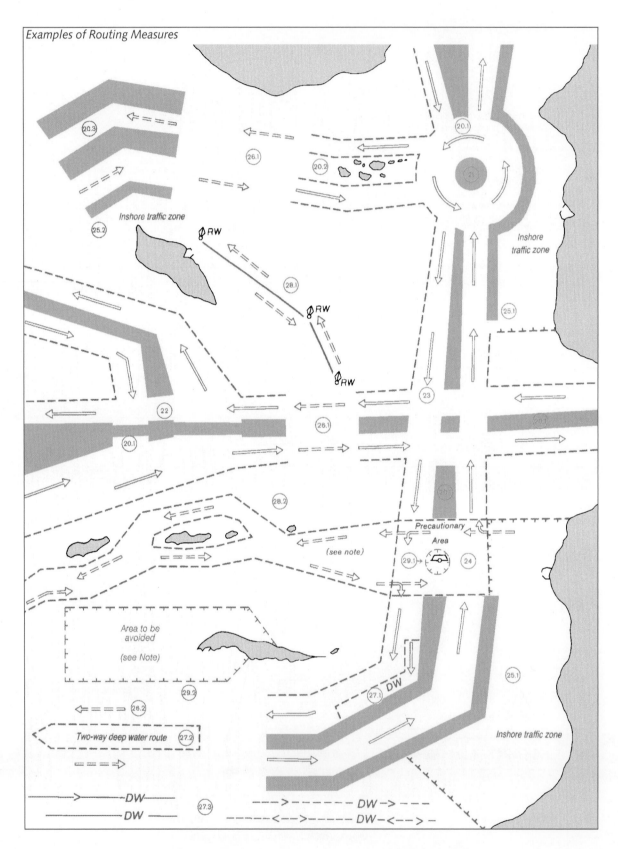

Examples of Routing Measures

M *Tracks, Routes*

	Examples of Routing Measures
(20.1)	Traffic separation scheme, traffic separated by separation zone
(20.2)	Traffic separation scheme, traffic separated by natural obstructions
(20.3)	Traffic separation scheme, with outer separation zone, separating traffic using scheme from traffic not using it
(21)	Traffic separation scheme, roundabout
(22)	Traffic separation scheme, with "crossing gates"
(23)	Traffic separation schemes crossing, without designated precautionary area
(24)	Precautionary area
(25.1)	Inshore traffic zone, with defined end-limits
(25.2)	Inshore traffic zone without defined end-limits
(26.1)	Recommended direction of traffic flow, between traffic separation schemes
(26.2)	Recommended direction of traffic flow, for ships not needing a deep-water route
(27.1)	Deep-water route, as part of one-way traffic lane
(27.2)	Two-way deep-water route, with minimum depth stated
(27.3)	Deep-water route, centerline as recommended. One-way or two-way track.
(28.1)	Recommended route (often marked by centerline buoys)
(28.2)	Two-way route with one-way sections
(29.1)	Area to be avoided, around navigational aid
(29.2)	Area to be avoided, because of danger of stranding

Radar Surveillance Systems

30	**Radar Surveillance Station**	Radar Surveillance Station, used by many large port authorities.	⊙Ra
31	*Ra Cuxhaven*	Radar range (range of surveillance radar)	
32.1	– – – – – – Ra – – – – – –	Radar reference line. A midchannel line corresponding to lines incorporated in harbor radar displays. It is used as a positional reference so that harbor authorities may easily give a ship its position—relative to the line—when visibility is poor.	
32.2	Ra 270° – 090°	Radar reference line coinciding with a leading line. When a radar reference line coincides with a leading line, the radar abbreviation "Ra," in magenta, is added to the leading line.	

Radio Reporting Points

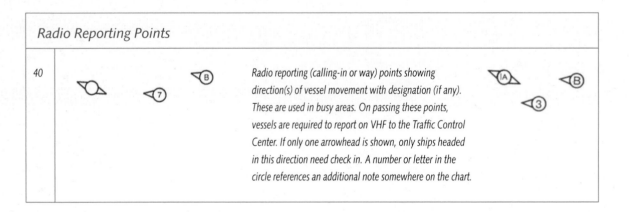

| 40 | | Radio reporting (calling-in or way) points showing direction(s) of vessel movement with designation (if any). These are used in busy areas. On passing these points, vessels are required to report on VHF to the Traffic Control Center. If only one arrowhead is shown, only ships headed in this direction need check in. A number or letter in the circle references an additional note somewhere on the chart. | |

Ferries

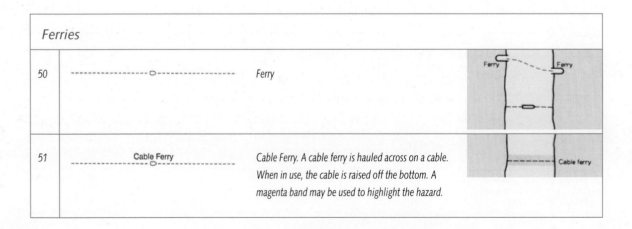

| 50 | – – – – –○– – – – – | Ferry | |
| 51 | Cable Ferry | Cable Ferry. A cable ferry is hauled across on a cable. When in use, the cable is raised off the bottom. A magenta band may be used to highlight the hazard. | |

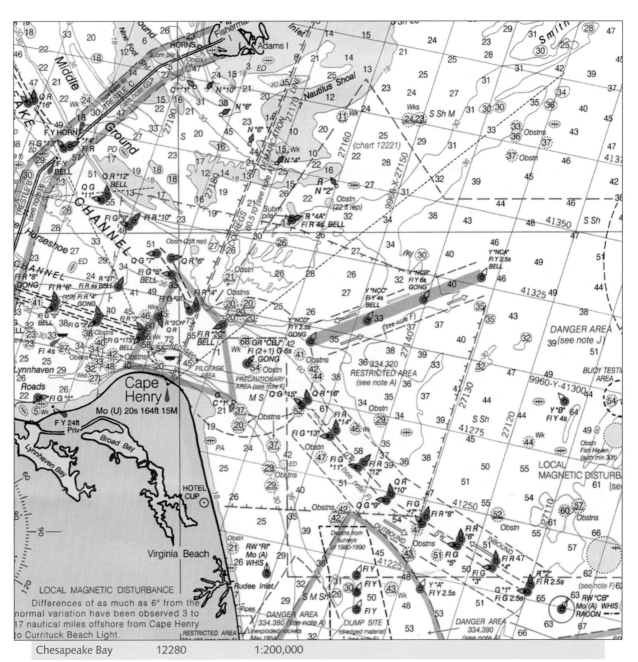

Chesapeake Bay   12280   1:200,000

The entrance to Chesapeake Bay. **Selected features:** *Note the two converging TSSs with a* **roundabout** *(traffic circle) area. The southern section has a well-buoyed deep-water (DW) channel down the center of the TSS. At its seaward end is a radar transponder buoy (RACON; see chapter 8). There are numerous* **wrecks** *and* **obstructions,** *many of them wire-dragged; a pilotage area (highlighted in magenta—ships are likely to be slowed or stopped and not very maneuverable); and various area limits defined in dashed and T-dashed magenta lines. The Cape Henry* **light description** *is a little unusual: "Mo (U) 20s 164ft 15M." "Mo (U)" means the flash pattern is Morse U, which is "dot, dot, dash." (For an explanation of the rest of the label, see chapter 8.)*

M *Tracks, Routes*

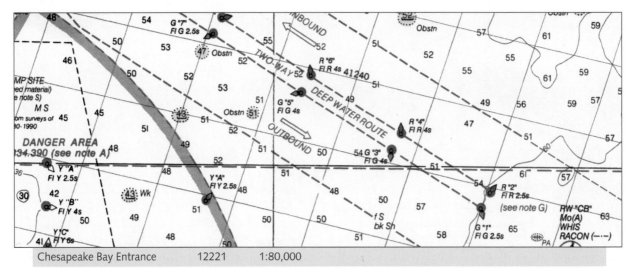

| Chesapeake Bay Entrance | 12221 | 1:80,000 |

A detail (at 1:80,000) of the deep-water (DW) route into the Chesapeake Bay shown on the previous chart (at 1:200,000), page 181.

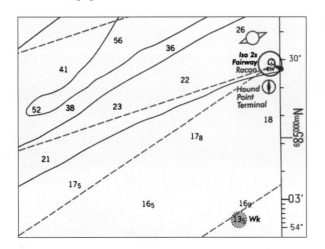

| Firth of Forth | NIMA 35082 | 1:25,052 |

Selected features: *Racon buoy, with red and white vertical stripes ("safe water"; see chapter 8) where the shipping lanes split.* **Radio calling-in point** (⃗O⃗) *for both inbound and outbound ships (arrowheads on both ends).* **Pilot boarding area** (◐).

	Supplementary National Symbols	
a	←→—DW—←→	Recommended track for deep draft vessels (track not defined by fixed marks)
b	←→—DW 83 ft—←→ DW 76 ft	Depth is shown where it has been obtained by the cognizant authority
c	– – – – – –	Alternate course
d	⟳	Established traffic separation scheme: Roundabout
e	○	If no separation zone exists, the center of the roundabout is shown by a circle

Section N: Areas and Limits

There are many types of areas within which certain activities are discouraged or prohibited, or from which certain classes of vessels are excluded. These are generally described as Restricted Areas. Within these areas, certain types of activities may be prohibited (e.g., anchoring prohibited or passage prohibited). Nevertheless, the use of the term *prohibited area* is discouraged by the IHO; the prohibitions within a *restricted area* should be defined in a label or note.

Various agencies, governmental and otherwise, have the authority to put these special restrictions on specific areas. Compliance with these restrictions is sometimes voluntary and sometimes mandatory; some apply all the time and some only at specified times or for specified vessels; and so on. Given the worldwide ratcheting up in security concerns since the attack on the World Trade Center in 2001 and the subsequent "war on terror," numerous new exclusion zones and other limits have been created and continue to be created and modified. The only way to stay abreast of this is with up-to-date charts, by tracking *Notices to Mariners*, and via informational websites.

In general, either dashed lines are used to define restricted areas or T-shaped dashes with the stems pointing toward the area in question. Sections of a boundary may incorporate another symbol (e.g., a submarine cable or pipeline symbol) to indicate the specific nature of the hazard or feature inside the area. Where the area includes some type of permanent physical obstruction, black is used. If the area designation is informational rather than applying to a permanent physical obstruction, or concerns an impermanent obstruction, magenta is used (e.g., state and international boundaries, 3- and 12-mile limits, fishing limits). A magenta screen may be added to either black or magenta boundaries or over the entire area in question to highlight it.

On NOAA's charts of U.S. waters, areas that are in some way restricted frequently have a label that includes a number (e.g., 165.501). This is a reference to the specific paragraph in the *Code of Federal Regulations (CFR) Title 33: Navigation and Navigable Waters*, the document in which the regulations for this area are defined (occasionally, the reference is to a second publication, *CFR 40: Protection of the Environment*). Title 33 can be found at http://ecfr.gpoaccess.gov, but in practice few will want to plough through it to find the explanation for a chart note. If the significance of the area is not self-evident, it is to be hoped that a note somewhere on the chart describes the regulations, but this is often not the case.

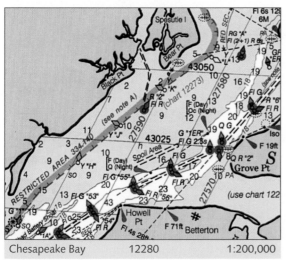

| Chesapeake Bay | 12280 | 1:200,000 |

T-shaped dashes and a magenta band to delineate a restricted area. The specific restrictions, or a source for them, will be found in note A.

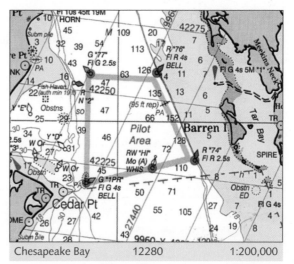

| Chesapeake Bay | 12280 | 1:200,000 |

Pilot-boarding area with no specific restrictions, but in which ships can be expected to be slowing and less maneuverable.

General

1.1		Maritime limit in general usually implying: Permanent obstructions. Note the use of black, implying a permanent physical obstruction within the area.	
1.2		Maritime limit in general usually implying: No permanent obstructions. Note the use of magenta, implying no permanent physical obstruction.	
2.1		Limit of restricted area. Note how the stems of the T-shaped dashes point toward the area in question.	Restricted Area
2.2	Entry Prohibited	(Screen optional.) Limit of prohibited area (no unauthorized entry).	PROHIBITED AREA / PROHIB AREA

Anchorages, Anchorage Areas

10		Anchorage (large vessels)		
		Anchorage (small vessels)		
11.1	A N53 14	Anchor berths	14	
11.2	N53 14	Anchor berths, swinging circle may be shown	3	D17
12.1		Anchorage area in general		Anchorage
12.2	No 1	Numbered anchorage area	Anchorage No 1	
12.3	Oaze	Named anchorage area	Neufeld Anchorage	

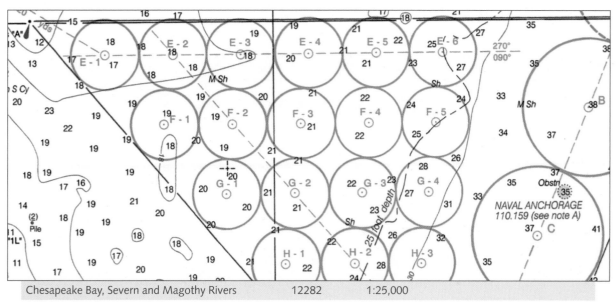

Chesapeake Bay, Severn and Magothy Rivers   12282   1:25,000

Naval anchorage off Newport, Virginia.

12.4	⚓ DW ⚓ ⚓	Deep Water Anchorage area, Anchorage area for Deep Draft Vessels	DW Anchprage
12.5	⚓ Tanker ⚓ ⚓	Tanker anchorage area	Tanker Anchorage
12.6	⚓ 24h ⚓ ⚓	Anchorage for periods up to 24 hours	
12.7	⚓ ⚓ ⚓	Explosives anchorage area. Note the flare symbol attached to a black dot, representing a bomb.	Explosives Anchorage
12.8	⚓ ⊕⚓ ⚓	Quarantine anchorage area	QUAR ANCH Quarantine Anchorage QUARANTINE ANCHORAGE
12.9	⚓ Reserved (see Note) ⚓ ⚓	Reserved anchorage	

Note: Anchors as part of the limit symbol are not shown for small areas. Other types of anchorage may be shown.

Under the rules of navigation, "a seaplane on the water shall, in general, keep well clear of all vessels and avoid impeding their navigation." This can make takeoff and landing somewhat difficult! In specified seaplane areas, the conventional right-of-way hierarchy is modified.

13		Seaplane landing area. Note the flying symbol (wings) inside the boundary line.
14		Anchorage for seaplanes. Note the flying symbol (wings) added to the top of the anchor symbol.

Restricted Areas

20		Anchoring prohibited	**ANCH PROHIB** Anch Prohibited	**ANCH PROHIB**
21		Fishing prohibited	Fish Prohibited	**FISH PROHIB**
22	*or* *or*	Limit of nature reserve: Nature reserve, Bird sanctuary, Game preserve, Seal sanctuary		
23.1	Explosives Dumping Ground	Explosives dumping ground	Explosives Dumping Ground	**Explosives Dumping** Ground
23.2	Explosives Dumping Ground (disused)	Explosives dumping ground (disused). Foul (explosives).	Explosives Dumping Ground	Explosives Dumping Ground
24	Dumping Ground for Chemicals	Dumping ground for chemical waste	Dump Site	Dumping Ground
25	Degaussing Range	Degaussing range. An area within which a ship's magnetic field can be measured through instruments and sensing cables on the seabed (the cable symbol may be added to the perimeter of the area). Anchoring and trawling should be avoided.	Degaussing Range	Degaussing Range

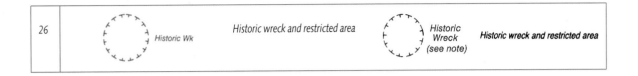

| 26 | | Historic Wk | Historic wreck and restricted area | | Historic Wreck (see note) | Historic wreck and restricted area |

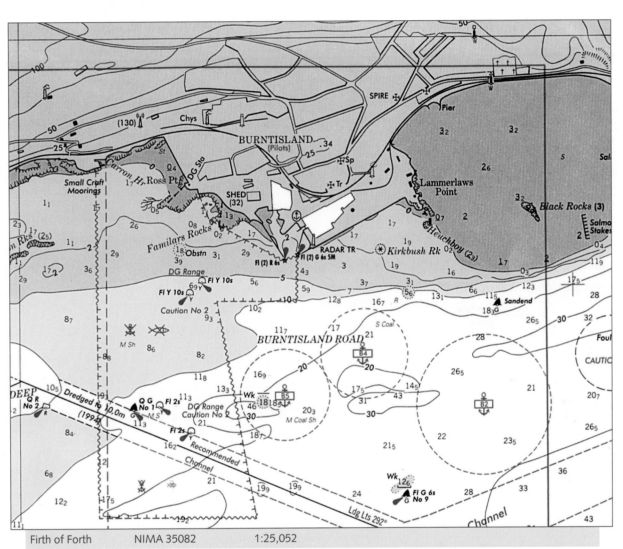

Firth of Forth   NIMA 35082   1:25,052

*A variety of cautionary and restricted areas: **Channel sides** (dashed magenta where there are no hazards, changing to black where the channel is physically restricted and has been dredged). A **degaussing area** (T-dashes interspersed with the submarine cable symbol) labeled "DG Range" (also including "no fishing" and "no anchoring" symbols). **Designated anchorages**, numbered (B2, B4, etc.). A **foul** area (to the east: note that this is in black because it represents a physical hazard). The leading lights label, together with its bearing (Ldg Lts 292°). This will be True degrees.*

*Miscellaneous drying heights (underlined), out-of-position heights (in parentheses), and heights above the high-water datum (bold, in parentheses). **Salmon stakes** to the east, which are below the level of the high-water datum (italic typeface). The **radar tower** (RADAR TR) in the center of the chart (capitals, so it is conspicuous). The **port captain's** (harbormaster's) **office**. Two **church** symbols, one with a tower (Tr) and one with a spire (Sp), a third with SPIRE spelled out in capitals (conspicuous), and a fourth with no label attached. A **range on shore** with white markers (W) in the northeast quadrant, with a **cemetery** next to the forward half of the range.*

Military Practice Areas

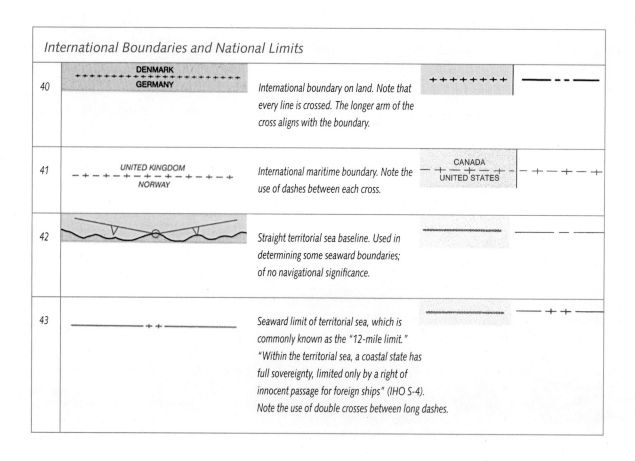

| 30 | Firing danger area. The bomb symbol points toward the area. |

| 31 | Entry Prohibited | Military area, entry prohibited | PROHIBITED AREA · Prohibited Area |

| 32 | Mine-laying practice area. The area may contain unexploded mines. Note the mine symbol pointing toward the area. |

| 33 | SUBMARINE EXERCISE AREA (see Note) | Submarine transit lane and exercise area |

| 34 | Minefield (see Note) | Minefield |

International Boundaries and National Limits

| 40 | DENMARK / GERMANY | International boundary on land. Note that every line is crossed. The longer arm of the cross aligns with the boundary. |

| 41 | UNITED KINGDOM / NORWAY | International maritime boundary. Note the use of dashes between each cross. | CANADA / UNITED STATES |

| 42 | Straight territorial sea baseline. Used in determining some seaward boundaries; of no navigational significance. |

| 43 | Seaward limit of territorial sea, which is commonly known as the "12-mile limit." "Within the territorial sea, a coastal state has full sovereignty, limited only by a right of innocent passage for foreign ships" (IHO S-4). Note the use of double crosses between long dashes. |

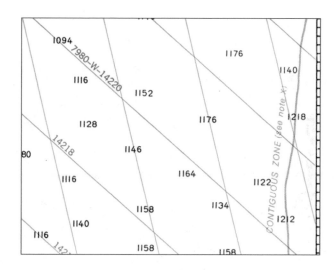

Contiguous zone (generally magenta), which is up to 24 miles beyond the territorial sea baseline. It represents the limit of a state's customs, fiscal, immigration, and/or sanitary jurisdiction.

44	———————— + ————————	Seaward limit of contiguous zone, "a zone adjacent to the territorial sea where the coastal state may exercise control to prevent infringement of its customs, fiscal, immigration, and/or sanitary regulations" (IHO S-4). It may not extend more than 24 miles beyond the territorial sea baseline (N43).	━━━━━━━━ + ━━
45	— ⋈ — — — ⋈ — — ⋈ – – – ⋈ –	Limit of fishery zone. This may extend as far as 200 miles beyond the territorial sea baseline (see N42). If a country has more than one fisheries limit (with different sets of regulations), the line for the inner one is dashed and the outer one is solid. The fish symbol may or may not be used.	–⋈–
46	———— UK Continental Shelf ————	Limit of continental shelf	
47	———— EEZ ————	Limit of Exclusive Economic Zone. This may extend as far as 200 miles beyond the territorial sea baseline (see N42); it is generally synonymous with the limit of the fishery zone (see N45).	–⋈–
48	– –⊖– – – – – –⊖– –	Customs limit	
49	– –‿_ Harbour Limit _‿– –	Harbor limit	– –‿_ Harbor Limit _‿– –

HYDROGRAPHY: N *Areas, Limits*

Various Limits

60.1		Limit of fast ice, Ice front (ice attached to the land)	
60.2		Limit of sea ice (pack ice)—seasonal	
61	Log Pond	Log pond	Log boom
62.1	Spoil Ground	Spoil ground	Spoil Area
62.2	Spoil Ground (disused)	Spoil ground (disused)	Spoil Area Discontinued
63	Dredging Area	Dredging area. When at work, vessels engaged in dredging are restricted in their ability to maneuver. There may be floating pipes, barges, and other apparatus in the area.	
64	Cargo Transhipment Area	Cargo transhipment area	
65	Incineration Area	Incineration area, in which chemical waste may be burned by special ships; they may appear to be on fire or in distress.	

Supplementary National Symbols

a	COLREGS demarcation line	
b	Limit of fishing areas (fish trap areas)	
c	Dumping ground	Dumping Ground
d	Disposal area (Dump site)	Disposal Area 92 depths from survey of JUNE 1972 85
e	Limit of airport	
f	Reservation line (Options)	
g	Dump site	Dump Site

O Hydrographic Terms

A mariner is usually not especially concerned with most of these terms, of which there are many, and there is no way to remember all the abbreviations. If it becomes important, you'll just have to look them up.

O Hydrographic Terms

1		Ocean		25	Shl	Shoal
2		Sea		26	Rf, Co rf	Reef, Coral reef
3	G	Gulf		27		Sunken rock
4	B	Bay, Bayou		28	Le	Ledge
5	Fd	Fjord		29		Pinnacle
6	L	Loch, Lough, Lake		30		Ridge
7	Cr	Creek		31		Rise
8	Lag	Lagoon		32	Mt	Mountain, Mount
9	C	Cove		33	SMt	Seamount
10	In	Inlet		34		Seamount chain
11	Str	Strait		35	Pk	Peak
12	Sd	Sound		36		Knoll
13	Pass	Passage, Pass		37		Abyssal hill
14	Chan	Channel		38		Tablemount
15		Narrows		39		Plateau
16	Entr	Entrance		40		Terrace
17	Est	Estuary		41		Spur
18		Delta		42		Continental shelf
19	Mth	Mouth		43		Shelf-edge
20	Rd	Roads, Roadstead		44		Slope
21	Anch	Anchorage		45		Continental slope
22	Apprs	Approach, Approaches		46		Continental rise
23	Bk	Bank		47		Continental borderland
24				48		Basin

○ *Hydrographic Terms*

49		*Abyssal plain*
50		*Hole*
51		*Trench*
52		*Trough*
53		*Valley*
54		*Median valley*
55		*Canyon*
56		*Sea channel*
57		*Moat, Sea moat*
58		*Fan*
59		*Apron*
60		*Fracture zone*
61		*Scarp, Escarpment*
62		*Sill*
63		*Gap*
64		*Saddle*
65		*Levee*
66		*Province*
67		*Tideway, Tidal gully*
68		*Sidearm*

Other Terms		
80		*projected*
81		*lighted*
82		*buoyed*
83		*marked*
84	anc	*ancient*
85	dist	*distant*
86		*lesser*
87		*closed*
88		*partly*
89	approx	*approximate*
90	Subm, subm	*submerged*
91		*shoaled*
92	exper	*experimental*
93	D, Destr	*destroyed*

Aids and Services

Lights, Buoys, Beacons, Fog Signals, Radar, Radio, Electronic Position-Fixing Systems, Services, and Small-Craft Facilities

THE SECTIONS on AIDS AND SERVICES in *INT-1* cover a fairly mixed bag of information. *Familiarity with the first two sections—Section P: Lights, and Section Q: Buoys, Beacons—is essential.* Section R (Fog Signals) adds more detail; Section S (Radar, Radio, Electronic Position-Fixing Systems) is mostly obsolete. Section T is principally of interest to shipping, and Section U provides a framework (underutilized at present) for the inclusion on charts of peripheral information of interest to small-boat owners (e.g., marina information).

Together, P, Q, R, and S cover what are known as Aids to Navigation (ATONs in coast guard parlance), frequently referred to as *navaids*. The information contained on a chart about navaids is supplemented by information published in light lists (issued by all hydrographic offices; in the U.S., this publication lists all official navaids, unlit as well as lit). A light list for any area being cruised is a useful addition to the navigator's toolbox, particularly because it provides a physical description of each light and buoy, which can help with daytime identification.

If a navaid is on land or in some way rigidly fastened to the bottom (e.g., a beacon mounted on a piling), any label uses vertical lettering. If its position is accurately known, NOAA uses capital letters in its label; otherwise, the initial letter of each word is capitalized (position approximate). All floating navaids have labels with italicized letters (see chapter 5).

Section P: Lights

A light in the context of this section refers to a major light, such as a lighthouse, lightship, or large buoy with a powerful light. Less powerful lights associated with buoys and smaller beacons are discussed in the next section (Q).

Light Structures and Major Floating Lights

INT-1 calls for the position of a light to be indicated by a five-point star, with two star sizes recommended—the larger being used for more important lights. NOAA typically uses a bold dot, which, notes IHO S-4, "is permissible but is not recommended because the star symbol is more distinctive (dots are used for spot heights, posts, small islets, etc.)."

On large-scale charts, the following characteristics of lights are given in the following order:

- Flash character (characteristic), which describes the sequence and timing of the flashes (see P10.1 to P10.11).

- Color, which is shown using standard abbreviations (see P11.1 to P11.8). If no color is given, it is assumed to be white.

- Period, which is the total time, in seconds, it takes to go through one full pattern of flashes,

Computing the Range of a Light

To compute the geographic range of a light, we need to know both the height of the light (h_1) and the height of eye of the observer (h_2). The range (in nautical miles) is then computed as follows:

$$D = 1.17(\sqrt{h_1} + \sqrt{h_2})$$

Where:
D = geographic distance in nautical miles
h_1 = height of light (in ft.)
h_2 = height of eye of observer (in ft.)

(If h_1 and h_2 are in meters, use 2.07 as the multiplier to keep the result in nautical miles.)
Using the Cuckolds light (Boothbay Harbor, Maine), which has the characteristics "Gp FL (2) 6sec 59ft 12M HORN," and assuming a height of eye of 9 feet (about right from the cockpit of most cruising boats), we have the following equation:

$$D = 1.17 \times (7.68 + 3) = 12.5 \text{ miles}$$

In this case, the geographic range (12.5 miles) from our small boat is almost the same as the nominal range (12 miles). On a clear night, we should be able to pick out the light almost as soon as it comes over our horizon. Of course, if visibility is reduced, we will not see the light at this distance.

Geographic range also can be looked up in a

Geographic Range Table

HEIGHT		DISTANCE, nm	HEIGHT		DISTANCE, nm
Feet	Meters		Feet	Meters	
5	1.5	2.6	110	33.5	12.3
10	3.0	3.7	120	36.6	12.8
15	4.6	4.5	130	39.6	13.3
20	6.1	5.2	140	42.7	13.8
25	7.6	5.9	150	45.7	14.3
30	9.1	6.4	200	61.0	16.5
35	10.7	6.9	250	76.2	18.5
40	12.2	7.4	300	91.4	20.3
45	13.7	7.8	350	106.7	21.9
50	15.2	8.3	400	121.9	23.4
55	16.8	8.7	450	137.2	24.8
60	18.3	9.1	500	152.4	26.2
65	19.8	9.4	550	167.6	27.4
70	21.3	9.8	600	182.9	28.7
75	22.9	10.1	650	198.1	29.8
80	24.4	10.5	700	213.4	31
85	25.9	10.8	800	243.8	33.1
90	27.4	11.1	900	274.3	35.1
95	29.0	11.4	1,000	304.8	37
100	30.5	11.7			

Note: nm = nautical miles. Courtesy Navigator Publishing

table showing the distance of visibility of objects at sea (see opposite page). The light's height and the height of eye of the observer are looked up separately (not added together), and then the two visibility numbers that have been extracted from the table are added together.

Looking at the table for the Cuckolds light, the nearest height to 59 feet (h_1) is 60 feet, which gives a geographic range of 9.1 miles; the nearest height to 9 feet (h_2, the height of the observer) is 10 feet, which gives a range of 3.7 miles.

D (geographic range) = 9.1 + 3.7 =
12.8 miles

This is a little on the high side because both height numbers have been rounded up.

Finally, we need to note that the height of the Cuckolds light given on the chart is calculated from the chart's high-water datum, which is MHW. On other charts, it may be calculated from another datum—this must be checked in the small print. In any event, at most states of the tide, the height of the light above sea level is greater than its charted height, and the geographic range is commensurably increased (e.g., at low tide with a 10 ft. tide, the light will be 69 ft. above the water level, extending its geographic range to 13.2 miles—which is somewhat above its nominal range; in this case, the nominal range is the limiting factor).

In practice, in many cases the nominal (charted) range of a major lighthouse substantially exceeds its geographic range when viewed from a small boat—in other words, the light will not come into view (come over the horizon) until well after the chart tells us it is visible. Its loom (the glow it makes in the sky) may be visible long before the light is over the horizon, especially on a night with low-lying clouds (the light reflects off the underside of the clouds). It is not unusual to be able to pick out the loom of a powerful light from 20 or 30 miles away.

together with the intervals between them ("a full sequence of phases"). Seconds are abbreviated to a small (lowercase) "s" or to "sec" on NOAA charts.

- Height (elevation), which is the height of the *light itself* (not the top of the structure in which it is housed) above the high-water datum in use on the chart (stated in a note somewhere on the chart; see chapter 3). On INT charts, the elevation is expressed in meters, using a small (lowercase) "m"; on charts in imperial units, it is expressed in feet ("ft").

- Visibility (range), which on older charts meant the *geographical range* (the distance a light could theoretically be seen, limited only by the curvature of the earth, assuming that the observer had a height of eye of 5 meters); NOAA used this until 1972. Many lights rated this way are, in fact, not powerful enough to be seen this far off, in which case the *luminous (nominal) range* is used, as it is on all new charts. This is the distance a light can be seen on a clear night, assuming that the observer is high enough to see it (i.e., the light is not obscured by the curvature of the earth; it may well be for a powerful light—see the sidebar). In either case, the range is expressed in nautical miles, using a capital (uppercase) "M." If there is more than one light, the lesser range may be shown, or else both ranges are shown separated by a slash (e.g., 15/10M). If there are more than two lights, the longest and shortest range may be given, separated by a hyphen (e.g., 15-7M).

- Number or letter, which is the assigned numbers or letters of the light structure (if any). These are painted on the side of the structure.

- Ancillary information (e.g., the addition of a foghorn).

For example, the Point Judith light in Rhode Island is 65 feet high, with a composite group occulting white light (explained later in this chapter) that goes through a full cycle every 15 seconds. The light has a nominal range of 16 miles, and there is a foghorn. It is labeled as follows:

Oc (1+2) 15s 65ft 16M HORN

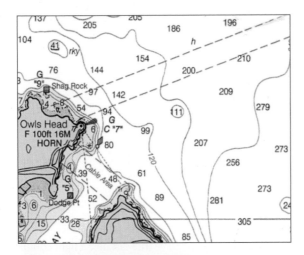

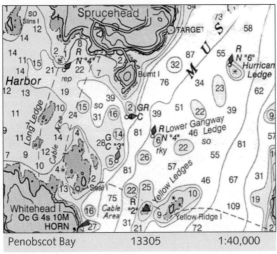

Penobscot Bay	13305	1:40,000

Maine lighthouses, NOAA style (i.e., no star symbol). **Selected features:** *Owls Head, F 100ft 16M HORN— Fixed white (because no color is given), 100 feet above the high-water datum, range of 16 miles, with a foghorn. Whitehead Island, Oc G 4s 10M HORN—Occulting green with a 4-second cycle, range of 10 miles, with a foghorn; no height is given (somewhat unusual).*

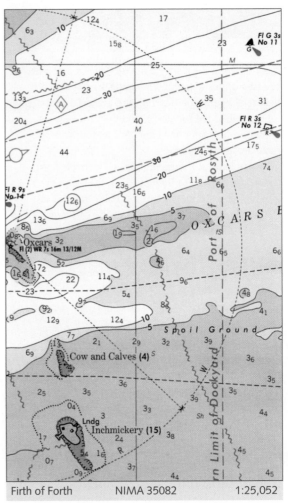

Firth of Forth	NIMA 35082	1:25,052

INT-1 style light symbol, using a star. Fl(2) WR 7s 16m 13/12M. This light flashes twice every 7 seconds. It has a white and a red sector (labeled W and R on the perimeter of the circle). It is 16 meters above the high-water datum. The white light is visible for 13 miles, the red for 12 miles. Note also the calling-in symbol for ships just to the north of the light, the disused submarine cable, and the dockyard limit, all in magenta (informational, with no physical obstruction).

There may or may not be full stops (periods) between the various components on the label.

Small-scale charts may omit some of this information because of a lack of space to display it. On major lights, IHO S-4 recommends that the height be dropped first, followed by the period, the range, and then the other details, leaving just a light symbol. In harbors and restricted channels, the range is dropped first, followed by the elevation, the period, and then the other details.

Most lights and lighted buoys have a "flare" attached to the charted symbol to indicate that it is lit (sometimes the label substitutes). Regardless of the color of the light, the flare is magenta. The color of the light is stated in the label (if it is other than white).

P Lights

Light Structures, Major Floating Lights

Several of the following illustrations have labels for the color of the structure (e.g., BRB = black, red, black; BY = black, yellow), and in each case the symbol has a "topmark" of some type. These colors and topmarks are not intrinsic to the feature being illustrated; they are examples of additional information about the feature that may be shown on the chart. The meaning is explained in section Q.

1	★ ★ Lt LtHo	Major light, minor light. Note the magenta flare, to indicate the presence of a light (of any color).
2		Lighted offshore platform. In some areas platforms have white and red lights flashing Morse code "U"—Mo(U)—which signifies "you are standing into danger." ■ PLATFORM (lighted)
3	BY ★ BnTr	Lighted beacon tower ○ Marker (lighted) BY
4	R BRB ★ Bn	Lighted beacon R
5	R ★ Bn	Articulated light, buoyant beacon, resilient beacon ○ Art R
6		Light vessel; Lightship; Major floating light
7		Unmanned light-vessel; light float
8		LANBY (Large Automated Navigational Buoy).

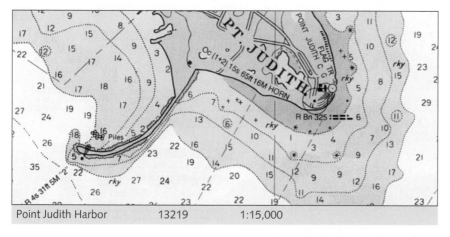

Point Judith Harbor   13219   1:15,000

Point Judith Light, Rhode Island—Oc (1+2) 15s 65ft 16M HORN. Composite occulting (1+2) every 15 seconds, 65 feet above the high-water datum, 16-mile range, with a foghorn. It also has a radio beacon transmitting Morse P (dot, dash, dash, dot) and Morse J (dot, dash, dash, dash).

P *Lights*

Light Characters (Characteristics)

	Abbreviation		Class of Light	Illustration	Period shown
	International	National			
10.1	F	F	Fixed		F
	Occulting (total duration of light longer than total duration of darkness)				
10.2	Oc	Oc; Occ	Single-occulting		Oc
	Oc (2) *Example*	Oc (2); Gp Occ	Group-occulting		Oc (2)
	Oc (2+3) *Example*	Oc (2+3)	Composite group-occulting		Oc(2+3)
	Isophase (duration of light and darkness equal)				
10.3	Iso	Iso	Isophase		Iso
	Flashing (total duration of light shorter than total duration of darkness)				
10.4	Fl	Fl	Single-flashing		Fl
	Fl (3) *Example*	Fl (3)	Group-flashing		Fl (3)
	Fl (2+1) *Example*	Fl (2+1)	Composite group-flashing		Fl (2+1)
10.5	LFl	LFl	Long-flashing (2s or longer)		L Fl
	Quick (repetition rate of 50 to 79—usually either 50 or 60—flashes per minute)				
10.6	Q	Q	Continuous quick		
	Q (3) *Example*	Q (3)	Group quick		
	IQ	IQ	Interrupted quick		
	Very quick (repetition rate of 80 to 159—usually either 100 or 120—flashes per min)				
10.7	VQ	VQ	Continuous very quick		VQ
	VQ (3) *Example*	VQ (3)	Group very quick		
	IVQ	IVQ	Interrupted very quick		
	Ultra quick (repetition rate of 160 or more—usually 240 to 300—flashes per min)				
10.8	UQ	UQ	Continuous ultra quick		
	IUQ	IUQ	Interrupted ultra quick		
10.9	Mo (A) *Example*	Mo (A)	Morse Code		
10.10	FFl	F Fl	Fixed and flashing		F Fl
10.11	AL.WR	AlWR	Alternating. The "WR" stands for white and red.		AlWR

P *Lights*

Colors of Lights

	Abbreviation		
	International	National	
11.1	W	W	White (only on sector- and alternating lights)
11.2	R	R	Red
11.3	G	G	Green
11.4	Bu	Bu	Blue
11.5	Vi	Vi	Violet
11.6	Y	Y	Yellow
11.7	Y Or	Y Or	Orange
11.8	Y Am	Y Am	Amber

Colors of lights shown on:
Standard charts
Multicolored charts
Multicolored charts at sector lights

Period—the time taken to exhibit a full sequence of phases

12	90s Example	Period in seconds	90s

Elevation

| 13 | 12 m
Example | Elevation of light given in meters or feet above
the high-water datum (not the sounding datum) | 12 m, 36 ft |
|---|---|---|---|

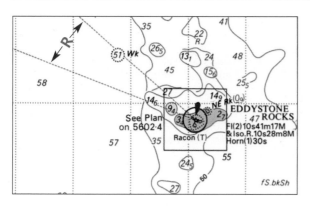

Eddystone Rocks lighthouse. There is an all-around white light with a sectored red light.

Fowey to Plymouth	BA 5602.3	1:75,000

P Lights

Range

Note: Charted ranges on most charts are nominal (luminous) ranges given in nautical miles; however, on some older charts, it may be geographical range.

14	15 M Example	Light with single range	15 M	15 M
	15/10 M Example	Light with two different ranges. NOS: only lesser of two ranges is charted	10 M	15/10 M
	15-7 M Example	Light with three or more ranges. NOS: only least of three ranges is charted	7 M	15-7 M

Disposition

15	(hor)	horizontally disposed	(hor)
	(vert)	vertically disposed	(vert)

Examples of a Full Light Description

16

Example of a light description on a metric chart
Fl(3)WRG.15s13m7-5M

FL(3) Class or character of light: in this example, a group-flashing light, regularly repeating a group of three flashes.

WRG. Colors of light: white, red, and green, exhibiting the different colors in defined sectors.

15s Period of light in seconds, i.e., the time taken to exhibit one full sequence of 3 flashes and eclipses: 15 seconds.

13m Elevation of focal plane above MHW, MHWS, MHHW, or, where there is no tide, above MSL: 13 meters.

7-5m Luminous range in sea (nautical) miles: the distance at which a light of a particular intensity can be seen in "clear" visibility, taking no account of earth curvature. In those countries (e.g., U.S., U.K.) where the term "clear" is defined as a meteorological visibility of 10 sea (nautical) miles, the range may be termed "nominal." In this example, the ranges of the colors are: white 7 miles, green 5 miles, red between 7 and 5 miles.

Example of a light description on a feet or fathoms chart
Al.Fl.WR.30s110ft23/22M

Al.Fl. Class or character of light: in this example, exhibiting single flashes of differing colors alternately.

WR. Colors of light shown alternately: white and red all-round (i.e., not a sector light)

30s Period of light in seconds, i.e., the time taken to exhibit the sequence of two flashes and two eclipses: 30 seconds.

110ft Elevation of focal plane above MHW, MHWS, MHHW, or, where there is no tide, above MSL: 110 feet.

23/22M Range in sea (nautical) miles. Until 1971 the lesser of geographical range (based on a height of eye of 15 feet) and luminous range was charted. Now, when the charts are corrected, luminous (or nominal) range is given. In this example, the luminous ranges of the colors are: white 23 miles, red 22 miles.

P *Lights*

Lights Marking Fairways (leading lights, lights in line, and direction lights)

A *fairway* is that part of a river or harbor that constitutes the main navigable channel for vessels of a larger size. This is the usual course followed by vessels entering or leaving a harbor. It is also often called a *ship channel*. Different types of lights are used to help ships keep to the channel, including leading lights and various sectored lights (which exhibit different flash patterns and/or colors over different sectors).

Leading lights, particularly when there are two lights in line, are particularly useful because they provide an unequivocal and unambiguous indication of the track to be followed—the lights are either in line or they are not. However, at some point on approaching the lights, you will run out of the channel; this is typically indicated by a dashed line on the chart rather than a solid line.

Leading lights may be any color (typically white) and any flash pattern, although occulting ("Oc": the total duration of light is longer than that of darkness) and isophase ("Iso": there is an equal duration of light and darkness) are common. They vary tremendously in visibility (some can be seen for miles, others over relatively short distances). If there is a pair of lights, the rear one will be higher than the forward one.

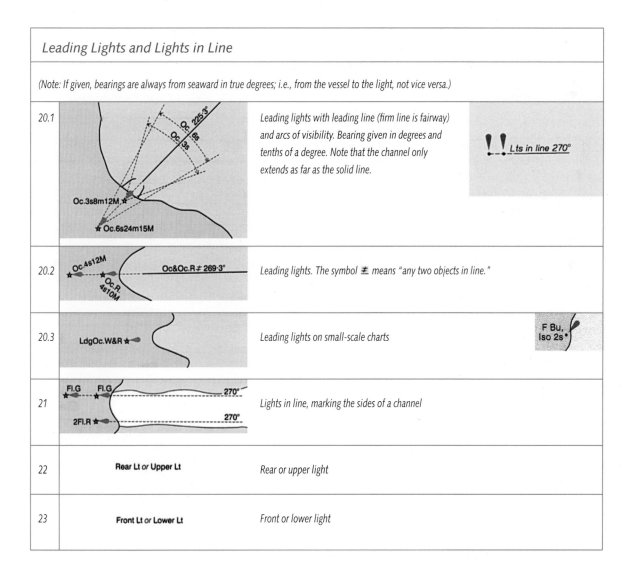

Leading Lights and Lights in Line

(Note: If given, bearings are always from seaward in true degrees; i.e., from the vessel to the light, not vice versa.)

20.1		Leading lights with leading line (firm line is fairway) and arcs of visibility. Bearing given in degrees and tenths of a degree. Note that the channel only extends as far as the solid line.
20.2		Leading lights. The symbol ⋢ means "any two objects in line."
20.3		Leading lights on small-scale charts
21		Lights in line, marking the sides of a channel
22	**Rear Lt *or* Upper Lt**	Rear or upper light
23	**Front Lt *or* Lower Lt**	Front or lower light

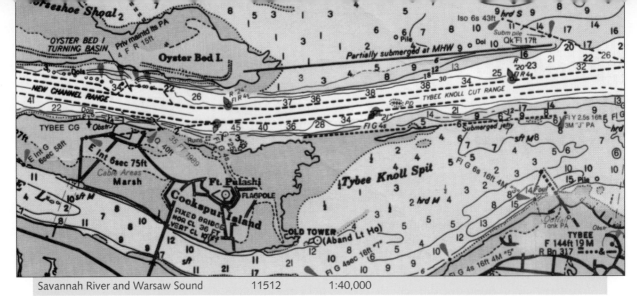

Savannah River and Warsaw Sound | 11512 | 1:40,000

There is lots going on with this chart, making it somewhat difficult to read despite its relatively large scale (1:40,000). In particular, it is a little difficult to decipher the leading lights for the Tybee Knoll Cut Range (they are left of center, Q 40ft and E.Int 6 sec 75ft). Note the dashed line where the range line runs out of the channel. **Additional features:** *The* **breakwater** *to the north, partially submerged at Mean High Water (MHW). The* **submerged jetty** *to the south. Various shoals, piles, and dolphins. The* **dangerous wreck** *in the channel (PD = Position Doubtful; it definitely exists, but its location is uncertain). The* **abandoned lighthouse** *(positioning dot and capitals, so its position is accurate and it is conspicuous). The* **uncertain coastline** *(high-water line) at some points around the marsh (dashed line). The use of the black coastline symbol to delineate the visible* **edge of the marsh** *(the visible high-water line from the perspective of a navigator).*

Direction Lights

Direction lights are a particular variant of a sector light (defined in the next paragraph) with a very narrow sector marking a direction to be followed that may be flanked by darkness, a lower light level, or light of a different color. Commonly, the sector intended for navigation is white with red and green to port and starboard (which side is red and which green depends on whether this is IALA Region A or B; see section Q), or simply red on both sides. If you see the red or green light, you know you have strayed out of the channel; if there is both red and green, you know on which side you have strayed. If the central line of a direction light is charted, to distinguish it from a leading line, it is labeled "Dir." The light itself may also be labeled "Dir" to indicate that it has a particularly precise cutoff. A moiré effect light is a special type of direction light with a black line displayed against a yellowish light.

The term *sector light* is used generically for any light that does not have all-around visibility. This includes an all-around light with an obscured sector (something in the way; see P43) and one in which there is an all-around white light with a separate colored light with a limited sector (see P42). In all cases, a light is presumed to be all-around unless the chart shows something different.

	Direction Lights	
	(Note: If given, bearings are always from seaward in true degrees; i.e., from the vessel to the light, not vice versa.)	
30.1	⋆ Dir 269° Fl(2)5s10m11M	Direction light with narrow sector and course to be followed, flanked by darkness or unintensified light
30.2	Oc.12s6M ⋆ Dir 299° Dir 255·5° ⋆ Fl(2)15s11M	Direction light with course to be followed, uncharted sector is flanked by darkness or unintensified light

P Lights

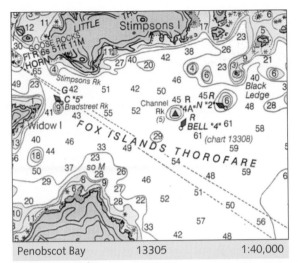

Penobscot Bay   13305   1:40,000

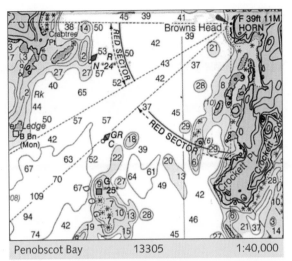

Penobscot Bay   13305   1:40,000

Goose Rocks Light: Fl R 6s 51ft 11M—a red flashing light with a cycle of 6 seconds, 51 feet high, and visible for 11 miles. It has a very narrow white sector that serves as a direction light to enter Fox Islands Thorofare.

Browns Head light: F 39ft 11M HORN—a white fixed light with red sectors on either side, 39 feet high, and visible for 11 miles. It serves as a direction light, delineating the passage between the beacon on Fiddler Ledge ("Mon" stands for "Monument") and the rocks to the south (green beacon, number 25).

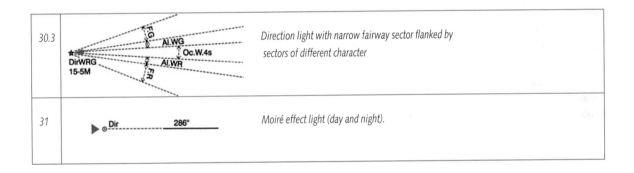

| 30.3 | | Direction light with narrow fairway sector flanked by sectors of different character |
| 31 | | Moiré effect light (day and night). |

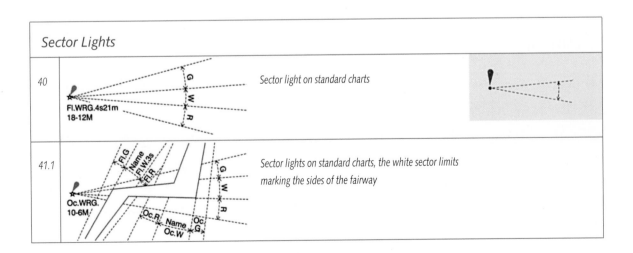

Sector Lights		
40		Sector light on standard charts
41.1		Sector lights on standard charts, the white sector limits marking the sides of the fairway

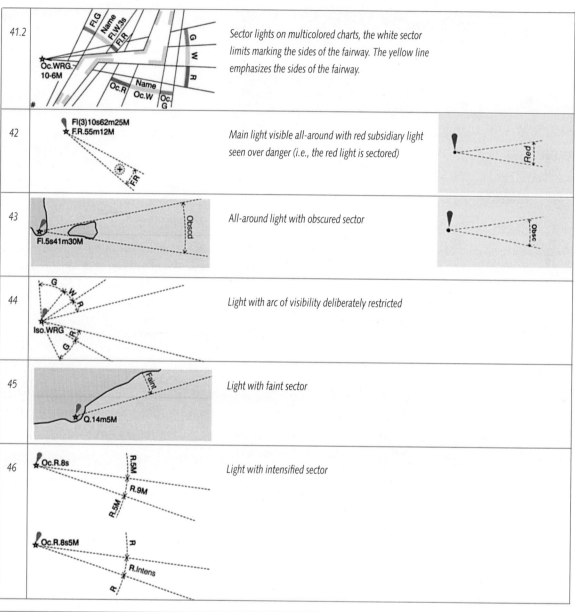

41.2		Sector lights on multicolored charts, the white sector limits marking the sides of the fairway. The yellow line emphasizes the sides of the fairway.
42	Fl(3)10s62m25M F.R.55m12M	Main light visible all-around with red subsidiary light seen over danger (i.e., the red light is sectored)
43	Fl.5s41m30M	All-around light with obscured sector
44	Iso.WRG	Light with arc of visibility deliberately restricted
45	Q.14m5M	Light with faint sector
46	Oc.R.8s R.5M R.9M R.5M Oc.R.8s5M R R.Intens R	Light with intensified sector

Lights with Limited Times of Exhibition

50	F.R(occas)	Lights exhibited only when specially needed (for fishing vessels, ferries) and some private lights ("occas" = occasionally)	Occas F R (occas)
51	Fl.10s40m27M (F.37m11M by day)	Daytime light (charted only where the character shown by day differs from that shown at night)	F Bu 9m 6M (F by day)
52	Q.WRG.5m10-3M Fl.5s(in fog)	Fog light (exhibited only in fog, or if the character changes in fog)	

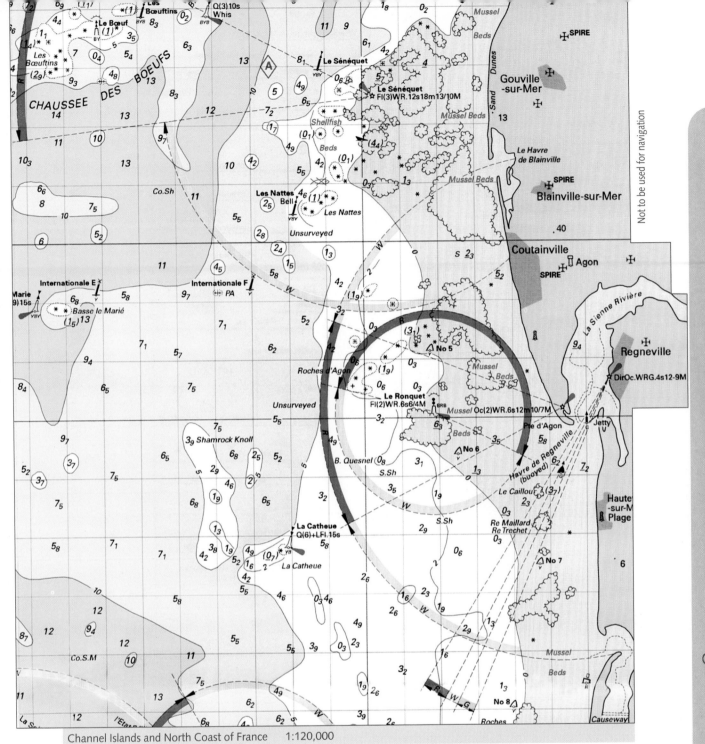

Channel Islands and North Coast of France   1:120,000

Not to be used for navigation

Complex sectored lights are more common in Europe than in the Americas. Here we have a series of lights on the north coast of France. The light at Regneville is a directional light (Dir), with a narrow red and green sector either side of the white sector to indicate when a vessel is out of the channel (this is IALA Region A, so the red sector is on the left-hand side of the channel when approaching from seaward; in IALA Region B it would be on the right-hand side—see later in this chapter). **Additional features:** *A number of* **cardinal marks**, *identifiable by their topmarks (two triangles, one above the other, in various arrangements) and lateral buoyage for IALA Region A (see later in this chapter for an explanation of cardinal and lateral marks).* **DirOc.WRG.4s 12-9M** = *Directional occulting light; white, red, and green; 4-second period; with the most powerful light (the white, since it is listed first), having a range of 12 miles, and the least powerful (the green) a range of 9 miles.* **Note also:** *An* **isolated danger mark.** *Three different* **rock symbols** *(drying, awash, and submerged).* *A* **radar reflector symbol** *(Q 11) on the cardinal mark for Le Boeuf rock (NW quadrant). Also try to locate the following: drying heights; "no fishing" symbol; unsurveyed areas; a dangerous submerged wreck; a locator symbol for tidal stream information; church symbols. Note that the depth conventions are not those of the IHO—the deeper water is the darker blue.*

P *Lights*

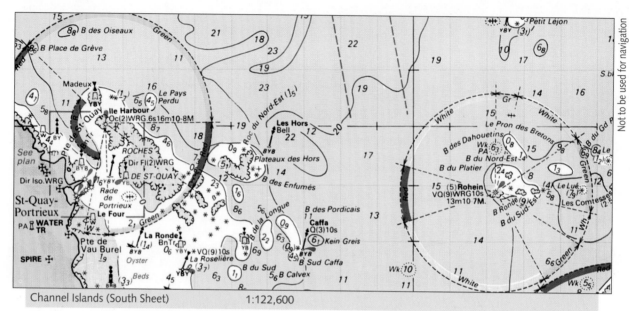

Channel Islands (South Sheet)   1:122,600

Complex sectored lights off the north coast of France. The Rohein light has eight distinct sectors, with a very quick (VQ) flash pattern.

53	⭐ Fl.5s(U)	Unwatched (unmanned) light with no standby or emergency arrangements (U = unwatched/unmanned)		
54	(temp)	Temporary light		
55	(exting)	Extinguished light		

Special Lights				
60	⭐ AeroAl.Fl.WG.7·5s11M	Aero light	❗ AERO	❗ AERO Al WG 7½s 108m 13M
61.1	⭐ AeroF.R.353m11M RADIO MAST (353)	Air obstruction light of high intensity		❗ AERO F R 77m 11M
61.2	(89) 🗼 (R Lts)	Air obstruction lights of low intensity (it is the absence of the light flare that indicates the low intensity)		⊙ TR (R Lts)
62	Fog Det Lt	Fog detector light		Fog Det Lt

63	(illuminated)	Floodlight, floodlighting of a structure	
64	F Iso F.R	Strip light (found along piers and in similar places)	
65	F.R (priv)	Private light other than one exhibited occasionally	Priv / F R (priv)

Supplementary National Symbols				
a	Riprap surrounding light		c	Group-Short Flashing
b	Short-Long Flashing		d	Fixed and Group Flashing

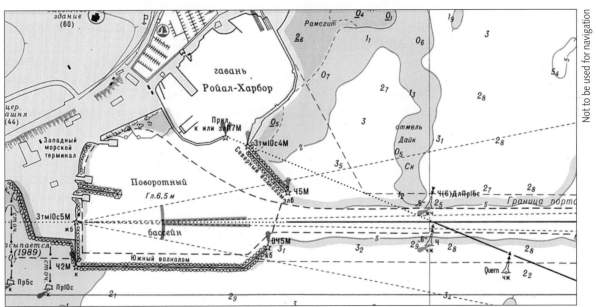

Despite the labels on this Russian chart (of Ramsgate, England) being incomprehensible to anyone who cannot read the Cyrillic script, because the symbology is international, it is possible to work out most of it! In a pinch, this chart could be used for navigation without understanding the language.

Q Buoys, Beacons

Section Q: Buoys, Beacons

Buoys are floating navaids. Beacons are rigidly attached to the ground or the seabed. Day beacons are beacons without lights.

The shapes, numbers, coloring, topmarks, and other features of buoys and beacons are designed to comply with a particular system of buoyage. As early as 1889, there were attempts to make these consistent on an international basis, standardizing on red conical buoys to starboard when approaching a port from seaward, and black can buoys to port (this type of system is known as a *lateral system* as opposed to a *cardinal system* or some other system—see below).

Unfortunately, when lights were first introduced, some European countries placed red lights on the black buoys because they already had red lights on the port side of harbor entrances. In 1936, the international Geneva Convention specified red lights to port and white to starboard; however, the United States (which was using red to starboard) and other countries were not signatories. World War II prevented ratification of the Geneva Convention. When navaids were reestablished in Europe starting in 1946, the convention was generally followed but with significant differences in interpretation from one country to another, resulting in nine different systems in use.

In 1965, the International Association of Lighthouse Authorities (IALA) established a committee to harmonize the existing rules. In 1971, the MV *Brandenburg* struck the wreckage of the *Texaco Caribbean* in the Dover Strait (between England and France) and sank, despite the fact that the wreck was appropriately marked. A few weeks later, the MV *Niki* hit the wreckage and sank. A total of fifty-one lives were lost, which prompted the IALA to action.

Five types of marks were defined—lateral, cardinal, isolated danger, safe water, and special—with specific rules for each. These rules apply to all fixed and floating marks, except for certain specialized navaids already discussed: lighthouses, sectored lights, leading lights and marks, and lightships and their substitutes (light floats and LANBYs).

Of the five types of mark, the most common are those using the lateral system. Referring to this system, IHO S-4 notes: "By 1976 the rules for System 'A' (red to port) were completed and implementation began in 1977. The rules for System 'B' (red to starboard) were completed early in 1980, but were so similar to those for 'A' that the two were combined to become 'The IALA Maritime Buoyage System.' Within the single system, lighthouse authorities are allowed the choice of using red to port or red to starboard on a regional basis, the two regions being known as Regions A and B. The new IALA System rules were adopted in November 1980." Generally speaking, System A is used in Europe, Asia, Africa, and Australasia; System B is used in the Americas including the Caribbean.

Lateral System

The core concept in the lateral system is one in which a vessel is considered to be approaching a harbor, river, estuary, or some other waterway from seaward. The shapes, numbers, colors, and flash characteristics (if lit) of buoys and beacons vary according to whether they are on the right-hand or the left-hand side of the vessel. In areas where there is no clear definition of what constitutes an approach from seaward, the relevant authority makes an arbitrary determination of the "direction" of the buoyage (e.g., the Intracoastal Waterway in the United States; see the accompanying sidebar). Where confusion seems possible, an arrow indicating the General Direction of Buoyage is sometimes placed on a chart.

IALA Systems A and B are almost identical with the exception of a reversal of the port and starboard colors and numbering systems. The shapes, topmarks, and so forth remain the same; however, System A has green buoys and beacons (and odd numbers) to the right and red (with even numbers) to the left, whereas System B has red to the right with even numbers

(continued on page 213)

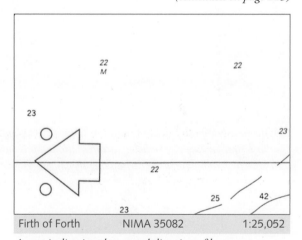

Firth of Forth   NIMA 35082   1:25,052

Arrow indicating the general direction of buoyage.

LATERAL MARKS — REGION A

This diagram is schematic and in the case of pillar buoys in particular, their features will vary with the individual design of the buoys in use.

PORT HAND

Colour: Red.
Shape: Can, pillar or spar.
Topmark (when fitted): Single red can.
Retroreflector: Red band or square.

STARBOARD HAND

Colour: Green.
Shape: Conical, pillar or spar.
Topmark (when fitted): Single green cone point upward.
Retroreflector: Green band or triangle.

DIRECTION OF BUOYAGE

LIGHTS, when fitted, may have any rhythm other than composite group flashing (2+1) used on modified Lateral marks indicating a preferred channel. Examples are:

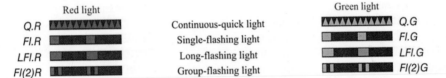

Red light			Green light
Q.R	Continuous-quick light		Q.G
Fl.R	Single-flashing light		Fl.G
LFl.R	Long-flashing light		LFl.G
Fl(2)R	Group-flashing light		Fl(2)G

The lateral colours of red or green are frequently used for minor shore lights, such as those marking pierheads and the extremities of jetties.

PREFERRED CHANNELS

At the point where a channel divides, when proceeding in the conventional direction of buoyage, a preferred channel is indicated by

Preferred channel to starboard

Colour: Red with one broad green band.
Shape: Can, pillar or spar.
Topmark (when fitted): Single red can.
Retroreflector: Red band or square.

Preferred channel to port

Colour: Green with one broad red band.
Shape: Conical, pillar or spar.
Topmark (when fitted): Single green cone point upward.
Retroreflector: Green band or triangle.

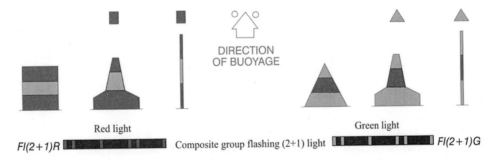

DIRECTION OF BUOYAGE

Red light   Green light

Fl(2+1)R   Composite group flashing (2+1) light   Fl(2+1)G

NOTES

Where port or starboard marks do not rely on can or conical buoy shapes for identification, they carry the appropriate topmark where practicable.

Even numbers are to port, odd to starboard, increasing from seaward.

Lateral Marks, Region A

LATERAL MARKS — REGION B

This diagram is schematic and in the case of pillar buoys in particular, their features will vary with the individual design of the buoys in use.

PORT HAND

Colour: Green.

Shape: Can, pillar or spar.

Topmark (when fitted): Single green can.

Retroreflector: Green band or square.

STARBOARD HAND

Colour: Red.

Shape: Conical, pillar or spar.

Topmark (when fitted): Single red cone, point upward.

Retroreflector: Red band or triangle.

LIGHTS, when fitted, may have any rhythm other than composite group flashing (2+1) used on modified Lateral marks indicating a preferred channel. Examples are:

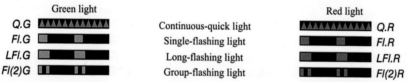

Green light		Red light
Q.G	Continuous-quick light	Q.R
Fl.G	Single-flashing light	Fl.R
LFl.G	Long-flashing light	LFl.R
Fl(2)G	Group-flashing light	Fl(2)R

The lateral colours of red or green are frequently used for minor shore lights, such as those marking pierheads and the extremities of jetties.

PREFERRED CHANNELS

At the point where a channel divides, when proceeding in the conventional direction of buoyage, a preferred channel is indicated by

Preferred channel to starboard

Colour: Green with one broad red band.

Shape: Can, pillar or spar.

Topmark (when fitted): Single green can.

Retroreflector: Green band or square.

Preferred channel to port

Colour: Red with one broad green band.

Shape: Conical, pillar or spar.

Topmark (when fitted): Single red cone point upward.

Retroreflector: Red band or triangle.

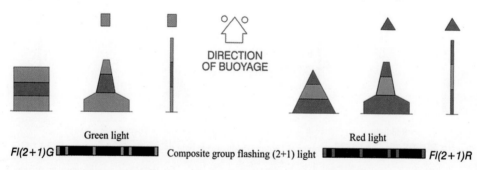

Green light		Red light
Fl(2+1)G	Composite group flashing (2+1) light	Fl(2+1)R

NOTES

Where port or starboard marks do not rely on can or conical buoy shapes for identification, they carry the appropriate topmark where practicable.

Even numbers are to starboard, odd to port, increasing from seaward.

Lateral Marks, Region B

Q *Buoys, Beacons*

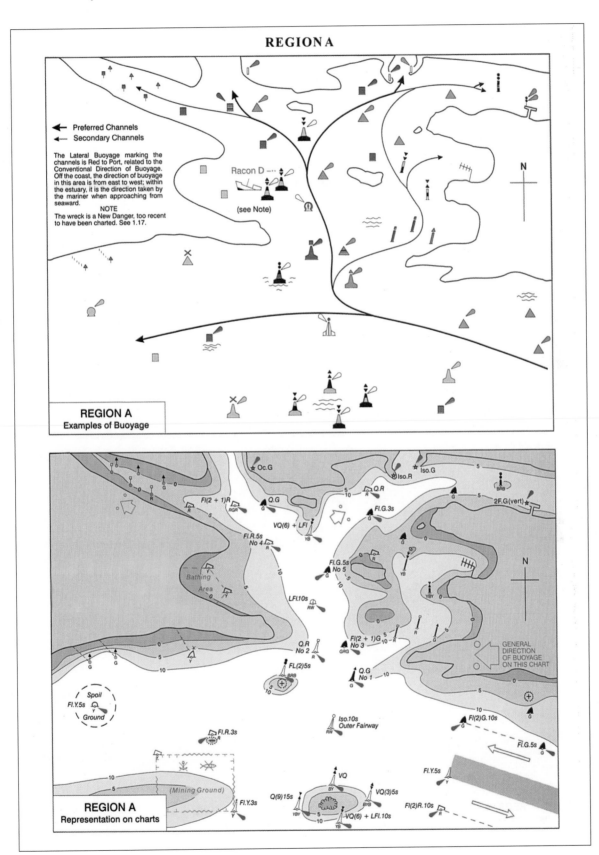

Preferred Channels, Region A

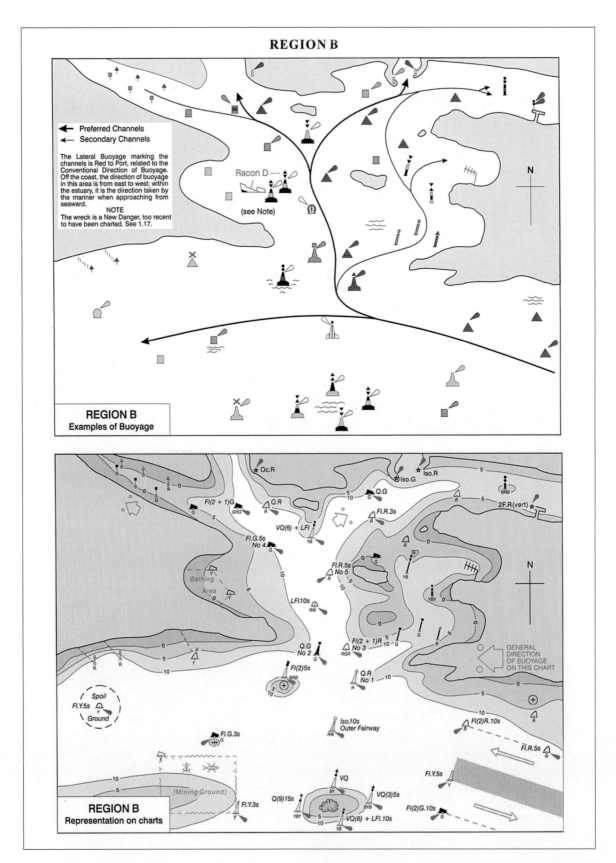

REGION B

REGION B
Examples of Buoyage

Preferred Channels
Secondary Channels

The Lateral Buoyage marking the channels is Red to Port, related to the Conventional Direction of Buoyage. Off the coast, the direction of buoyage in this area is from east to west; within the estuary, it is the direction taken by the mariner when approaching from seaward.

NOTE
The wreck is a New Danger, too recent to have been charted. See 1.17.

Racon D

(see Note)

REGION B
Representation on charts

Preferred Channels, Region B. In Region B red marks are typically even numbered, green are odd (reverse of what is shown).

AIDS AND SERVICES: Q *Buoys, Beacons*

(hence the "red, right, returning" mnemonic) and green to the left, with odd numbers.

Solid red and green colors are reserved for the lateral system and are not found on other types of marks (although red bands are used on both safe-water and isolated danger marks). Red and green lights are also reserved for the lateral system. Quick or very quick flashing lights are used for danger marks and to emphasize bends in channels; composite group flashing (2+1) is used on preferred channel marks where a channel divides, with the color of the light indicating whether the preferred channel is to port or starboard. Other than this, the lights may be any rhythm.

Cardinal System

Isolated offshore buoys do not fit the general framework of an "approach direction"; therefore, a second system of buoyage is used, known as the *cardinal system*. The idea is to set up a buoy or mark in such a way as to indicate on what side a hazard can be safely passed: a southern cardinal mark is set to the south of a hazard and must be passed to its south; a northern cardinal mark is set to the north of a hazard and must be passed to its north. The cardinal system is the same for both IALA Regions A and B, although it is rarely used in Region B. (NOAA's *Nautical Chart Manual* states, "the USCG will not use cardinal buoys in the foreseeable future.")

Black double-cone topmarks are an important feature of the cardinal system. For a north mark, both cones point up; for a south mark, they point down. North and south are easy to remember; east and west are a little more difficult. For east, they form a diamond; for west, an hourglass (which may be thought of as a wineglass; hence, "W").

Cardinal marks have yellow and black horizontal bands. The topmarks "point" to the black band—i.e., if both cones point up (N), the black band is on top; if both point down (S), the black band is on the bottom; if they point top and bottom (E), the yellow band is between black bands; if they point in to each other (W), the black band is between yellow bands.

Cardinal marks have quick or very quick flashing white lights that can be associated with a clock face. North marks are continuous; east marks have three flashes in a group (3 o'clock); south marks have six flashes in a group (6 o'clock) followed by a long flash; and west marks have nine flashes in a group (9 o'clock).

South cardinal mark (left)—the topmarks both point down; and west (right)—the topmarks point in to each other.

The Intracoastal Waterway

In addition to the IALA's System A and System B, modified systems may be employed on specific bodies of water (e.g., U.S. rivers that flow into the Pacific). Of these, the most important for U.S. sailors is that employed on the Intracoastal Waterway (ICW), which stretches from Maine in the northeast, south along the Atlantic seaboard, around Florida, and west around the Gulf of Mexico to Texas.

The IALA Region B system is used in the United States and on the ICW with the modification that it is assumed that the "red, right, returning" rule (see the text) is applied from north to south along the Atlantic coast and from east to west along the Gulf of Mexico coastline. The various waterway marks (buoys and beacons) often have some part colored yellow, which differentiates them from the other IALA System B marks. When you are headed south along the Atlantic coast, red marks are to starboard and green to port; when headed north, the opposite applies. Yel-low triangles go with red marks, yellow squares with green marks, and yellow bars with nonlateral aids (safe water marks, isolated danger marks, and range marks).

The ICW frequently intersects and utilizes stretches of water (e.g., river estuaries) that are governed by the standard IALA Region B rules. If such a stretch of water on the U.S. East Coast is approached from seaward from the south, those stretches that come under the standard IALA Region B rules have the red and green markers on opposite sides of those stretches governed by the ICW rules. Failure to appreciate at which point the switch occurs from one system to the other quickly puts you aground. We discovered this when coming into Fort Lauderdale (Florida) from seaward, and then heading north up the ICW—we left the first red waterway mark to starboard and promptly got stuck.

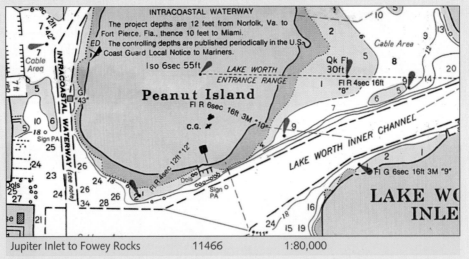

The sea is to the east. On entering Lake Worth inlet, from east to west, the red marks are to starboard (IALA Region B), but as soon as the turn is made to starboard to go north up the Intracoastal Waterway (ICW), the red marks are to port and the green to starboard (the waterway is considered to run north to south).

Isolated Danger, Safe Water, and Special Marks

Isolated danger, safe water, and special marks are used extensively in both IALA Region A and Region B. Isolated danger marks are placed on or over isolated dangers with a limited extent and safe water all around. They use red and black horizontal bands with black double-sphere topmarks. If lit, they have a white light showing a group of two flashes (two spheres, two flashes).

Safe-water marks are used to indicate that there

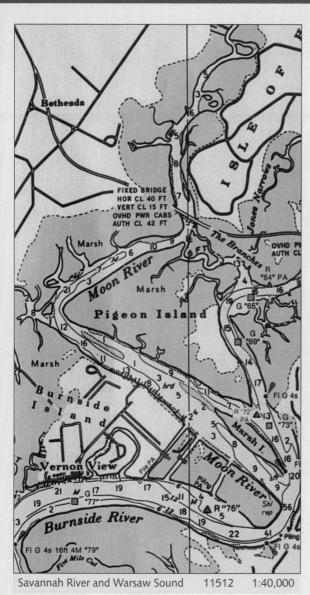

Savannah River and Warsaw Sound   11512   1:40,000

Note that the beacons are "red, left, returning" going upriver, despite the fact that this is IALA Region B, because this is part of the Intracoastal Waterway (ICW), which is considered to run north to south in this area.

areas (e.g., spoil grounds, military firing ranges, cables, recreational areas), TSSs where the use of lateral marks might cause confusion, and similar situations. In other words, there is no physical danger to navigation (boats can pass either side of the mark), but a mariner needs to be alerted to some other danger. They are yellow with a single yellow "X" as a topmark; when lit, it is a yellow light with any flash pattern other than those reserved for the cardinal system, isolated dangers, and safe-water marks.

Features Common to All Buoys and Beacons

The following conventions are followed in both IALA Regions A and B:

> The position of a buoy or beacon is indicated by a small circle (without a central dot) in the middle of the base of the symbol. (The exception is the use of triangles and squares to denote beacons on many NOAA charts, in which case the position is presumed to be at the center of the symbol.) Note that the circle is purely symbolic in terms of the circle that will be made by the buoy as it moves around its mooring (the watch circle); *it does not reflect the real-life watch circle, which may be larger* (especially if the buoy is in deep water or in an area of large tides so that at low tide it has significant scope). The buoy position on a chart is at best approximate and should, in

Yellow special mark. This is a pillar buoy.

is navigable water throughout the area. They are used as centerline, midchannel, or landfall buoys. They have red and white vertical stripes and, if lit, either a white light with an occulting, isophase, single long flash, or a Morse "A" (dot, dash) pattern.

Special marks are used to demarcate various

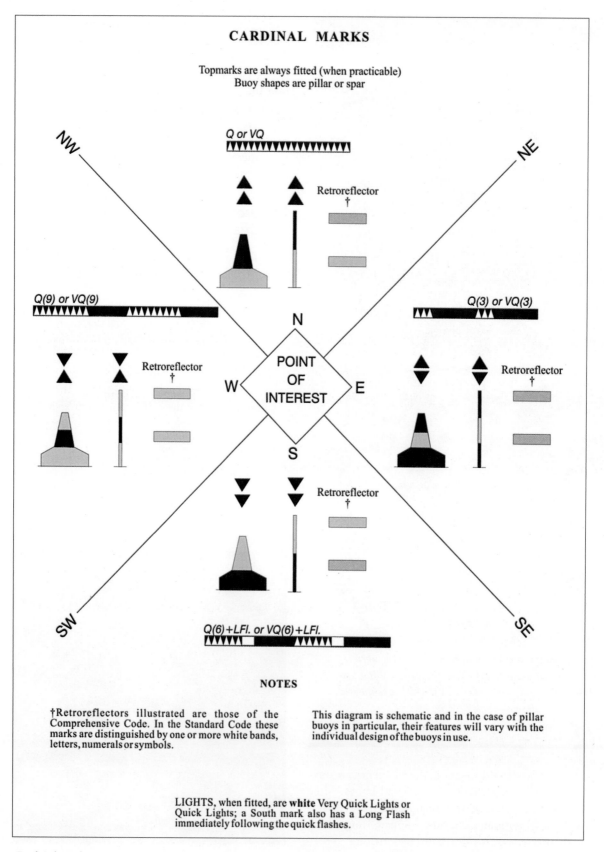

CARDINAL MARKS

Topmarks are always fitted (when practicable)
Buoy shapes are pillar or spar

Q or VQ

NW

NE

Retroreflector †

Q(9) or VQ(9)

Q(3) or VQ(3)

Retroreflector †

N

POINT OF INTEREST

W   E

S

Retroreflector †

SW

SE

Q(6)+LFl. or VQ(6)+LFl.

NOTES

†Retroreflectors illustrated are those of the Comprehensive Code. In the Standard Code these marks are distinguished by one or more white bands, letters, numerals or symbols.

This diagram is schematic and in the case of pillar buoys in particular, their features will vary with the individual design of the buoys in use.

LIGHTS, when fitted, are **white** Very Quick Lights or Quick Lights; a South mark also has a Long Flash immediately following the quick flashes.

Cardinal marks.

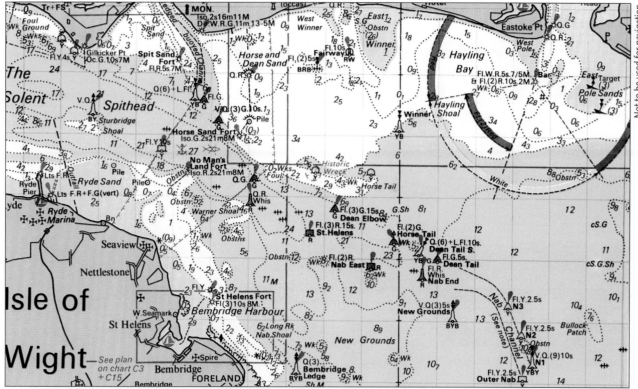

*A mix of lateral and cardinal marks. This is Region IALA A, so when approaching a channel (the Nab Channel) from seaward, the green lateral buoys are to starboard and the red to port (as opposed to red to starboard and green to port in IALA Region B). Otherwise the two regions are similar: nun buoys to starboard, cans to port; even numbers on red buoys, odd on green; etc. **Additional features:** The **cardinal buoys** on this chart can be identified by their topmarks, which also indicate on what side they should be passed. **Note also:** a vertically striped red and white, spherical, **safe-water buoy** (center top). Various yellow **spherical buoys** (special marks). A number of **wrecks**, stranded (in the NE quadrant) and sunk, some considered dangerous (with a dotted line around them) and some not (the sunk wreck symbol with no dotted line). Nonstandard water colors.*

some sense, be considered unreliable (buoys can get moved by storms and other forces).

- The buoy symbol is generally a stylized representation of what it looks like as seen from the side (i.e., in elevation). The principal shapes are as follows:

  1. conical/"nun" (looks like a pointed cone; typically used for unlit buoys to starboard)

  2. can/cylindrical (looks like a cylinder on end; typically used for unlit buoys to port)

  3. spherical (the part above the waterline is shaped like a sphere; typically used as unlit safe-water or midchannel buoys)

  4. pillar (typically a lattice tower mounted on a flat base; used almost anywhere, commonly as a base on which to mount a light)

  5. spar (in the form of a pole or a long cylinder,

floating upright; used almost anywhere, commonly with a light)

  6. barrel (looks like a cylinder on its side; used only as a special mark)

  7. the term *super buoy* is used for very large buoys of any shape.

- A variety of topmarks are used. In the lateral system, triangular topmarks are used to starboard, square to port, and spherical on safe-water and isolated danger marks. The cardinal system uses two triangles in different configurations (see Q130.3).

- In the case of beacons, the only shape that has any significance is the topmark.

- Buoy symbols are generally shown on a chart as italic (hydrographic feature), which distinguishes them from beacons (shown vertical; a

Q *Buoys, Beacons*

Lighted green pillar buoy with a gong in its base.

Unlit green can buoy.

Red and white (safe-water) pillar buoy on station. Note the single spherical topmark.

A red pillar buoy on station.

A beacon used as a range marker.

Q Buoys, Beacons

topographic feature because they are rigidly fixed to the seabed or land).

- Italic text is used on any label for a buoy (hydrographic feature) and vertical letters for a beacon (topographic feature) (see chapter 5).

- Green buoys and beacons are given odd numbers, red even numbers. The numbers increase from seaward as you move upstream.

- The following characteristics of buoys may be given, usually (but not always) in the following order: color (omitted if black); shape (if unlit); numbers or letters; flash character (if lit); and fog signal (if so equipped). The following examples are from Muscongus Bay, Maine, United States (note the use of italics throughout because they are floating aids):

1. *R "20M" Fl R 4s WHISTLE* (a red buoy, shape unspecified, number 20M, flashing red every 4 seconds, with a whistle-type foghorn)

2. *R N "14"* (a red nun buoy, number 14)

3. *R G* (red and green; no other information)

4. *N R G* (nun, red and green; no other information)

5. *C "1"* (can buoy, number 1; no other information)

6. *G "1" Fl G 6s BELL* (a green buoy, shape unspecified, number 1, flashing green every 6 seconds, with a bell-type foghorn)

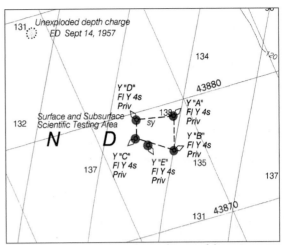

Yellow buoys as special marks, in this case delineating a Surface and Subsurface Scientific Testing Area. The buoys are privately maintained (Priv). Note the unexploded depth charge, Existence Doubtful (ED).

- Lighted buoys and beacons generally have a flare added to the symbol (NOAA uses the flare on beacons but puts a magenta circle or disc around the position circle on buoys). This flare or disc is magenta for both red and green lights; the light color will be identified in a label (if no color is given, it is white). Green buoys have green lights; red buoys have red lights; a buoy marking a split in a channel has a light with a color that indicates the preferred side on which to leave the buoy (port or starboard); and a safe-water buoy generally has a white light.

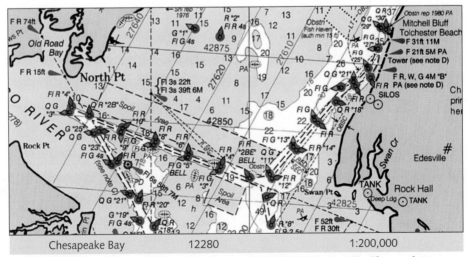

A mass of buoys marking channels in the Chesapeake Bay (IALA Region B). Chart scale is 1:200,000. This chart is hard to read! There are range lights, a direction light, a sectored light, numerous lit buoys, various stranded and sunken wrecks, a spoil area and fish haven, and numerous other details. I would want a larger-scale chart before entering these waters.

Q *Buoys, Beacons*

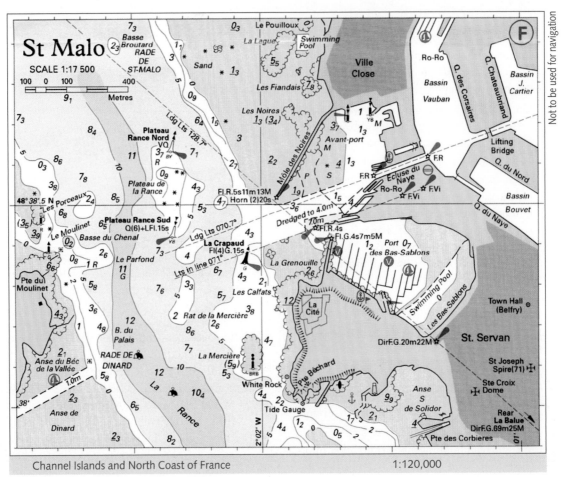

Buoyage in IALA Region A. Mostly cardinal marks, but also an isolated danger mark (in the center south) with black, red, black (BRB) horizontal stripes and two spherical topmarks, and a couple of mooring buoys. Nonstandard water colors.

Q *Buoys, Beacons*

	Buoys and Beacons		
1		Position of buoy	
2		Green and black. Note that black is used on charts as the default color for green if green is not used. NOAA frequently uses a colored diamond to identify the color of red and green buoys.	

3		Single colors other than green and black. Note that the default color for red is to leave the symbol uncolored (white). NOAA frequently uses a colored diamond to identify the color of red and green buoys.	
4		Multiple colors in horizontal bands; the color sequence is from top to bottom	
5		Multiple colors in vertical or diagonal stripes; the darker color is given first	
6		Retroflecting material. Note: Retroflecting material may be fitted to some unlit marks. Charts do not usually show it. Under IALA Recommendations, black bands will appear blue under a spotlight.	

Lighted Marks

7		Lighted marks on standard charts. Note the magenta circle used for buoys on NOAA charts in lieu of a flare.	
8		Lighted marks on multicolored charts	

Topmarks and Radar Reflectors

9		IALA System buoy topmarks (beacon topmarks shown upright). The significance of these topmarks is explained in Q130.3.	
10		Beacon with topmark, color, radar reflector, and designation. Note the use of vertical letters because it is rigidly attached to the ground or seabed.	

| 11 | | Buoy with topmark, color, radar reflector, and designation. Note the use of italics for a floating navaid. Note: Radar reflectors on floating marks are usually not charted. | | |

Buoy Shapes

20			Conical buoy, Nun buoy	N		
21			Can or cylindrical buoy	C		
22			Spherical buoy	SP		
23			Pillar buoy	P		
24			Spar buoy, Spindle buoy	S		
25			Barrel buoy			
26			Super buoy			

Light Floats

| 30 | Fl.G.3s Name | Light float as part of IALA System. A light float is an unmanned light vessel. | | Fl G 3s Name |
| 31 | Fl.10s | Light float (unmanned light vessel) not part of IALA System | | Fl(2) 10s 11M |

Q *Buoys, Beacons*

Mooring Buoys

40	⚓ # ⚓ # ⚓ # ⚓	Mooring buoys. Note the "mooring ring" in the top of the buoy symbol, not to be confused with the positioning circle in its base.	⚓
41	⚓ Fl.Y.2·5s	Lighted mooring buoy (example)	⚓	⚓ Fl Y 2s
42	(trot, with berth numbers ① ②)	Trot, mooring buoys with ground tackle and berth numbers	
43	⚓ 〰〰〰〰〰〰	Mooring buoy with telegraphic or telephonic communication	
44	Small Craft Moorings	Numerous moorings (example)	⚓ (5 buoys) Moorings

Special-Purpose Buoys

50	⚓ DZ	Firing danger area (danger zone) buoy	
51	⚓ Target	Target	
52	⚓ Marker Ship	Marker Ship	
53	⚓ Barge	Barge	
54	⚓	Degaussing range buoy (see N25)	
55	⚓	Cable buoy	⚓ Tel
56	⚓	Spoil ground buoy	⚓

57	⚲ Y	Buoy marking outfall	⚲
58	▱ ODAS	ODAS-buoy (Ocean-Data-Acquisition System). Data-collecting buoy of super-buoy size (buoys for collecting weather and oceanographic data). Also LANBY (Large Automated Navigational Buoy) and SPM (Single Point Mooring) for tankers.	▱ ODAS
		Special-purpose buoys	BW or ⚲Y ⚲ BW or ⚲Y ⚲
59	⚲ Y	Wave recorder, Current meter	
60		Seaplane anchorage buoy	⚲ AERO
61		Buoy marking traffic separation scheme	
62	⚲ Y	Buoy marking recreation zone	

Seasonal Buoys

70	⚲ (priv) Y	Buoy privately maintained (example)	⚲ Priv (maintained by private interests, use with caution)
71	⚲ (Apr-Oct) Y	Temporary buoy (example)	

Beacons

80	⬥ ⊙Bn	Beacon in general, characteristics unknown or chart scale too small to show	□Bn ⬥ Bn
81	⬥ BW ⊙Bn BW	Beacon with color, no distinctive topmark	□ RW ▲ ⬛ ⬥ BW
82	⬥ R ⬥ BY ⬥ BRB	Beacons with colors and topmarks (examples)	⬥ R ⬥ BY

Q *Buoys, Beacons*

83	BRB	BRB	Beacon on submerged rock (topmark as appropriate). Note the submerged rock symbol incorporated into the base.

Minor Impermanent Marks Usually in Drying Areas (Lateral Mark of Minor Channel)

90	⊥		Stake, Pole. A stake or pole is moderately substantial, as compared to a withy (see Q92).	∘ Pole • Pole	⊥
91	**PORT HAND** Υ	**STARBOARD HAND** ↟	Perch, Stake. A perch is a staff placed on top of a buoy, rock, or shoal.	∘ Stake • Stake	⊥
92	⊼	⇞	Withy. A withy is a stick or branch pushed into the seabed.		

Minor Marks, Usually on Land

100	⚶	Cairn. A cairn is a man-made pile of rocks.	⊙CAIRN ⌀cairn	⊙CAIRN ⌀cairn △ ⚶
101	▫ Mk	Colored or white mark		

Beacon Towers

110	☖ ▐ ☖ ▲ ☖ ☗ R G R G BY BRB	Beacon towers without and with topmarks and colors (examples)	▫ RW	☖ ▐ ☖ ▲ R G R G
111	⛫	Lattice beacon		

Q Buoys, Beacons

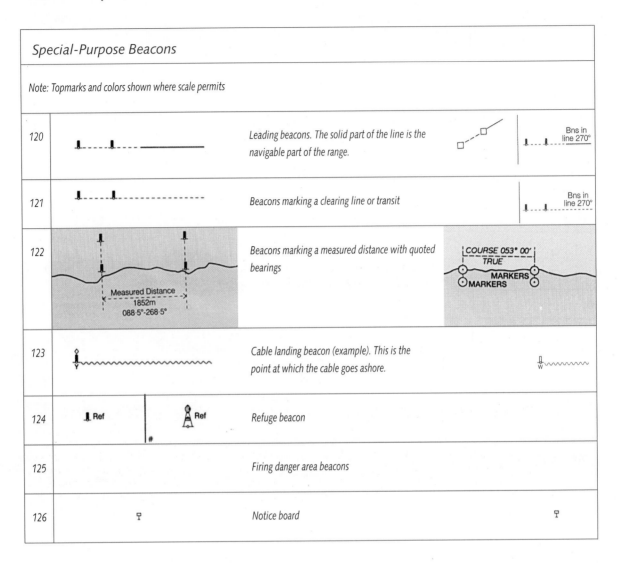

Special-Purpose Beacons

Note: Topmarks and colors shown where scale permits

120		Leading beacons. The solid part of the line is the navigable part of the range.	Bns in line 270°
121		Beacons marking a clearing line or transit	Bns in line 270°
122	Measured Distance 1852m 088·5°-268·5°	Beacons marking a measured distance with quoted bearings	COURSE 053° 00' TRUE MARKERS MARKERS
123		Cable landing beacon (example). This is the point at which the cable goes ashore.	
124	Ref / Ref	Refuge beacon	
125		Firing danger area beacons	
126		Notice board	

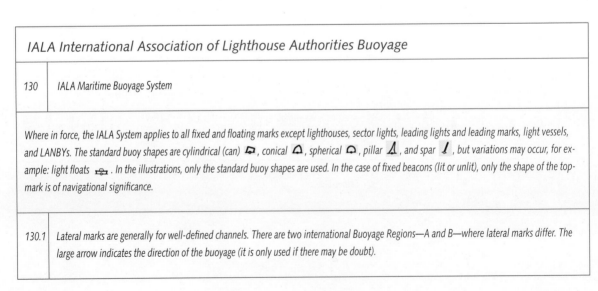

IALA International Association of Lighthouse Authorities Buoyage

130	IALA Maritime Buoyage System

Where in force, the IALA System applies to all fixed and floating marks except lighthouses, sector lights, leading lights and leading marks, light vessels, and LANBYs. The standard buoy shapes are cylindrical (can) , conical , spherical , pillar , and spar , but variations may occur, for example: light floats . In the illustrations, only the standard buoy shapes are used. In the case of fixed beacons (lit or unlit), only the shape of the topmark is of navigational significance.

130.1	Lateral marks are generally for well-defined channels. There are two international Buoyage Regions—A and B—where lateral marks differ. The large arrow indicates the direction of the buoyage (it is only used if there may be doubt).

AIDS AND SERVICES: Q *Buoys, Beacons*

Q Buoys, Beacons

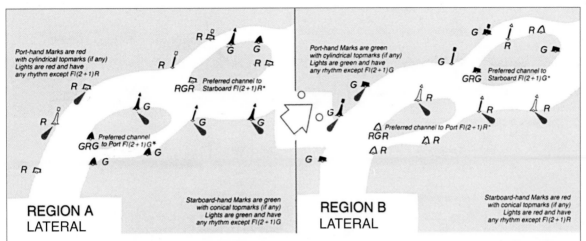

A preferred channel buoy may also be a pillar or a spar. All preferred channel marks have horizontal bands of color. Where for exceptional reasons an Authority considers that a green color for buoys is not satisfactory, black may be used.

130.2 Direction of Buoyage. The direction of buoyage is that taken when approaching a harbor from seaward or along coasts, the direction determined by buoyage authorities, normally clockwise around landmasses.

 Symbol showing direction of buoyage where not obvious.

130.3 Cardinal Marks indicating navigable water to the named side of the marks.

All marks are the same in Regions A and B. Cardinal marks are distinguished both by coloration (yellow and black horizontal bands) and by a pair of triangular topmarks, one on top of the other. A north cardinal mark has a black band above a yellow band, with both triangular topmarks pointing upward (to the north). A south cardinal mark has the yellow band above the black, with both topmarks pointing down (to the south). An east cardinal mark has black bands at the top and bottom, with yellow in between; the top topmark points upward, the bottom down (together, they form a diamond). A west cardinal mark has yellow bands at the top and bottom, with black in between; the two topmarks point in toward one another. Note that in all cases, the two topmarks point toward the location of the black band(s), which helps to remember the banding on the marks.

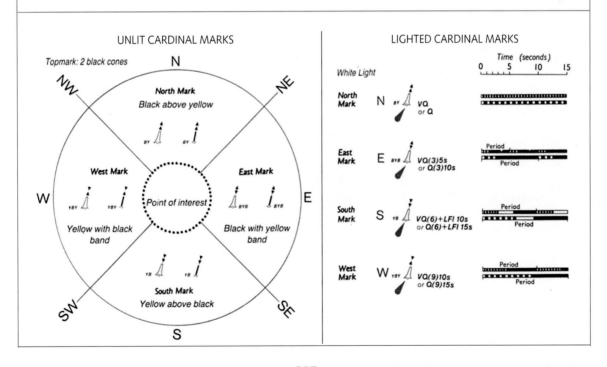

130.4	Isolated Danger Marks stationed over dangers with navigable water around them. The topmark consists of two black spheres, one above the other. Body: black with red horizontal band(s).
	BRB BRB | BRB BRB Fl(2) *white light*

130.5	Safe-Water Marks such as midchannel and landfall marks. If a topmark is used (it frequently is not), it is a single sphere. The light may be isophase (Iso), occulting (Oc), Morse "A" (Mo(A)), or long flashing with a period of 10 seconds. Body: red and white vertical stripes.
	RW RW RW | RW RW RW Oc, or Iso, or L Fl 10s, or Mo (A) *white light*

130.6	Special Marks not primarily to assist navigation but to indicate special features. Body (shape optional): yellow . Topmark (if any): yellow "X". Yellow light (rhythm optional). In special cases, yellow can be in conjunction with another color.
	Y Y Y | Y Y Y Fl.Y etc.

On NOAA charts, BEACONS with IALA System topmarks are charted by upright symbols, e.g., ⬥ ⬥ ⬥ ⬥ (minor beacon) or on smaller-scale

charts: ₒBn ★Bn Beacon towers are charted: ⬧ ⬧ ⬧ ⬧ etc.

RADAR REFLECTORS on buoys and beacons are not generally charted.

LIGHT FLOATS: The IALA System is not usually applied to large light floats (replacing manned lightships) but may be applied to smaller light floats.

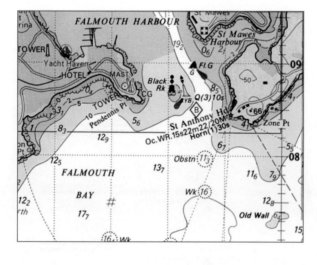

Three different types of buoys next to each other: lateral (◣), cardinal (♦), and isolated danger (♦).

Falmouth to Fowey	BA 5602.2	1:75,000

Q *Buoys, Beacons*

	Supplementary National Symbols	
a	Bell buoy	⚲BELL ◁BELL
b	Gong buoy	⚲GONG ◁GONG
c	Whistle buoy	⚲WHIS ◁WHIS
d	Fairway buoy (RWVS) (Red and White Vertical Stripes)	⚲RW
e	Midchannel buoy (RWVS)	⚲RW
f	Starboard-hand buoy (entering from seaward-U.S. waters)	⚲R "2"
g	Port-hand buoy (entering from seaward-U.S. waters)	⚲"1" ⚲"1"
h	Bifurcation, Junction, Isolated danger, Wreck, and Obstruction buoys. The top color indicates the preferred channel; that is, when approaching from seaward, if it is red, in IALA Region B it is preferred to leave the buoy to starboard; if green, to leave it to port.	⚲RB ⚲BR ⚲RG ⚲GR
i	Warping buoy	⚲
j	Quarantine buoy	⚲Y
k	Explosive anchorage buoy	⚲Explos Anch
l	Compass adjustment buoy	⚲Deviation
m	Fish trap (area) buoy (BWHB) (Black and White Horizontal Bands)	⚲BW
n	Anchorage buoy (marks limits)	⚲W
o	Checkered	⚲ Chec
p	Diagonal bands	⚲ Diag
q	Black	B
r	Triangular beacon	▲R Bn △RG Bn
	Black beacon	☐B Bn
	Square and other shaped beacons	■G Bn ☐GR Bn ☐W Bn ☐B Bn
	Color unknown	☐Bn
s	Mooring buoy with telegraphic communications	⚓Tel ⚓Tel
t	Mooring buoy with telephonic communications	⚓T ⚓T
u	Lighted beacon	⊥

Section R: Fog Signals

Fog signals are fairly short-range aids and are, for various reasons, unreliable position indicators. Several different types are in use, most of which are self-evident (e.g., a bell) but some of which are not, as follows:

- horn
- bell
- whistle
- gong
- explosive: the short report produced by the sound of an explosion

- diaphone: a low-pitched sound, generally ending in a "grunt" produced by the release of compressed air
- siren: a higher-pitched sound produced by the release of compressed air through a rotary device

Fog signals on land are usually timed to go off in a particular sequence over a specified period. This is often noted on the chart similar to light-flash characteristics and periods. Many fog signals mounted on buoys (e.g., bells and gongs) use energy from the waves and, therefore, are erratic and do not function in a flat sea.

General						
1	(((°	⊿	⊙	Position of fog signal. Type of fog signal not stated	Fog Sig)))	)))

Types of Fog Signals, with Abbreviations			
10	Explos	*Explosive*	*GUN*
11	Dia	*Diaphone*	*DIA*
12	Siren	*Siren*	*SIREN*
13	Horn	*Horn (nautophone, reed, tyfon)*	*HORN*
14	Bell	*Bell*	*BELL*
15	Whis	*Whistle*	*WHIS*
16	Gong	*Gong*	*GONG*

Examples of Fog Signal Descriptions				
20	Fl.3s70m29M Siren Mo(N)60s ‡	*Siren at a lighthouse, giving a long blast followed by a short one (Morse "N"), repeated every 60 seconds*	Fl 3s 70m 29M Siren Mo(N)60s	
21	‡ Bell	*Wave-actuated bell buoy*	BELL	BELL
22	Q(6)+LFl.15s Horn(1)15sWhis YB ‡	*Light buoy, with horn giving a single blast every 15 seconds, in conjunction with a wave-actuated whistle*	Q(6)+LFl 15s HORN(1) 15s WHIS	Q(6)+LFl 15s HORN WHIS YB
	‡ *The fog signal symbol may be omitted when a description of the signal is given.*			

S *Radar, Radio, Electronic Position-Fixing Systems*

Section S: Radar, Radio, Electronic Position-Fixing Systems

This section is primarily concerned with technology aimed at shipping rather than the recreational boater, or else technology that is fast becoming obsolete (e.g., few recreational boats carry radio direction finding [RDF] equipment these days; Decca and Omega have been phased out; and funding for Loran-C was terminated in the U.S. in 2010, although at the time of writing—2011—it was reported to still be operational). It should be noted that in Europe Loran-C is being updated to "enhanced" Loran, otherwise known as eLoran, to provide an alternative to GPS should the GPS system fail.

Section S begins with several types of devices related to radar, as follows:

- A coast radar station is a shore-based station that a ship can contact by radio to obtain a position.

- A *ramark* transmits continuously on radar frequency, producing a line on a ship's radar display that indicates the bearing to the ramark.

- A radar transponder beacon (racon) is a beacon that emits a characteristic signal when activated by the emission of a ship's radar, creating an image that indicates the racon's position.

Next is a section that discusses RDF (S10–S16). As noted, few recreational boaters carry this equipment and, in general, the facilities associated with it are being phased out. Decca (S20–S25) is history (as of March 31, 2000). Loran-C was set for decommissioning in the United States in 2000. On January 1, 2000, the government announced it would keep it going in its waters as a backup to GPS (there was considerable concern about relying solely on GPS), but funding was terminated in 2010; as noted above, in Europe Loran-C is being upgraded to eLoran (which has a positional accuracy of around 8 m) as an alternative to GPS, with the intention of keeping it at least until 2022. S30 to S37 provides information on the lattice overlay on charts associated with Loran-C. Omega (S40–S42) is also history, canceled on September 30, 1997.

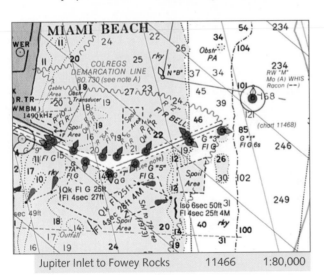

| Jupiter Inlet to Fowey Rocks | 11466 | 1:80,000 |

Racon marking the entrance to the channel into Miami. Note that this is a safe-water buoy (red and white vertical stripes) with the white light flashing Morse A [Mo(a)—dot, dash], which is a common flash pattern for safe-water buoys. At the inner end of the channel is the symbol for a radio beacon, but with no further identification or details given.

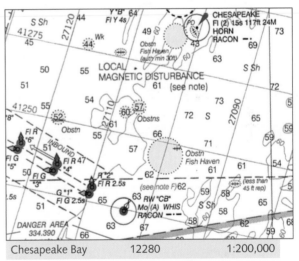

| Chesapeake Bay | 12280 | 1:200,000 |

Racons at the mouth of Chesapeake Bay. Note that the northern one is a fixed structure (vertical type), whereas the southern one is a safe-water buoy (italic letters; red and white vertical stripes). The PD (Position Doubtful) alongside the northern one refers to the dangerous wreck symbol, not the beacon ("PD" is sloped; if it referred to the beacon, it would be upright). There are various other wrecks and obstructions, some wire-dragged depths, a TSS, parts of three other area boundaries (one dashed and highlighted with a magenta band, one simply dashed, and one T-dashed), a local magnetic disturbance, and a Loran-C lattice overprint (the diagonal lines).

	Radar			
1	⊙ Ra	Coast radar station, providing range and bearing service on request	⊙ Ra	
2	⊙ Ramark	Ramark, radar beacon transmitting continuously	⊙ Ramark	
3.1	⊙ Racon(Z) (3cm)	Radar transponder beacon, with Morse identification, responding within the 3 cm (X-) band	⊙ RACON	
3.2	⊙ Racon(Z) (10cm)	Radar transponder beacon, with Morse identification, responding within the 10 cm (S-) band		
3.3	⊙ Racon(Z)	Radar transponder beacon, responding within the 3 cm (X-) and the 10 cm (S-) band		
3.4	Racon Obscd Racon(P)	Radar transponder beacon with sector of obscured reception		
	Racon(Z) ⊙ Racon(Z)	Radar transponder beacon with sector of reception		
3.5	Racon ⊙ — Racon ⊙ Racons ≠ 270°	Radar transponder beacons with bearing line		
	Racon ★ — Racon ★ Lts ≠ 270° Racons ≠ 270°	Radar transponder beacons coincident with leading light		
3.6	Racon Racon	Floating marks with radar transponder beacons	RACON (—) R "2" Fl R 4s	Racon
4	ᨆ	Radar reflector. The radar reflector symbol is no longer used on NOAA charts.	ᨆ Ra Ref	ᨆ
5	ᨆ	Radar-conspicuous feature	ᨆ Ra (conspic)	ᨆ

S *Radar, Radio, Electronic Position-Fixing Systems*

Radio

10	(symbol) Name RC	Circular (nondirectional) marine or aero-marine radio beacon	(symbol) R Bn, RC
11	(symbol) RD 269·5° RD	Directional radio beacon with bearing line	(symbol) RD 072°30' RD
	(symbol) RD Lts≠270° RD 270°	Directional radio beacon coincident with leading lights	
12	(symbol) RW	Rotating-pattern radio beacon	(symbol) RW
13	(symbol) Consol	Consol beacon	(symbol) CONSOL Bn 190 kHz MMF ▀▀. / (symbol) CONSOL
14	(symbol) RG	Radio direction-finding station	(symbol) RDF
15	(symbol) R	Coast radio station providing QTG service	○ R Sta / (symbol) R
16	(symbol) Aero RC	Aeronautical radio beacon	(symbol) AERO R Bn

Electronic Position-Fixing Systems

Decca

20	AB AC AD	Identification of Lattice Patterns	AB AC AD
21	————————	Line of Position (LOP)	————
22	————————	Line of Position representing Zone Limit (or, on larger scales) other intermediate LOPs	
23	— — — — —	Half-lane LOP	
24	— — — — — ·	LOP from adjoining Chain (on Interchain Fixing Charts)	

| 25 | *(6) A12* | Lane value, with Chain designator (Interchain charts only) and Zone designator. | *A 12* |

Note: A Decca Chain Coverage Diagram is given when patterns from more than one Chain appear on a chart. LOPs are normally theoretical ones; if Fixed Error is included, an explanatory note is given.

	Loran-C		
30	7970–W 7970–X	Identification of Loran-C-Rates	9960–Y 9960–Z
31		Line of Position (LOP)	
32		LOP representing time difference value of an integral thousandths (microseconds)	
33		LOP beyond reliable groundwave service area	
34		LOP from adjoining Chain	
35		LOP from adjoining Chain beyond reliable groundwave service area	
36	7970–X 33000	LOP labeled with rate and full microsecond value	9960–Z–58000
37	050	LOP labeled with final three digits only	050

Note: A Loran-C Chain Diagram may be given if rates from more than one Chain appear on a chart.
An explanatory note is given if LOPs include propagation delays.

Omega								
40	AB	AC	BC	Charted station pairs		DF	CF	AC
41				Line of Position (LOP)				
42	297	AB–300		Lane values		DF-702		
	Note: A cautionary note draws attention to the need to consult Propagation Prediction Correction (PPC) tables. An explanatory note draws attention to the unreliability of LOPs within 450 n miles of a transmitter.							

Satellite Navigation Systems								
50	WGS	WGS 72	WGS 84	World Geodetic System, 1972 or 1984		WGS	WGS 72	WGS 84
	Note: A note may be shown to indicate the shifts of latitude and longitude, in hundredths of a minute, which should be made to satellite-derived positions (which are referred to WGS) to relate them to the chart.							

Section T: Services

Section T contains miscellaneous information on various types of pilot, coast guard, and signal stations. This is primarily of interest to ships rather than recreational boaters.

T *Services*

Pilotage				
1.1	⬥	Boarding place, position of a Pilot-Cruising Vessel	Pilots ⬥	⬥
1.2	⬥ Name	Boarding place, position of a Pilot-Cruising Vessel, with name (e.g., District, Port)		⬥ Name
1.3	⬥ Note	Boarding place, position of a Pilot-Cruising Vessel, with note (e.g., for Tanker, Disembarkation)		⬥ (see note)
1.4	⬥ H	Pilots transferred by helicopter		
2	■ Pilot look-out	Pilot office with Pilot look-out, Pilot look-out		
3	■ Pilots	Pilot office	⊙ PIL STA	■ Pilots
4	Port Name (Pilots)	Port with Pilotage Service		

Coast Guard, Rescue Stations				
10	■ CG ⊙ CG P CG	Coast Guard station. The addition of a name for a coast guard station generally implies an important station with a 24-hour-a-day watch-keeping capability.	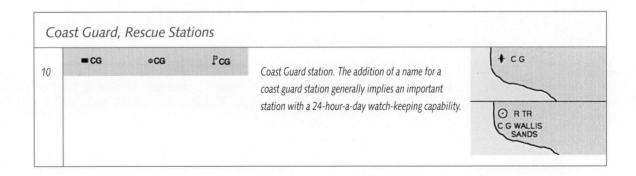	

11	▬CG✦ ◉CG✦ ℙCG✦	Coast Guard station with Rescue station. The rescue station symbol is the black oval with a line across it.	
12	✦	Rescue station, Lifeboat station, Rocket station (LSS = Life Saving Station)	✦ ✦ LS S
13	🛥✦ ✦	Lifeboat lying at a mooring	
14	Ref	Refuge for shipwrecked mariners	

Signal Stations

20	◉SS	Signal station in general (SS = Signal Station)	⊙S S
21	◉SS(INT)	Signal station, showing International Port Traffic Signals	
22	◉SS(Traffic)	Traffic signal station. Port entry and departure signals	
23	◉SS(Port Control)	Port control signal station	○ HECP
24	◉SS(Lock)	Lock signal station	
25.1	◉SS(Bridge)	Bridge passage signal station	
25.2	⚓F. Traffic Sig	Bridge lights, including traffic signals	
26	◉SS	Distress signal station	
27	◉SS	Telegraph station	
28	◉SS(Storm)	Storm signal station	S Sig Sta

29	⊙ SS(Weather)	Weather signal station, Wind signal station	⊙ NWS SIG STA	*National Weather Service signal station*
30	⊙ SS(Ice)	Ice signal station		
31	⊙ SS(Time)	Time signal station		
32.1	‡	Tide scale or gauge	○ Tide gauge	
32.2	⊙ Tide gauge	Automatically recording tide gauge		
33	⊙ SS(Tide)	Tidal signal station		
34	⊙ SS(Stream)	Tidal stream signal station		
35	⊙ SS(Danger)	Danger signal station		
36	⊙ SS(Firing)	Firing practice signal station		

Supplementary National Symbols		
a	Bell (on land)	○ BELL
b		
c	Marine police station	○ MARINE POLICE
d	Fireboat station	○ FIREBOAT STATION
e	Notice board	무
f	Lookout station; Watch tower	⊙ LOOK TR ▲
g	Semaphore	Sem
h	Park Ranger station	◉

U *Small-Craft Facilities*

There is an ever-increasing tendency to add to charts information of interest to small-boat owners. To date, other than the marina symbol, no international symbology has been developed in connection with this tendency; therefore, self-explanatory labels are used.

U *Small-Craft Facilities*

	Small-Craft Facilities	
1.1	⚓	Boat harbor, Marina
1.2		Yacht berths without facilities
2		Visitors' berth
3		Visitors' mooring
4		Yacht club, Sailing club
5		Slipway
6		Boat hoist
7		Public landing, Steps, Ladder
8		Sailmaker
9		Boatyard
10		Public house, Inn
11		Restaurant
12		Chandler
13		Provisions
14		Bank, Exchange office
15		Physician, Doctor
16		Pharmacy, Chemist
17		Water tap
18		Fuel station (petrol, diesel)
19		Electricity
20		Bottle gas
21		Showers

22	Launderette	
23	Public toilets	
24	Post box	
25	Public telephone	
26	Refuse bin	
27	Car park	
28	Parking for boats and trailers	
29	Caravan site	
30	Camping site	⛺
31	Water police	
32	Marina facilities	

International

Marina Facilities may be tabulated on harbour charts and large-scale coastal charts. ● indicates that the facility is available at the marina itself. Laundrettes etc. located outside the marina are not included. The facilities may not be available outside normal working hours. All marinas have water, toilets and rubbish disposal.

MARINA FACILITIES

	Diesel	Petrol	Bottle gas	Electricity	Repairs	Scrubbing berth	Boat hoist	Launching slip	Chandlery	Provisions	Laundrette	Bar	Showers	VHF Radio	Telephone Numbers
Bank's Quay	●	●	●	●				●	●				●	●	(02013) 4299
Beach Harbour Yacht Club	●	●	●	●				●	●	●			●	●	(0202) 707321
Grain Wharf Yacht Centre	●	●	●	●				●	●	●		●	●	●	(09295) 2650
Quay East								●	●				●		(0202) 685335

United States

No	LOCATION	TIDES	DEPTH	APPROACH-FEET (REPORTED)	ALONGSIDE-FEET (REPORTED)	ELECTRICITY-MOORINGS-BERTHS (TRANSIENT)	RAMP SURFACED-NATURAL	REPAIRS HULL-MOTOR-RADIO	MARINE RAILWAY-FEET	LIFT CAPACITY-TONS	BOAT RENTAL CANOE-ROW-MOTOR	CHARTER-HOUSE-SAIL	FOOD-LODGING-CAMPING	PUMP-OUT STATION	TOILETS-SHOWERS-LAUNDRY	WINTER STORAGE WET-DRY	NAUTICAL-CHART SALES	WATER-ICE	GROCERIES	BAIT-TACKLE-HARDWARE	DIESEL-OIL-GASOLINE
1	LAS VEGAS BOAT			80	20		S	HM					M		F C	T	P	WD	C	W I	GH BT	G
2	LAKE MEAD MAR			80	15	B E	S	HM					M		FL		T	P	WD	C	W I	DG
3	HEMENWAY HARBOR			80			S															
4	TEMPLE BAR HAR			80	15		SN						M	H	FLC		TSL P	WD	C	W I	GH BT	G
5	ECHO BAY RESORT			35	35	BM	S	M					M	H	FLC		TSL P	WD	C	W I	GH BT	G
6	OVERTON BEACH			100			S						M		F C		TSL	WD		W I G	BT G	
7	CALLVILLE BAY M			100	40		S						M	H	F C		TS P	WD		W I G	B	G

(+) DENOTES HOURS LATER   (-) DENOTES HOURS EARLIER
THE LOCATIONS OF THE ABOVE PUBLIC MARINE FACILITIES ARE SHOWN ON THE CHART BY LARGE PURPLE NUMBERS.
THE TABULATED "APPROACH - FEET (REPORTED)" IS THE DEPTH AVAILABLE FROM THE NEAREST NATURAL OR DREDGED CHANNEL TO THE FACILITY.
THE TABULATED "PUMPING STATION" IS DEFINED AS FACILITIES AVAILABLE FOR PUMPING OUT BOAT HOLDING TANKS.
(H) APPROACH DEPTH FLUCTUATES WITH LAKE LEVELS.

Part 3

Appendix

Index to *INT-1*

Section letters and numbers refer to chapters 6 to 8.

Glossary and Acronyms

A.817 (19) a standard of the IMO governing electronic charts and equipment used to display them.

AIS Automatic Identification System—an automated tracking system for identifying, locating, and displaying information between vessels.

ARCS Admiralty Raster Chart Service—a raster chart format developed and controlled by the British Admiralty.

ATON Aid to Navigation—buoys, beacons, fog signals, lights, and so forth serving the interests of safe navigation.

BA British Admiralty, the agency responsible for charting U.K. waters.

Bathymetric lines lines of equal depth (like contour lines on land).

Beacon lighted or unlighted aid to navigation rigidly attached to the earth's surface.

BSB File Format raster chart format developed in the U.S. by MapTech in conjunction with NOAA.

Cable one tenth of a nautical mile (i.e., 200 yd.).

Can buoy an unlit buoy of which the part above the waterline has the shape of a cylinder on end.

Cardinal point the four principal directions of the compass (north, south, east, and west).

Cardinal system a system of buoyage that marks dangers by reference to the cardinal points.

Cartography the art, science, and technology of making maps and charts.

CCOM Center for Coastal and Ocean Mapping, University of New Hampshire

Chart Datum (CD) (short for Chart Sounding Datum) a permanently established surface to which soundings or tide heights are referenced.

Contour a line joining points of equal vertical distance above or below a datum.

Controlling depth the least depth in the approach or channel to an area such as a port, governing the maximum draft of vessels that can enter.

CUBE Combined Uncertainty and Bathymetric Estimator—algorithm used to interpret sounding data.

Datum (geodetic) a set of parameters specifying the reference surface or the reference coordinate system, used in the calculation of points on earth.

Degaussing neutralization of the magnetic field of a vessel by means of suitably arranged electric coils permanently installed in the vessel.

Deviation the angle between magnetic north and compass north, expressed as degrees east or west of magnetic north. Deviation changes in different places and on different headings.

DGPS differentially corrected GPS.

Diurnal having a period or cycle of approximately one tidal day (i.e., the ebbs and floods are approximately 12 hours each, as opposed to 6 hours, which results in a semidiurnal tide).

DMA Defense Mapping Agency (renamed National Imagery and Mapping Agency, NIMA, in 1995), a division of the U.S. Department of Defense that provides mapping and charting support (primarily charts of non-U.S. waters).

Dolphin a substantial mooring post or buffer.

Drying heights heights above chart sounding (low-water) datum of those features that are periodically covered and uncovered.

Ebb tidal current moving away from land or down a tidal stream (opposite of flood).

Ebb tide the portion of the tide between high water and the following low water.

EC electronic chart that does not meet the requirements for an ENC.

ECDIS Electronic Chart Display and Information System—a navigation system that displays electronic charts in a manner that complies with the requisite standards.

ECS Electronic Chart System—a generic term for electronic charts and equipment that do not comply with the ECDIS/RCDS standards.

EEZ see *Exclusive Economic Zone*.

Electronic chart very broad term to describe the data, the software, and the electronic system, capable of displaying electronic chart information.

Elevations heights of natural and artificial objects above an adopted reference plane (as opposed to the ground or seabed; see *Height*).

Ellipsoid see *Spheroid*.

eLoran enhanced Loran, an advanced development of the Loran system being deployed in Europe.

ENC Electronic Navigational Chart—the database, standardized as to content, structure, and format, issued for use with ECDIS on the authority of government-authorized hydrographic offices.

Exclusive Economic Zone (EEZ) a zone contiguous to the territorial sea over which countries claim economic control (typically 200 miles or, if less than 200 miles, the midpoint between two countries).

Fairway the main navigable channel in a river, harbor, and so forth.

Fathom 6 feet.

Feature real-world object or phenomenon represented on a chart.

Fishing zone the offshore zone in which a country claims exclusive fishing rights, generally the same as the EEZ.

Flood tidal current moving toward land or up a tidal stream (opposite of ebb).

Flood tide the portion of the tide between low water and the following high tide.

Foreshore the strip of land between the low-water (sounding) datum and the high-water (shoreline) datum.

Form lines broken lines representing contour lines that are sketched to give a sense of the shape of terrain, rather than an accurately measured representation.

Foul area an area of numerous uncharted hazards to navigation or anchoring.

Geodetic datum the adopted position, in latitude and longitude, of a single point to which the mapped or charted features of an entire region are referred.

Geographic range the theoretical distance a light can be seen as limited by the curvature of the earth; it varies according to the height of the light and the observer.

Geoid the real-life surface of the earth if all heights are reduced to sea level.

Gnomonic chart also called a Great Circle Chart—a chart constructed on the gnomonic projection and often used for transferring great-circle routes to Mercator charts.

GPS global positioning system—a space-based radio-positioning, navigation, and time-transfer system operated by the U.S. government. GPS to which differential corrections have been applied is known as differential GPS (DGPS). Wide Area Augmentation System (WAAS) is another technology for increasing the precision of a GPS signal.

Great circle the line of intersection of the surface of a sphere and any plane that passes through the center of the sphere.

Hachures short lines used to indicate the slope of the ground or the seabed.

Height the vertical distance of an object above the ground or seabed (as opposed to a reference plane; see *Elevations*).

HO Hydrographic Office.

Hydrography the science that deals with the measurement of the physical features of the oceans, seas, rivers, and lakes.

IALA International Association of Lighthouse Authorities.

IEC International Electrotechnical Commission.

IHB International Hydrographic Bureau—the permanent secretariat of the IHO.

IHO International Hydrographic Organization—international coordinating organization for national hydrographic offices.

IMO International Maritime Organization—the specialized agency of the United Nations responsible for measures to improve the safety of international shipping and to prevent marine pollution from ships.

ISO International Standards Organization—the organization of the European Community charged with producing common product standards.

Isobath a line connecting points of equal depth.

Isogonal (isogonic) line of equal magnetic variation (magnetic "contour").

LANBY (LNB) Large Automated Navigational Buoy (Large Navigational Buoy).

Large-scale chart a chart that covers a small area in a lot of detail.

LAT Lowest Astronomical Tide.

LIDAR Light Detection And Ranging, a laser-based survey technique for charting shallow waters from aircraft.

LLWLT Lower Low Water Large Tide (see also LNT).

LNT Lowest Normal Tide (see also LLWLT).

Luminous range (nominal range) the greatest distance a light can be seen in clear conditions without considering the effect of the curvature of the earth.

M-4 IHO publication, *Chart Specifications of the IHO and Regulations of the IHO for International (INT) Charts.* Renamed S-4.

Magnetic variation the difference at any given location between true north and magnetic north, expressed as degrees east or west of true north; it changes over time and in different places.

MBES multibeam echo-sounder.

Mercator chart a chart based on the Mercator projection, which is used for almost all coastal charts. (Note: it is obtained by mathematical formulas and therefore is technically not a projection but a representation.)

Meridians lines of longitude.

Metadata background data about the information displayed on a chart.

MHHW Mean Higher High Water.

MHW Mean High Water.

MHWS Mean High Water Springs.

MLLW Mean Lower Low Water.

MLW Mean Low Water.

MLWS Mean Low Water Springs.

MSL Mean Sea Level.

Navaids navigational aids. See also *ATON*.

Neap tides tides of a below-average tidal range that occur when the moon is midway between new and full.

NGA National Geospatial Intelligence Agency.

NMEA 0183 a combined electrical and data-transfer specification developed by the National Marine Electronics Association in the U.S.

NMEA 2000 the replacement for NMEA 0183.

NOAA National Oceanic and Atmospheric Administration, which is responsible, through NOS, for charting U.S. waters.

Nominal range see *Luminous range*.

NOS National Ocean Survey, the division of NOAA that is responsible for charting U.S. waters.

Notice to Mariners a periodic notice issued by maritime administrations regarding changes in aids to navigation, dangers to navigation, important new soundings, and other information that affects charts, light lists, and other nautical publications.

Nun buoy an unlit buoy of which the part above the waterline has the shape of a cone pointing upward.

OS Ordnance Survey, the United Kingdom's shoreside survey agency.

Overscale to display a chart at a larger scale than its compilation scale.

PDBS Phase Differencing Bathymetric Sonar—an emerging technology for charting shallow water.

Period the interval of time between the commencements of the identical aspect in two successive cycles of a rhythmic light.

Pillar buoy a buoy composed of a central structure (often latticework) mounted on a flat base.

Pixel Picture Element—the smallest element resolvable by electronic devices such as scanners, display devices, and plotters.

POI Points of Interest.

Polygon a non-self-intersecting, closed chain defining the boundary of an area.

RACON Radar Transponder Beacon—a radio-navigation system that transmits a signal displayed on radar screens.

Raster a regular array of pixels with information pertaining to each element (pixel) or group of elements.

RCDS Raster Chart Display System—a system that displays raster charts in accordance with IHO Special Publication No. 61.

RDF Radio Direction Finder—radio-receiving equipment that is used to determine the direction from which the signal is coming.

RNC raster navigational chart that complies with S-61 and is issued by a national hydrographic office.

RTCM Radio Technical Commission for Maritime Services.

S-4 (see M-4).

S-52 IHO Special Publication 52, *Specifications for Chart Content and Display Aspects of ECDIS*.

S-57 IHO Special Publication 57, *IHO Transfer Standard for Digital Hydrographic Data*.

S-61 IHO Special Publication 61, *Raster Chart Display Systems*, setting standards for raster-chart displays.

S-100 a new standard being developed by the IHO as a replacement for S-57.

Scale the ratio between the linear dimensions of a chart, map, or drawing and the actual dimensions represented.

Semidiurnal having a period or cycle of approximately one half of a tidal day (i.e., the ebbs and floods are approximately 6 hours each).

Slack water the state of a tidal current when its speed is near zero.

Small-scale chart a chart that covers a large area in little detail.

SOLAS Safety of Life at Sea—an international maritime safety treaty, first drafted in response to the sinking of the *Titanic*.

Sounding Datum see *Chart Datum*.

Spheroid (ellipsoid) a flattened sphere used to define a horizontal chart datum.

SPM Single Point Mooring—generally for oil tankers, and often well out to sea.

SPOR Shoreline Plane of Reference—the high-water datum used to define the coastline.

Spring tides tides of above-average tidal range as a result of the influence of a new or full moon.

SSS sidescan sonar

Territorial sea the water area bordering a nation over which it has exclusive jurisdiction (typically, the 12-mile limit or the midpoint between two countries if it is less than the 12-mile limit).

UGC user-generated content.

UKHO United Kingdom Hydrographic Office.

USCG United States Coast Guard.

Variation see *Magnetic variation*.

Vector direct connection between two points, either given as two sets of coordinates (points), or by direction and distance from one given set of coordinates.

WAAS Wide Area Augmentation System—a technology for improving the accuracy of GPS signals.

Watch circle the circle described by a buoy as it moves around its mooring.

WEND Worldwide Electronic Navigational Chart Database—a common worldwide network of ENC datasets, based on IHO standards, designed specifically to meet the needs of international maritime traffic using ECDISs that conform to the IMO Performance Standards.

WGS World Geodetic System—a global geodetic reference system developed by the United States for satellite position-fixing and recommended by IHO for hydrographic and cartographic use.

Wire-drag survey a survey using a submerged cable to determine least depths in a given area.

Zoom a method of enlarging (zooming in) or reducing (zooming out) graphics displays on a screen.

Common Chart Abbreviations

aband Abandoned
ABAND LT HO Abandoned lighthouse
abt About
AERO Aeronautical
AERO R Bn, Aero RC Aeronautical radio beacon
AERO R Rge Aeronautical Radio Range
AIS Automatic Identification System
Al, Alt Alternating light
ALC Articulated Loading Column
ALL Admiralty List of Lights and Fog Signals
ALRS Admiralty List of Radio Signals
alt Altitude
ALWP Adopted Average Low Water Plane
Am Amber
anc Ancient
Anch Anchorage
Anch prohib Anchorage prohibited
Annly Annually
Ant Antenna
approx Approximate
Apprs Approaches
Arch Archipelago
Art Articulated light
ASD Admiralty Sailing Directions
ASL Archipelagic Sea Lane
Astro Astronomical
ATT Admiralty Tide Tables

AUTH Authorized
Aux Auxiliary light
Ave Avenue
AWOIS Automated Wreck and Obstruction Information System
B Black
Bdy Mon Boundary monument
Bk. Bank
bk Broken
Bkhd Bulkhead
Bkw Breakwater
Bld, Blds Boulder, Boulders
Bldg Building
BM Benchmark
Bn, Bns Beacon(s) (in general)
Bn Tr, BnTrs Beacon Tower(s)
Bo Boulder(s)
Bol Bollard
Br Breakers
brg Bearing
Bu Blue
BWHB Black and white horizontal bands
BWVS Black and white vertical stripes
C. Cape
C Can, Cylindrical (buoy)
C Coarse
ca Calcereous
CALM Catenary Anchor Leg Mooring
Cap Capitol
Cb Cobbles
CD Chart Datum

cd Candela
Cem Cemetery
CFR Code of Federal Regulations
CG Coast Guard
Ch Church
Chan Channel
Chem Chemical
CHY, chy, chys Chimney(s)
CICSS Committee on the International Chart, Small Scales
Cl Clearance
cm Centimeter(s)
Co Coral
Co Hd Coral head
COLREGS International Regulations for Preventing Collisions at Sea, 1972
concr Concrete
Consol Consol beacon
conspic Conspicuous
const Construction
corr Correction
cov Covers
Cr. Creek
Cswy Causeway
CT HO, Ct Ho Courthouse
CUP, Cup Cupola
CUS HO, Cus Ho Customhouse
Cy Clay
decrg Decreasing
deg Degrees
dest Destroyed
dev Deviation
DG, DG Range Degaussing Range

DGPS Differential Global Positioning System
DIA Diaphone
Dir Direction
Discol Discolored water
discontd Discontinued
dist Distant
Dk Dock
dm Decimeter(s)
DMA Defense Mapping Agency
DMAHTC Defense Mapping Agency Hydrographic/Topographic Center
Dn, Dns Dolphin(s)
Dol Dolphin
dr Dries
DW Deep water
dwt Dead Weight Tonnage
DZ Danger Zone
E East
ED Existence doubtful
Ed Edition
EEZ Exclusive Economic Zone
E Int Isophase Light (equal interval)
Entr Entrance
Est Estuary
explos Explosive
Exting Extinguished light
f Fine
F Fixed light
Facty Factory
FAD Fish Aggregating Device
FCZ Fishery Conservation Zone
F Fl Fixed and flashing (light)
F Gp Fl Fixed and group flashing (light)
Fl Flash, flashing (light)
Fla Flare stack (at sea)
fm, fms Fathom, fathoms
Fog Det Lt Fog detector light
Fog Sig Fog signal station
FP Flagpole
F Racon Fixed frequency radar transponder beacon
FS Flagstaff
Fsh Stks Fishing stakes
Ft Fort
ft Foot, feet
F TR Flag tower
G Gravel

G Green
GCLWD Gulf Coast Low Water Datum
glac Glacial
GMT Greenwich Mean Time
Govt Ho Government house
Gp Group
Gp Fl Group flashing
Gp Occ Group occulting
GPS Global positioning system
Grd, grd Ground
Grt Gross Register Tonnage
GT Gross Tonnage
h Hard
h Hour
H Helicopter
HAT Highest Astronomical Tide
Hbr Harbor
Hbr Mr Harbor master
Hd Head, Headland
HHW Higher High Water
Hk Hulk
Hn. Haven
HO House
Hor Horizontal lights
HOR CL Horizontal clearance
Hosp Hospital
Hr. Harbor
Hr Mr Harbor Master
HW High Water
HWL High Water Line
I. Island, islet
IALA International Association of Lighthouse Authorities
ICW Intracoastal Waterway
IHB International Hydrographic Bureau
IHO International Hydrographic Organization
(illum) Illuminated
IMO International Maritime Organization
incrg Increasing
INT International
Intens Intensified
I Q, I Qk, Int Qk Interrupted quick
Irreg Irregular
Iso Isophase
ITZ Inshore Traffic Zone

IUQ Interrupted ultra quick
IVQ Interrupted very quick
km Kilometer(s)
kn Knot(s)
L. Lake, Loch, Lough
Lag. Lagoon
LANBY Large Automated Navigation Buoy
LASH Lighter Aboard Ship
LAT Lowest Astronomical Tide
Lat Latitude
lat Latitude
LD Least Depth
Ldg Landing
Ldg Lt Leading light
Le. Ledge
LFl Long-flashing light
LL List of Lights
LLW Lower Low Water
LLWD Lower Low Water Datum
LNB Large Navigational Buoy
Lndg Landing
LNG Liquefied natural gas
LNM Local Notice to Mariners
long, Long Longitude
LOOK TR Lookout station, Watch tower
LORAN Long-range navigation
LPG Liquefied Petroleum Gas
LS Lightship
LSS Lifesaving station
Lt, Lts Light(s)
LT HO, Lt Ho Lighthouse
Lt V Light-vessel
LW Low Water
LWD Low Water Datum
LWL Low Water Line
m Medium
m Meter(s)
m Minute(s) of time
M Mud
M Nautical mile (see also *NM*)
Mag Magnetic
Maintd Maintained
Mg Mangrove
MHHW Mean Higher High Water
MHW Mean High Water
MHWL Mean High Water Line
MHWN Mean High Water Neaps
MHWS Mean High Water Springs

MICRO TR Microwave tower
min Minute(s) of time
Mk Mark
MLLW Mean Lower Low Water
MLW Mean Low Water
MLWL Mean Low Water Line
MLWN Mean Low Water Neaps
MLWS Mean Low Water Springs
mm Millimeter(s)
Mo Morse code light, Fog signal
MON Monument
MR Marine Reserve
MRCC Maritime Rescue and Coordination Center
Ms Mussels
MSL Mean Sea Level
Mt Mountain, Mount
MTL Mean Tide Level
MWL Mean Water Level
N North
N Nun, Conical (buoy)
NAD 27 North American Datum of 1927
NAD 83 North American Datum of 1983
NE Northeast
NGA National Geospatial Intelligence Agency
NIMA National Imagery and Mapping Agency
NM Nautical Mile
No Number
NOAA National Oceanic and Atmospheric Administration
NOS National Ocean Service
Np Neap Tides
NSICC North Sea International Chart Commission
NT Net Tonnage
NTM Notices to Mariners
NW Northwest
OBSC Obscured light
Obscd Obscured
Obs Spot Observation spot
Obstn Obstruction
Obstr Obstruction
Oc, Occ Intermittent, Occulting light, Occultation
Occas Occasional light
OD Ordnance Datum

ODAS Ocean Data Acquisition Systems
Or Orange
OVHD PWR CAB Overhead power cable
P Pebbles
PA Position Approximate
Pass. Passage
PD Position Doubtful
Pen Peninsula
PIL STA, Pil Sta Pilot Station
Pk. Peak
PO Post Office
Pos Position
Priv Privately maintained
priv Private, Privately
Priv maintd Privately maintained
Prod Well Production Well
Prohib Prohibited
proj Projected
Prom Promontory
prom Prominent
PSSA Particularly Sensitive Sea Area
Pt Point
Pyl Pylon
Q, Qk Fl Quick flashing light
R Coast radio stations QTG service
R Red
R Rock
Ra Radar Range, Radar Reference Line, Coast Radar Station
RACON Radar transponder beacon
Ra (conspic) Radar conspicuous object
RA DOME, Ra Dome Radar Dome
Ramark Radar Beacon
Ra Ref Radar reflector
RBHB Red and black horizontal bands
R Bn Radio beacon (see also *Ro Bn*)
RC Non-directional Radiobeacon
RD Directional Radiobeacon
RDF Radio direction finder
RDF, Ro DF Radio direction-finding station (see also *RG*)
Rds. Roads, Roadstead
Ref Refuge
Refl Retroreflecting material
Rep, rep Reported

Restr Restricted
Rf. Reef
RG Radio Direction-Finding Station
RGE, Rge Range (navigation aid)
Rge Range (coast feature)
Rk Rock (coast feature)
Rk, rky Rock, Rocky (bottom characteristic)
Rky, rky Rocky (coast feature)
R Lt Red light
(R Lts) Air Obstruction Lights (low intensity)
R MAST Radio mast
Ro Bn Radio beacon (see also *R Bn*)
RoRo Roll-on Roll-off ferry terminal
RR Railroad
R TR Radio tower
Ru Ruins
RW Rotating radiobeacon
RW Bn Red and white beacon
RWVS Red and white vertical stripe
s Second(s) or time
S Sand
S South
SALM Single Anchor Leg Mooring
SAR Search and Rescue
SBM Single Buoy Mooring
Sch School
SD Sailing Directions
SD Sounding Datum
SD Sounding Doubtful
Sd Sound
sec Second
sf Stiff
S Fl Short flashing light
Sh Shells
shl Shoal
Si Silt
Sig Signal
Sig Sta Signal station
SIREN Siren, fog
S-L Fl Short-long flashing light
SMt Seamount
so Soft
SOLAS Safety of Life at Sea
SP Spherical (buoy)
Sp Spire
Sp Spring Tides
S'PIPE Standpipe

SPM Single Point Mooring
SPOR Shoreline Plane of Reference
S Sig Sta Storm signal station
SS Signal Station
St Stones
Sta Station
std Standard
St M, St Mi Statute mile
Str Strait
sub Submarine
Subm, subm Submerged
Subm ruins Submerged ruins
Subm W Submerged well
SW Southwest
SWOPS Single Well Oil Production
   System
sy Sticky
t Ton, tonne
TD Time difference
Tel Telephone, Telegraph
(temp) Temporary
Tk Tank
TLS Traffic Lane Separation

TR, Tr, Trs Tower(s)
TSS Traffic Separation Scheme
TV TR Television tower (mast)
ULCC Ultra Large Crude Carrier
Uncov Uncovers, dries
unev Uneven
Unexam Unexamined
Unintens Unintensified
UQ Continuous ultra quick
USCG United States Coast Guard
USGS United States Geological
   Survey
UT Universal Time
UTC Coordinated Universal Time
UTM Universal Transverse Mercator
v Volcanic
var Variation
Vel Velocity
Vert Vertical lights
VERT CL Vertical clearance
Vi Violet
Vil Village
VLCC Very Large Crude Carrier

Vol Volcanic
VQ, V Qk Fl Very quick flashing
   light
VS Vertical stripes
VTS Vessel Traffic Service
W West
W White
Water Tr Water tower
WD Wire drag
Wd Weed
WGS 72 World Geodetic System
   of 1972
WGS 84 World Geodetic System
   of 1984
Whf Wharf
WHIS Whistle, fog
Wk, Wks Wrecks, Wreckage
W Or White and orange
Y Yellow (also amber and orange at
   times)
yd, yds Yard(s)

Bibliography

Primary Sources

Publication S-4, Chart Specifications of the IHO and Regulations of the IHO for International (INT) Charts (Ed. 4.1.0, Feb 2011). Published by the IHB.

Chart 5011 (INT-1): Symbols and Abbreviations Used on Admiralty Charts (4th ed., 2008). U.K. Hydrographic Office (Taunton, Somerset), © Crown 2008.

Chart No. 1: United States of America: Nautical Chart Symbols, Abbreviations, and Terms (10th ed., 2000). U.S. Department of Commerce. *Chart No. 1* is included almost in its entirety in this book.

Nautical Chart Manual (7th ed., 1992; corrected to May 2002). U.S. Department of Commerce, Office of Coast Survey.

Nautical Chart User's Manual (1997). A NOAA book that has not been published but is available on the NOAA website.

Other Sources (organized by publishing body)

NP 100, The Mariner's Handbook (1999 ed.). Published by the British Admiralty, Taunton, Somerset, England.

The International Hydrographic Review. A twice-annual publication of the International Hydrographic Bureau, 4 Quai Antoine 1er, B.P. 445-MC 98011, Monaco; info@ihb.mc; www.iho.shom.fr/.

IHO S-44, IHO Standards for Hydrographic Surveys, 5th ed., 2008.

IHO S-52, Specifications for Chart Content and Display Aspects of ECDIS, Oct. 2009.

IHO C-55, Status of Hydrographic Surveying and Nautical Charting Worldwide, 3rd ed., 2004, updated to 2011.

IHO S-57, IHO Transfer Standard for Digital Hydrographic Data, Edition 3.1, Nov. 2000.

IHO S-60, User's Handbook on Datum Transformations Involving WGS 84, 3rd ed., July 2003.

IHO S-61, Product Specification for Raster Navigational Charts (RNC) (1999).

IHO S-63, Data Protection Scheme, Ed. 1.1, March 2008.

IHO S-100, Universal Hydrographic Data Model, 2010. (Will replace S-57.)

ISO 19379: 2003. *International Organization for Standardization, Ships and Marine Technology—ECS Databases—Content, Quality, Updating, and Testing.* Geneva, Switzerland.

The Hydrographic Journal. Published four times a year by the Hydrographic Society, University of East London, Longbridge Road, Dagenham, Essex RM8 2AS, England.

NOAA Hydrographic Surveys Specifications and Deliverables (June 2000). Available on the NOAA website.

Miscellaneous technical papers from the NOAA website.

Center for Coastal and Ocean Mapping (CCOM), Annual Report, 2010, and miscellaneous technical papers.

Geodesy for the Layman (5th ed., 1983). U.S. Department of Commerce, NOAA, Rockville, Maryland. This and the following book provide a good general introduction to the subject.

Basic Geodesy (Sept 1977). U.S. Department of Commerce, NOAA, Rockville, Maryland.

World Geodetic System 1984; Its Definition and Relationship with Local Geodetic Systems (Sept. 1991). Defense Mapping Agency, U.S. Department of Defense, TR 8350.2.

The American Practical Navigator ("Bowditch", 1995 ed.). Published by the Defense Mapping Agency.

RTCM 10900.4, Radio Technical Commission for Maritime Services Standard for Electronic Chart Systems (ECS). Version 5 was released in 2011. Arlington, VA.

A Story of Maps (1949). Lloyd A. Brown (Boston: Little, Brown). A good general history of mapmaking and chart-making.

General Index

Numbers in **bold** refer to pages with illustrations

A

accuracy
  astronomical observation compared to ellipsoid-derived, 19
  charting revolution and increase in, 8
  of charts, 33–35
  of data, 8
  of depth information, 12
  of DGPS, 8, 29, 33
  digitization of existing charting products and, 8
  of electronic charts, 42–**49**, 50–52, **51**
  of GPS, 12, 22, 29, 50
  limits of, understanding of, 10, 12
  nautical surveys, 19–**22**
  of navigation tools, 10
  positional accuracy of chart features, 90
  of position fixes, 19
  satellite-based navigation systems, 10, 20–22
  of soundings, 29, **30**, 59–61, **60**, **69–71**, 80–81
  of surveys, 12–**19**, 29–35, **30**, 59–61, **60**
acronyms, 252–55
ActiveCaptain, 78, 79, **80**
Admiralty Raster Chart Service (ARCS) format, 73

aerial photography overlays, **48**, 75, **77**, 79
aids and services. *See also* buoys and beacons
  fog signals, 88, **230**
  lights and lit structures, 88, **193–207**
  organization and structure of section, 87, 88, 193
  pilotage services, **182**, **183**, **236**
  radar, radio, and electronic position-fixing systems, 88, **231–35**
  rescue stations, **236–37**
  signal stations, **237–38**
  small-craft facilities, 239–40
  supplementary national symbols, **207**, **229**, **238**
aids to navigation (ATONs). *See also* buoys and beacons; lights and lit structures
  charted information about, 193
  numbering and labeling conventions, 193
  sounding data and charting of, 36–37
airports (airfields), 117, **126**
Airy, George, 15
Airy 1830 ellipsoid, 15, **16**
AIS (Automatic Identification System), 76
Amazon River, 70
anchorages and anchorage areas, **184–86**

Annapolis
  charts of, **65**, **109**, **117**, **136**
  sounding datum for chart, **66**
ARCS (Admiralty Raster Chart Service) format, 73
areas and limits, 88, 94, **183–90**
astronomical observations and position fixes, 12–**14**, 15–**18**, 19, 20, **21**
Australia
  accuracy of chart information for, 34
  symbology update from hydrographic office in, **86**
Automatic Identification System (AIS), 76

B

Bahamas
  accuracy of chart information for, 34
  charts for navigation in, 74, 75, **77**, 79
bare rocks, 118, **160**
barometric pressure, 70
baselines, 12–16, **13**, 20, **21**
Bay Islands reef, 29
Bay of Fundy, tide table for, **66**
beacons. *See* buoys and beacons
bearings, 112–13
Belize
  accuracy of chart information for, 34
  chart of, **93**

pared to ellipsoid-derived, 19
astronomical observations and,
  12–14, 15–18, 19, 20, 21
discrepancies and position errors
  between surveys, 15, 16, 18,
  19, 20–24, 45, 50–52
electronic position-fixing systems,
  231, 233–35
real-time positioning, 13
positions, distances, directions, and
  compasses, 87, 110–16
powerlines, charting of, 67, 126,
  127, 128, 133
private sector, charts from, 8, 72, 73,
  74–78, 86–87. *See also specific
  chart-producing companies*
Puerto Rico, charts of, 106, 153

Q

Queen Elizabeth II, 59, 107

R

radar installations, symbols for, 131
radar overlays, 79
radar reflectors, 221–22
radar stations, 231, 232
radar surveillance systems and stations, 180
radar transponder beacon (racon),
  231, 232
radio beacons, 233
radio direction finding (RDF) equipment and stations, 231, 233
radio reporting (calling-in) points,
  180, 182
Radio Technical Commission for
  Maritime Services (RTCM), 75
railways, symbols for, 125, 128, 133,
  136
ramarks, 231, 232
Ramsgate, chart of, 107, 207
ranges, charting of, 133, 139
Raster Chart Display System
  (RCDS) mode, 73, 101
raster charts
  concept of and characteristics of,
    39–42, 52–58
  notes on, 48–49
  paper charts compared to, 88

production of, 42
quilting together, 47
real-time positioning with, 13
resolution issues, 42–44
standards for, 73, 74
standards for, development of, 8
switching between vector and, 42
updates and corrections to, 50
vector charts compared to, 52–58
zoom function, overzooming, and
  display of, 44–47, 45, 46,
  53, 55, 56, 58
Raster Navigational Chart (RNC),
  73, 74, 76
raster scans of smooth sheets, 36,
  37, 39
Raymarine chart and display technology, 75
RCDS (Raster Chart Display System) mode, 73, 101
*Recommended Minimum Standards
  for Electronic Charting Systems*
  (RTCM), 75
reefs
  avoiding, 22–24, 23
  charting of, 163, 167
  coral, growth of, 29, 30
  Cork Clipper loss on, 23, 24,
    51–52
  surveys and changes to, 29
Regional Electronic Chart Coordinating Centre (RENC), 37–38
*Regulations of the IHO for Interna-
  tional (INT) Charts and Chart
  Specifications of the IHO* (IHO
  S-4)
  buoyage system rules, 208
  coastline features and perspective
    on, 117
  lights and lit structures, informa-
    tion about, 196
  numbering and labeling recom-
    mendations, 92
  publications based on, 85–86
  routing measures, 176
  soundings placement on charts, 41
  source diagrams, purpose of, 107
  standard publication in, 85–86
  vertical datum, 61, 62, 63
relief and contour heights, 120
Renaud, M. J., 85

RENC (Regional Electronic Chart
  Coordinating Centre), 37–38
rescue stations, 236–37
restricted areas, 183, 186–88
rhumb-line course, 28
Rio Dulce, wind and water levels
  near, 69, 70
Rivers Tamar, Lynher, and Tavy,
  chart of, 128
RNC (Raster Navigational Chart),
  73, 74, 76
roads, symbols for, 125
rocks
  charting of and symbols for, 82,
    86, 88, 117–18, 133, 153,
    160–63, 167
  numbering and labeling conven-
    tions, 92–93
  surveys and accuracy of location
    of, 20
routes and tracks, 88, 173–82
RTCM (Radio Technical Commission for Maritime Services), 75
ruins, charting of, 136, 138, 139
Rule of Twelfths, 145
Russia, charts from, 19, 42, 81, 107,
  207

S

Safety of Life at Sea (SOLAS) convention, 72, 73
safe-water marks, 214–15, 217, 228
San Francisco, 59, 60
Santee Basin, chart of, 65
Santiago Harbor, Cuba, 21
satellite-based navigation systems. *See
  also* differential GPS (DGPS);
  GPS (global positioning system)
  accuracy of, 10, 20–22
  charting of and symbols for, 235
  discrepancies and position errors
    between surveys and, 18–19,
    20–24
Savannah River and Warsaw Sound,
  charts of, 99, 123, 133, 141,
  202, 215
seabed, nature of, 88, 157–59, 158
seamounts, 59, 60
Seattle, tide information for, 62, 66
seawalls, 134